Which Way Forward Indian Missions?

A Critique of Twenty-five Years
1972–1997

K. Rajendran

SAIACS Press

Which Way Forward Indian Missions?
A Critique of Twenty-Five Years 1972—1997
Copyright © Krishnasamy Rajendran, 1998

Requests for information should be addressed to:
SAIACS Press
Box 7747, Kothanur, Bangalore 560 077, INDIA

SAIACS Press is an imprint of SAIACS Publications

ISBN   81-900849-4-1

Managing Editor: Ian Payne
Editor: Beulah Wood
Layout: Ian Payne
Printing & Cover Design: Promotions India
Distribution: Mission Educational Books

Copies are available from:
1.   Mission Educational Books   2.   Mission Educational Books
      Lalgarh   P.O. Box 2299
      MADHUPUR (SP)   Ayanavaram
      Bihar 815 353   CHENNAI 600 023
      INDIA   INDIA
      Ph/Fax (91) 64—382 4566   Fax: (91) 44—626 4641

3.   SAIACS Press
      Box 7747, Kothanur
      BANGALORE 560 077
      INDIA
      Phone: (91) 80—846 5235   Fax: (91) 80—846 5412
      E-mail: saiacs@giasbg01.vsnl.net.in   Website: http://www.epinay.com/saiacs

DEDICATION

I dedicate this book to

—my mentors who discipled me

—my Indian missionary colleagues who labour hard in discipling
the peoples of this nation

—my wife Pramila, daughter Preeti and son Pradeep who have
strengthened me for mission.

And I thank God.

About the Author

Coming from Trichirapalli in Tamil Nadu, Krishnasamy Rajendran was studying in college when he listened to the words of a dying friend and accepted Christ. In 1970 he joined Operation Mobilisation, working with many OM missionaries all over India. In early 1978 he married Pramila, who was from Uttar Pradesh. Together they worked in church planting at Biharsharif, Bihar.

Late that same year, they joined the OM ship, Logos. Rajendran worked, at different periods over the next six years, as the Director of Programmes, Director of Conferences, Director of Training and Personnel. During this time they visited over forty countries, witnessing to many people, interacting with local Christians, hundreds of Christian leaders and learning about churches and missions in every country.

It was while they were on the Logos, that their daughter, Preeti, and son, Pradeep, were born—in Papua New Guinea and England respectively.

From 1984 until 1995 Rajendran led the missionary training programmes for OM India. This meant he was involved in pastoral care issues of missionaries and also interacted widely with other missions in India and across the world.

Sensing a need for further input, the family went in 1995 to study at the South Asia Institute of Advanced Christian Studies (SAIACS) in Bangalore. Pramila did an M.A. in Pastoral Counselling and Rajendran tackled a Doctor of Missiology. Graduating in 1998, Rajendran completed a dissertation on missions in India. This book is the fruit of that study.

Now living in Chennai, Rajendran is Assistant General Secretary of the India Missions Association, an association of over 100 missions with a combined missionary work force of more than 15,000.

Acknowledgements

This book is the fruit of my time at South Asia Institute of Advanced Christian Studies. I am grateful to God for the opportunity to study, think, interact and write during three years at SAIACS. When I packed my books and submitted my thesis, I regretted my formal study was over.

The leaders of Operation Mobilisation released me to study.

My prayer partners stood with me, trusted me and supported us as a whole family. Dr. Graham Houghton perceptively guided my studies and pointed me towards some missionary lives, which have been a highlight for me. Dr. Noel Jason pastored us as a family and we valued his expository teaching and insights. Dr. P. Augustine and his wife Sumathi inspired us as friends. The whole staff of SAIACS supported us. I am indebted to academic, library, kitchen, garden and the office staff for the vital atmosphere to concentrate.

I thank Mr. Ebenezer Sunder Raj of India Missions Association for access to documents and discussion of mission issues. I thank God also for the support of staff of IMA and OM. I am indebted to Dr Daniel Satyaraj, Carol Houghton, Marcia Michael, Angela Ball and Judith Payne for help in editing different chapters. I am obliged also to people I interviewed for their insights. Beulah Wood and Ian Payne have toiled in the final editing process.

I also thank Friends, my accountability group, David Shunmugam, John Abubakker and Chinnasamy Sekar for sharing and prayer each month. My own brothers K. Selvaraj, K. Jayakumar and sister K. Shanti who came to Christ one after another have been a tremendous encouragement. Pastor Dr. Booshanaraj Thomas and good friends of Bangalore Evangelical Free Church gave moral support.

I pray God will use this study to encourage improved care of missionaries, finer strategy and better evangelisation of India.

Index of Tables

Contents

4 Modern Indian Missions and their Decisions ... 55

5 Grouping for Co-operation 82

Abbreviations

ABCFM American Board of Commissioners for Foreign Missions.
AEF Asia Evangelical Fellowship.
AFC Ambassadors For Christ.
AGM Annual General-Body Meeting.
AGS Assistant / Associate General Secretary.
AIACHE All India Association for Christian Higher Education.
AICOME All India Congress on Missions and Evangelism.
ANM Advancing Native Mission, Bhubaneshwar
ATA Asian Theological Association.
BCM Bible Centred Ministries.
BGEA Billy Graham Evangelistic Association
BIC Brethren in Christ.
BJP Baratiya Janata Party.
B.Min. Bachelor in ministry degree.
BSP Bahujan Samaj Party
BYM Blessing Youth Mission which was also called FGYMA.
CARE The Cell for Aid and Relief to Evangelists.
CBCI Catholics Bishops Council of India.
CBCNEI Council of Baptist Churches of North East India.
CCC Campus Crusade For Christ.
CCS Centre for Communication Skills, Bangalore.
CEFI Child Evangelism Fellowship of India.
CEO Chief Executive Officer.
CeO Continuing Educational Opportunities.
CGAI Church Growth Association of India. [It was also called CGRC]
CGRC Church Growth Research Centre, [CGAI] Chennai.
CGMM Church Growth Missionary Movement, Madurai.
CIS Confederation of Independent States [Former USSR].
CLS Christian Life Service, a mission agency.
CLS Christian Literature Service
CMAI Christian Medical Association of India.
CMC Christian Medical College, Vellore.
CNEC Christian National Evangelism Commission.
CSM Corner Stone Ministries.
DAI Development Associates International.
DAWN Discipling a Whole Nation.
ECC Every Creature Crusade.
ECFA Evangelical Council for Financial Accountability
EFICOR Evangelical Fellowship of India Commission on Relief.
EGF Evangelical Graduate Fellowship [Part of UESI].
EHA Emmanuel Hospital Association.
ELFI Evangelical Literature Fellowship of India.
EMA Evangelical Missionary Alliance.
EMFI Evangelical Medical Fellowship of India.
ENFI Evangelical Nurses Fellowship of India.
ETAI Evangelical Trust Association of India.
ETANI Evangelical Trust Association for North India.
ETASI Evangelical Trust Association for South India.
FEUM Free Evangelical Urban Mission.
FES Friends Educational Society.
FECI Free Evangelical Church in India.
FFNI Friends For Neighbours in India, Vellore.
FMC Frontiers Missions Centre.
FMPB Friends Missionary Prayer Band, Chennai.
GCI Grace Counselling India.
GEMS Gospel Echoing Missionary Society.
GFA Gospel For Asia.
GMI Global Mapping International.
GMM Gujarat Missionary Movement.
GRCP The Grass Roots Church Planters.
GS General Secretary.
HUP Homogeneous Unit Principle.
IAE India Association of [Itinerant] Evangelists.
ICGM India Church Growth Mission, Madurai.
ICMA Indian Christian Media Association.

ICPF — Inter-Collegiate Prayer Fellowship.
IEA — India Evangelistic Association.
IEF — Indian Evangelical Fellowship.
IEHC — India Every Home Crusade.
IEM — Indian Evangelical Missions.
IEOM — Indian Evangelical Overseas Mission.
IET — Indian Evangelical Team.
IFVH — India Fellowship for Visually Handicapped.
IICCC — Indian Institute of Cross Cultural Communications.
IIM — Indian Institute of Missiology.
ILO — International Labour Organisation.
IMA — India Missions Association
IMAAN — Indian Missions Alliance Among Neighbours
IOM — India Outreach Mission, Nagpur.
IPEC — International Programme on Elimination of Child Labour.
JKLF — Jammu & Kashmir Liberation Front of Kashmir.
JVI — Joshua Vision India, Hyderabad.
KEF — Kashmir Evangelical Fellowship.
KEMF — Kerala Evangelistic Missionary Fund.
LAMP — Language Acquisition Made Practical.
LEF — Laymen Evangelical Fellowship.
LMM — Laymen's Missionary Movement.
LMS — London Missionary Society.
MAF — Missionary Aviation Fellowship.
MEM — [Young People's] Missionary Education Movement.
Mks — Missionary Kids.
MoU — Memorandum of understanding.
MP — Member of Parliament.
MSA — Missions Standard Association.
MSC — Missions Standard Cells.
MUF — Missionary Upholders Family.
MUT — Missionary Upholders Trust.
MVM — Maharastra Village Ministries.
NACSC — National Association for Christian Social Concerns.
NCCI — National Council of Churches in India.
NCE — National Consultation on Evangelism.

NICM — National Institute of Christian Management
NFEM — The National Forum for Evangelism and Missions.
NLCI — New Life Computers India, Bangalore.
NMM — Nagaland Missionary Movement.
NRI — Non-Resident Indian.
OBC — Other Backward Caste.
OFM — Orissa Follow-up Ministry.
OM — Operation Mobilisation.
PCM — Pentecostal-Charismatic Missions.
PF — Provident Fund.
PFI — Pentecostal Fellowship of India.
PIN — Postal Index Numbers.
PTS — Portable Training School.
RBM — Rural Blessing Mission, Wardha, Maharastra.
RSS — Rastriya Swayam Sevak.
SAC — South Asian Concern, U.K.
SABC — Southern Asia Bible College.
SC — Scheduled Castes.
SGM — Scripture Gift Mission.
SAIACS — South Asia Institute of Advanced Christian Studies.
SIBS — South India Biblical Seminary.
SISWA — South India Soul Winning Association.
SPCK — The Society for Promoting Christian Knowledge.
ST — Scheduled Tribes.
SVM — Student Volunteer Movement.
SVP — Student Volunteer Programme, arranged by UESI.
SWOT — Strengths, Weaknesses, Opportunities and Threats.
UBS — Union Biblical Seminary.
U.P. — Uttar Pradesh.
UTC — United Theological College.
UESI — Union of Evangelical Students of India.
UN — United Nations.
USCWM — United States Centre for World Missions.
VHP — Vishwa Hindu Parishad.
WLU — World Link University.
YCLT — Yavatmal College for Leadership Training.
YMCA — Young Men's Christian Association.
YWCA — Young Women's Christian Association.
YWAM — Youth With A Mission.

Foreword

The heritage and legacy of the Christian Church in South Asia reaches back to Thomas the apostle of our Lord. Still the present day Roman Catholic Church and the Churches of the Protestant confessions have their more immediate roots in what has been called, the modern missionary movement. To this end from the mid nineteenth century to about twenty years after Independence there were at any one time somewhere between 5000 and 7000 foreign missionaries at work all over the country. Since the mid-sixties their numbers have declined until the present when there are as few as 200 foreign missionaries who possess Residential Permit status left in India. One of the questions close to any serious missionaries heart and mind has always been, "who will take over when we leave," and more importantly, "what will happen when we leave?"

K.M. Panikkar, former Ambassador, has offered his prediction on the latter question in his, *Asia and Western Dominance*. He was convinced that once the prop of colonial power and the foreign missionary was withdrawn the Church would recede and in a decade or two collapse. As it has turned out just the opposite is the case. Perhaps there was a time when the Indian Church looked to the mission and the missionary to, "take care of the things." Thankfully no longer. In fact as the scaffolding of the missionary endeavour was dismantled and packed up, it was discovered that the building of the Indian Church was made of material of a far better quality than had been often imagined.

K. Rajendran's study is proof of the point. The relatively few foreign mission agencies have been replaced by a plethora of largely indigenous agencies and societies. His research shows, several hundred missions have been organised over the past two decades. More ismportantly these represented at least 15,000 Indian missionaries. Rajendran begins by reviewing the work of foreign mission. He considers their limitations, success and failures. The study of the post-Independence period is valuable for its sweep across the national landscape in what he calls, a nation in transition. Then he looks at the status of the present Indian missionary movement. Rajendran has provided us with a never before undertaken review and reflection on the entire scope of the present missionary endeavour. The issues he has looked at are real and will need to be reflected upon further by Indian mission leaders if the lofty aims before them are to be in any measure realised.

Essential reading for anyone wishing to be acquainted with this expansive and impressively effective movement that has so wonderfully replaced the earlier missionary effort and begun to build so marvelously upon the foundation that was laid by those who went before.

Graham Houghton, SAIACS, 22 February, 1999

Which Way Forward Indian Missions?
A Critique of Twenty-five Years 1972–1997

Introduction

In 1997 India celebrated the fiftieth year of independence. India has moved from where it was fifty years ago. So have Christian missions.

There is an old story of a rabbit and a tortoise running a race. The rabbit ran fast and too sure of his speed, slept on the way only to lose the race while the tortoise moved steadily with a goal in view. The tortoise won. The moral for us is that missions that run at a steady pace can keep the goal in view.

We must measure our achievement, evaluate the past and present in the light of today's challenges. Then we can move forward with purpose. This study analyses mission in India today.

Western pioneering Protestant missionaries gave the foundation for much of the success on which Indian missionaries now build. Growth has been spectacular over the past fifty years. Indian missionaries have grown from 543 in the year 1972 till in 1994 there were 12,000 missionaries. Still they come. India is the foremost among Two-Thirds World missionary-sending countries.

In the next fifty years missionaries and activities will increase. We will need more planning and direction, more pastoral care and contact, more training of leadership, and more varied evangelism. Mission leaders will be stretched. They must plan for growth. Some will be bitterly disappointed that they did not prepare themselves and their followers.

In the midst of growth, many missionaries suffer inadequate salaries, poor health care, inadequate education for their children, and lack pensions and housing plans on retirement. We need bold steps to counter these problems. Missionaries, mission leaders and all Christians need to solve them.

On the field, even theologically trained missionaries may lose motivation and direction. Many hit dry patches when they face opposition, lack of growth in their work, and relationship problems.

High dropout rates, especially of first-term missionaries are due to five pressure points, according to Tom Eckbald of South American Mission. These are: the problem of role identification, the broader participation required in culture and society, the need for initiative and self-management, the hard work and difficulties of evangelism and Church-planting, creativity and innovation.[1] Some missions arrange refresher courses once a year for missionaries. Could we do more? Or would this overtax the resources of the few Bible and missionary Colleges?

The author observed several pressing needs that demand discussion and action. They include mass conversion versus individual conversions, integration of converts into the life of the church, contextualisation, conflicts between evangelism and social work, the means to evangelise, accountability of missionaries and mission leaders, the place of lay people in missions, short-term missions, cross-cultural adaptations, and comity.

Mission bodies must plan strategically for corporate ownership, measure evangelism results, build trust for Indian and international partnership, provide and hold to standards for mission and missionary welfare. They must educate the church for missions, prompt continuous education for missionaries, initiate more women's work, prepare Indian missionaries for global ventures, draft and train future leadership and funding for missions.

Our missions have grown rapidly. Now we must appraise both our methods and our support systems to enhance our enterprise, the evangelisation of India.

END NOTES

1 Kayser, John G., "Training and Missionary Attrition", *Training for Cross Cultural Ministries*, Vol. 97, No 1, February 1997, pp. 6–7. Quoted from Tom Eckbald, "Tips for Urban Church Planters", *Urban Mission* 1 (1984), p. 18.

1

Early Endeavour and the Impact of Missionaries

To begin to evaluate Indian missions we need to briefly survey the positive contribution made by the early foreign missionaries, the task of this chapter, and to understand their limitations, the focus of chapter two.

Protestant missionaries arriving in India in the late eighteenth century precipitated revolution by preaching the Gospel, won people for Christ, discipled, established churches, advocated social change and even influenced the Freedom Movement by influencing the fathers of the new India.

Impact on Secular India

By the indirect influence of the missionaries, India remains today a secular rather than a sectarian nation. They campaigned against Sati[1], female infanticide, and the class of Thugs. They worked to alleviate the condition of Hindu widows and temple prostitutes and raise the age of marriage.

Raja Ram Mohun Roy's Hindu reformation was influenced by Christian missionaries and their teaching. William Carey, the Father of modern missions, worked against these when he introduced modern journalism, and published both Bengali and English newspapers and magazines. He stimulated a renaissance of Bengali literature. Carey's Enquiry and his personal example led to a major revolution in outlook and outreach of the Christian Church.

Christian Friedrich Schwartz, is an example. A German missionary at Tranquebar, Trichinopoly and then Tanjore he had much to do with the kings of Tanjore, was reputed to be of high integrity and widely trusted. He influenced Tulasi Raja and taught the raja's adopted son Serfogee Raja. Even Hyder Ali, a Muslim ruler, had a high regard for Schwartz who brought peace between the English and French rulers and dissolved misunderstandings. He helped preserve the throne of Tanjore by rescuing Serfogee and becoming his effective guardian. When Schwartz was dead, Serfogee recorded his gratitude in an inscription at Tanjore, and wished for more "missionaries who should resemble the departed Schwartz!"[2]

Years later a large number of white Christians associated with the
Indian freedom movement. Allan Octavian Hume was the first
president of the Indian National Congress. CF Andrews, Stanley
Jones, Fred B. Fisher Clifford Manshardt, Stokes – went a long way
towards changing the popular misconception that Christianity was
the other side of the Imperialist coin. Stanley Jones vocally supported the Indian freedom movement, struggling at times with the
ruling British Government. Jones was even willing to receive the
nationalists to his gathering. However Jones never lost sight of
introducing Christ to the people of India. Because of his influence
Ralph T. Templin formed Krishtagraha movement[3] which was
similar to Satyagraha movement started by Gandhiji. The ideology
of the Krishtagraha movement was to re-orientate Christianity
away from being pro-Western and toward achieving a soul of its
own, tied in closely to mother India. Jones as a front-line missionary sought to understand and interpret Gandhi sympathetically
from within the orthodoxy of the Christian Church.

CF Andrews was another missionary who had an enormous
influence upon Indians by his identification with Mahatma Gandhi
and Tagore.

Bishop Waskom Pickett, an American Methodist Bishop,
associated with Jawaharlal Nehru and Indira Gandhi. She attended
Bible studies at his home. In 1948 Nehru, fearing Gandhi would be
assassinated, trusted Pickett to convince Gandhi to leave Delhi.
Though Gandhi did not leave, he commented, "All my hopes for a
better India are being destroyed." Then Pickett expressed that "the
Christians were working for peace and patriotism." Gandhi voiced
the wish to publicly apologise to the Christians of India for not
being fair to them.[4] When Gandhi was assassinated, the first
memorial service anywhere in India, was held at Lucknow in a
large Methodist church. One of Gandhi's great grandsons, a well-
trained physician, was married in a Methodist Church at Ohio,
America. When his mother visited for the marriage, she hoped that
the whole family would be Christian.[5]

After Independence, Pickett took part in sorting out national
problems when there were community clashes between Sikhs and
Hindus.[6] When Bishop Pickett and Dr. Ambedkar become friends,
Ambedkar took many Christian books from Pickett and distributed them to many of his colleagues. After two years Ambedkar
asked him to baptise him secretly while he continued to be a
politician. He wanted Pickett to train and baptise 1000 of

Ambedkar's candidates, but they would not come under the authority of the Church and discipline. Pickett refused to baptise him unless it was publicly announced.[7]

In 1969, when Dr. Radha Krishnan hosted Bishop and Mrs. Pickett to luncheon, Radha Krishnan praised the impact of Indian Christians as keepers of law and order.[8] Such was the influence and participation of Bishop Waskom Pickett in the nation, especially with politicians.

Swami John Dharma Theerthan evaluated the impact of Christianity with these words. "The immediate effect of the impact of Christianity was a resurgence of moral and spiritual aspirations in opposition to all evils in the nation."[9] Khushwant Singh called missionaries helpers of the nation.[10]

Impact on the Growth of the Church in India

Stephen Neill in 1934 wrote euphorically of Indian Church growth, "In almost every corner of the country, the Christian Church has touched every stratum of society.[11] Singh agreed. "By 1921 the Protestants constituted 1.5 percent of the population of India, more than half of whom owed their Christianisation to American Missionary zeal."[12]

Ziegenbalg and others were known for training successors. Missionaries influenced Christians who carried on the beacon of evangelisation. Neill considered, "It was never the purpose of the wiser missionaries to reproduce in India a pale, dependent copy of their own form of Christianity; they foresaw a Church living an independent life, Indian in thought and worship and leadership."[13]

John P. Jones, a thinker and a strategist who served with the ABCFM[14] in Madurai for thirty-six years (1878–1914), challenged Indians in three extraordinary books to make Christianity their own in the Indian culture.[15] Jones habitually accompanied his Indian disciples in all evangelism, demonstrating how to explain the Gospel to people. He said, "A mission at best is a temporary thing. It should constantly aim to so nourish and strengthen the native Church as to make itself unnecessary."[16] He and many pioneers saw the good in their followers and discipled them to carry on the task of evangelisation as "Jesus saw His disciples not as what they were but what they were to become."[17]

Impact on the Down-trodden

Early missionaries worked hard to lift the poor, the down-trodden, the outcasts and the marginalised who were the victims of the Hindu philosophy of Varnashrama Dharma[18]. William Goudie, a Scottish Methodist missionary, was one. He gathered out-castes by scores and hundreds, and provided shepherding and instruction for them.[19] Today Goudie is remembered through institutions named after him at Ikkadu near Chennai.

In this way foreign Christian missionaries did a great deal for India in general and not just for Christians.

Impact on Indian Literature and Literacy

The contribution to Indian literacy by pioneering missionaries was exceptional. Missions started schools long before the government took a hand. Until a few years ago in many parts of India, ordinary schools were not open to the low-castes.[20] In Tranquebar the school pre-dated the church.[21]

"American missionaries compiled and published the earliest grammars and dictionaries of Punjabi, Hindi, Urdu and Marathi."[22] SH Kellogg pulled together more than a dozen dialects to create A Grammar of Hindi Language, which is still in use.[23] In South India, the Strict Baptist missionaries produced, alongside much other literary work, a Tamil dictionary and grammar.[24] Lucknow Christian College was the first institution in India to teach shorthand in English, Urdu and Hindi.[25]

There were thousands of mission schools, and in large areas every school was a mission school. JH Hodge, a Secretary of the National Christian Council of India, Burma and Ceylon prior to Indian Independence wrote, "Allied to education is that other outreach of influential missionary endeavour, the ministry of Christian literature."[26] Missionaries gave an enormous boost to mass education first in Bengal by teaching in the regional language.[27] In fact this is true for almost the whole of India.

Impact on Women's Education

In 1834, Caroline Atwater Mason wrote that only one percent of the Indian women could read and write.[28] "Reading and writing were practically confined to nautch girls and not for respectable women."[29] Despite local disbelief and pessimism the missionaries believed that the girls could be educated and transformed.

The Protestant missionaries' report of December twenty-eighth, 1707, at Tranquebar, said their Girls' school was the first Christian school for Indian girls, in all of India.[30] Hannah Marshman opened a school for girls at Serampore in 1800.[31] In 1870, Miss Isabella

Thoburn started a college on her verandah at Lucknow. Even the fathers of the girls said it was easier to teach their cows than their women. Miss Thoburn persisted, and eventually her graduates spread all over India, Burma, and Sri Lanka.[32] The college was probably the first women's college in all of Asia. With her came Dr. Clara Swain, the first woman medical missionary of any society, and the founder of the first hospital for women in all Asia.[33]

Rajaiah D. Paul reported in 1952 that seven percent of all those in teaching professions in India were Christians. He could recall the time when a hundred percent of the women employed as schoolteachers were Indian Christians.[34]

Ida Scudder, a missionary to South India, founded Vellore Christian Medical College in 1900 to train women as doctors and nurses, and men were admitted only in 1947. Dame Edith Brown did likewise at Ludhiana, Punjab. For years, while other communities refused to let their girls become nurses, Anglo-Indians and Christians made up almost the entire nursing profession in India. Many missionaries believed women were equal to men and should have the opportunity to learn, and their efforts at educating Indian women prompted a remarkable change on the Indian scene, helping women to think and contribute intelligently to society. By the 1994 census, women's literacy rate had grown to 39.42 percent compared to men's at 63.86 percent.[35] Missionaries had contributed to and inspired this progress.

Conclusion

Many scholars and thinkers have recognised the contribution to India of the earlier non-Indian missionaries. In 1928, Professor John Jesudason Cornelius of Lucknow said, "Christian missions have undoubtedly prepared the way for the mobilising of the thought power in India."[36] Swami Theerthan said, "The transformation that has been effected in the inner and outer life of the nation is one of the profoundest phenomena of human history."[37] Rajaiah D. Paul wrote, "The educated Hindu has for the most part been profoundly affected by Christianity and the education he has received, perhaps in a Christian school or a college.[38]

On this foundation missions march forward to the twenty-first century. Foreign missionaries are no longer physically present, but awareness of their work, the emerged Indian Church, and a healthy global partnership in missions will be the assets in moving into the twenty-first century.

END NOTES

1 In *Sati* a Hindu widow was burnt along with her deceased husband. Although not practised by all Hindus, the gruesome practice was perpetuated by many as religious fanaticism. It was outlawed in 1829 by the British Viceroy William Bentinct through the efforts of William Carey and Raja Ram Mohun Roy.

2 Stephen Neill, *Builders of the Indian Church* (London, Westminster: The Living Stone Press, 1934), p. 79.

3 Richard W. Taylor, *The Contribution of E. Stanley Jones.* (Madras: CLS, 1973), pp. 18–19.

4 Bishop JW Pickett, *My Twentieth Century Odyssey* (Bombay: Gospel Literature Service, 1980), pp. 150–151.

5 Ibid, p. 33, 154–155.

6 Ibid, p. 26.

7 Ibid, pp. 32–33.

8 Ibid, pp. 31–32.

9 Swami John Dharma Theerthan, *Choice Before India: Communism – Catastrophe; Sarvodya–Christ* (Trichur: Mission to Hindus, n.d.), p. 17.

10 Khushwant Singh, *India: an Introduction* (New Delhi: Vision Books), 1992, p. 75.

11 Neill, *Builders*, pp. 11–12.

12 Singh, *India*, pp. 75–76.

13 Neill, *Builders*, p. 15.

14 Harriet Wilder, *A Century in the Madura Mission–South India 1834–1934* (New York: Vintage Press, 1961), p. 16.

ABCFM –The American Board of Commissioners for Foreign Missions worked in Madura, Tamilnadu.

15 Books written by Dr John P. Jones are, [a] *India Its Life and Thought* (New York: The Macmillan Company, 1908). [b] *The Modern Missionary Challenge* (New York: Fleming H. Revell, 1910). [c] *India's Problem Krishna or Christ* (New York: Fleming H. Revell, 1903).

16 John P Jones, *India's Problem*, p. 223.

17 Chacko Thomas, former Director of M.V. Doulos, OM. Lecture, Lucknow, October 1988.

18 *Varnashrama Dharma* philosophy holds to four upper castes and does not allow backward castes and the untouchables into full society. This practice has kept untouchables in poverty, illiteracy, ignorance and 3000 years of bondage.

19 EW Thompson, *The Call of India* (London: The Wesleyan Methodist Missionary Society. 1912). p. 155.

20 Theerthan, *Choice Before India*, p. 16.

21 Stephen Neill, *Under Three Flags*, (New York: Friendship Press, 1954), p. 76.

22 Singh, India, p. 75.

23 Ibid, p. 269.

24 John K. Thorpe, *"Other Sheep" of the Tamil Fold. The Centenary Story of the Strict Baptist Mission 1861–1960* (London: S.B.M. Publications, 1961), pp. 34–36.

25 Pickett, *Odyssey.* p. 138.

26 JH Hodge, *Salute to India* (London: S.C.M., 1944), p. 98.

27 Moni Bagchee, "Christian Missionaries in Bengal", in [n.a.], *Christianity in India* (Madras: Vivekananda Prakashan, 1979), p. 191.

28 Caroline Atwater Mason, *Wonders of Missions* (London: Hodder & Stoughton Limited, 1922), p. 264.

29 CB Firth, *An Introduction to Indian Church History* (Madras: CLS, 1983), pp. 192–193.

30 Arno Lehmann, *It Began at Tranquebar* (Madras:CLS, 1956), p. 103.

31 Mason, *Wonders of Missions.* p. 265.

32 Margaret Carver Ernsberger, *India Calling* (Lucknow: Lucknow Publishing House, 1956), p. 2.

33 James K. Mathews, "The Mission to Southern Asia". James A. Engle & Dorcas Hall (Eds.), *The Christian Mission Today* (New York: Abingdon Press, 1960), p. 133.

34 Rajaiah D. Paul, *The Cross Over India* (London: SCM Press Ltd, 1952), p. 91.

35 Vasantharaj A., *A Portrait of India* (Madras: CGAI, 1995), p. 2.

36 John Jesudason Cornelius, "Movements Towards Christ in India," from Fennell P. Turner and Frank Knight Sanders (Eds.), *The Foreign Missions Convention at Washington 1925* (New York: Fleming H. Revell Company, 1925), p. 83.

37 Theerthan, *Choice Before India*, p. 17.

38 Paul, *The Cross Over India.* p. 89.

2

The Limitations of Foreign Missionaries

Alongside many positive achievements by missionaries in emancipation, education, and Christian values for the people of India, there were also limitations. This chapter, while acknowledging a great job done in communicating Christ, seeks to understand the human frailties. It was not just "how lovely are the feet of him who brings Good News,"[1] but what other burdens did those feet bring. Studying need neither magnify nor demean foreign missionaries but we ought to learn in order not to repeat the same mistakes.[2]

In evangelism the fixed factors are the message and the messengers. The variable factors are recipients, methods, resources, religions, intellectual capacities, social customs, development levels, national traits and temperaments.[3] Every method must be weighed. There is no one strategy. The variables crucially affected the success and failures of foreign missionaries. We as current missionaries analysing the predecessors in pre-independent India may hold respect and gratitude for past heroes and be thankful for all that is available to us today.

Limited Access to Information

If all the Western missionaries of the past had all the anthropological knowledge, information, communication, information technologies and care that the present day missionaries have, the earlier missionaries would have done far better and would have avoided many blunders. Indeed, mission history would have been different. Some of them did not even have newspapers and radios let alone satellite television, telephones, pagers, cellular phones or computers. Present Indian and Third World missionaries should be evaluated in the context of their greater access to knowledge and techniques acquired compared to the previous European missionaries. Present day missionaries have to be more accountable than any previous generation.[4]

It is said that some European missionaries held racial prejudice against blacks or coloured people. Today some coloured missionaries act the same way when dealing cross culturally with other races, tribes or castes. *Varnashrama* is the Indian brand of racism.

Indian missionaries should avoid such anthropological blunders by learning from the mistakes of others.

Disunity and Competition

In early 1600, the Jesuits had some hope of winning Jehangir, son of Emperor Akbar of the Moghul dynasty. But he was unhappy with the wrangling between the Portuguese Roman Catholics and Protestant English Ambassadors, Captain Hawkins and Thomas Roe.[5] In 1627 the Emperor Jehangir died. With him died hopes of Christianising India by converting its ruler. As a matter of fact no ruler of any princely state ever accepted the Christian faith.[6]

Disunity between the representatives of the Christian faith was endemic. Bishop Neill neatly summarised it thus. "The missionaries say that they have come just to preach Christ. All that they really want is to get people into their own little cages (after which) they will not even allow them to receive the Holy Communion together."[7] Obvious division in Christianity damaged the offer of Christ to Indians who were already filled with divergence and rifts.

Exaggerated or Caustic Reports

Missionaries reporting to their constituency were often both emotive and informative to raise concern, prayer and finance. At times they were condescending, lacking in empathy for their hosts, harsh, caustic, colourful and only partly factual.[8] The following is an example.

It is observed that children in heathen lands are like "wild asses, colts", ungoverned, ungovernable, idle and dissolute. Missionaries in contrast to pagan parents, govern and educate their children, make them learned, and can fit them also to be missionaries in their turns.[9]

Even if the above was true in only some situations, this attitude made missionaries feel and act superior, and thus annoy the ones to whom the Gospel was taken.[10] "Mistaken (old) concepts of missions repeated, believed and perpetuated ... . If they were ever true, are long since outdated."[11] "Those at home have ordinarily heard only one side of the missionary story, but how many national Christians from other lands have a chance to tell you how they view the situation?"[12] Bluntly Neill put it, "Christian history has been written far too much from the side of the operators, and far too little from that of the victims."[13] Stanley Jones wrote, "Christianity must be defined as Christ, not the Old Testament, not Western civilisation, but Christ Himself. Christ must not be seen as a Western Partisan but a Brother of Men.[14] This positive change of attitude helped the missionaries to build rapport with the nationals and learn mutually from each other.

Struggle with Host Cultures

Missionaries seldom identified with local cultures. Khushwant Singh observed that "many Christians continued bearing high sounding English names, their women wore a comical mixture of European and Indian dress. Their hymns translated sung to outlandish tunes (which) evoked more derision than reverence."[15] What Stephen Neill wrote in 1934 rang true, and still does. "Missionaries wished their converts to become as much like Englishmen as possible. Christianity in India today presents itself as an alien religion."[16] "To attend Sunday Churches in any of the greater churches in South India is an astonishing experience... Innovation, especially in Church worship is no more welcome in South India than it is in England."[17] Neill wanted to innovate and advocated careful adaptation and not throwing out everything from the past.

Jack C. Winslow, a friend of Gandhi, wrote that "missionaries with the Gospel brought unessential Western accompaniments."[18] Keshab Chandra Sen, deeply influenced by Christianity, founded *Prarthana Samaj*.[19] His devotion to Christ was remarkable but he felt that the missionaries were not presenting the Asian Christ.[20]. As far back as 1903, John P. Jones was distressed that modern Christianity was a product of Western thought, interpretation and life.[21] Rajaiah D. Paul in 1952 tried to re-define the Christian message in thought forms and in language that our countrymen would understand.[22] A Christian from Karnataka said a civilised Christian groom could not be married without a suit and a tie!

Reaching the High-Caste Hindus

Missionaries attempted in many ways to reach out to different sections of Indian people. Many concentrated among the elite and the high caste. This bore little fruit. Rupert Davis, surveying the growth of Methodism, observed that, "The early attempts at reaching the high-caste people had failed utterly, and it became a matter of policy to pursue evangelism by the indirect path of schools, colleges and hospitals."[23] The chief barrier was the Hindu caste system, because the higher castes could not care less. To them a Christian was synonymous with untouchable, an outcast.[24]

Indian Workers as "Agents"

Most missionaries treated their workers and evangelists well. However, the term used for the workers was "agents".[25] Graham Houghton describes four kinds of native agent. Readers with little training conducted services in small congregations. Catechists, who did some evangelism, nurtured and taught new believers. Pastors or Ministers were placed in charge of large congregations with pastoral oversight. And Native Missionaries shouldered responsibilities along with foreign missionaries, in some cases responsible on the same basis as their foreign counterparts.[26]

Some agents did not take good care of the new converts. Reports said some agents were mere hirelings, whose objects were monthly pay and pleasing their European masters.[27] William Goudie told a story of an agent who stole a watch from his room. He was caught by the police and brought a bad reputation to Christianity.[28] "With such information missionaries justified their presence and the leadership roles, and gathered around themselves dependent agents who merely fulfilled their expectations."[29] Though many missionaries were good to these workers, according to Stephen Neill, "Missionaries in the nineteenth century had to some extent yielded to the colonial complex..... Western man was the leader, and would remain so for a very long time, perhaps for ever."[30]

"Holy" People in Mission Compounds

The strength of missionary preaching was the call to Christianity. However, according to Bishop Lesslie Newbigin, "Converts were called upon to separate themselves radically from the society. But the 'churchly' society was rather a transplanted version of the medieval 'Christendom'.[31] "Missionaries, unable to distinguish in Hindu culture what was religious and what was social, taught the Christians to reject every Hindu custom indiscriminately."[32] This attitude made the Church dependent of the Western Missions and alienated it from the mainstream of Indian life.[33] In some cases new converts were extracted from their culture of necessity because their high caste families had threatened their lives. But extracting people from the community to the mission compound stopped 'people group' movements to Christ. Becoming a Christian, especially a mission compound person, created a mixed new Christian culture,[34] and cultural changes were dominated by the majority caste from which the converts came.

On the other hand, the lower strata of society, 'Dalits'[35] needed the identification, acceptance and protection of influential missionaries. "These (SC) converts had embraced Christianity to avoid stigma of caste and acquire human dignity."[36] "This they did to move up out of the caste system, to gain a new sense of one's own worth, dignity and self-respect."[37] Sadly, to this day "Dalit Christians have been seeking equality within the Church ... without any caste discrimination."[38] "The Christian missionary has been recognised as their true friend, ... for he has worked for their elevation and preached to them a Gospel of life an hope."[39] However, "the mission station approach encouraged insincere inquirers."[40] Even then, "The *Hindu* acknowledged the good work being done by Christian missionaries to ameliorate the problems of the Adi Dravidas."[41] Winslow, the biographer of Narayan Vaman Tilak and one of the founders of the Ashram Movement[42] confirmed this. "The outcaste communities of Mahars and Mangs ... found that emancipation within the shelter of the Christian Church... The early missionaries even unintentionally encouraged it.[43] The mission compound culture was perpetuated and nurtured by many of the missionaries who genuinely felt that the Christian community was "holy" or "separated", and thus their lives ought to be different in morality and in all other aspects of life.[44] In the process, "the mission station approach created an artificial world of almost total dependence upon the missionaries."[45] This made non-Christians feel Christians were almost traitors. Because Christians related to European missionaries, they were misunderstood as collaborators with the crushing colonisers. "The most unfortunate result of the separation of converts from their families was that this blocked the most effective channel for evangelism."[46] According to Houghton "this proved to be an impediment to its (the Gospel's) advance and plan to capture the heart of India."[47]

Lastly, some missionaries consciously did create compounds where they recreated and nurtured their own culture, housing and other habits to remind them of their own nation from where they came from. To maintain such status, they had to employ and train people. New converts became workers in the mission as cooks, waiters, teachers and in many other professions. Often, missionaries thought this was part of helping the converts become new creatures in Christ without the pressure from outsiders, the non-Christians. Mission compound culture has its negative repercussions still today.[48] A comparable situation is also found among some Indian missionaries in some states.[49]

Phil Parshall, a missionary to Bangladesh, said the remaining mission compounds should be dismantled to free missionaries to move into the community and share their incarnational testimony.[50]

At times upper castes pressurised early missionaries to accept the caste system. The mission at Tranquebar in 1706 cautiously respected castes and accepted its distinctions.[51] The country priests and the catechists there were of the higher castes.[52] This situation calls all today's South Indian and North Eastern Indian missionaries to be alert to withstand the pressures of the locals, especially when this is not biblical.[53]

Exclusivism and Non-Patriotism

HL Richard a researcher of Indian culture says, "Too often in the process of preaching Christ, missionaries were involved in public ridicule of Hinduism.[54] This caused problems at times in preaching the Gospel. "It must be admitted that missionaries generally share four things with colonial government agents: common nationality and culture, common race, administrative authority, and a position of privilege.[55] Many a young missionary-minister with little or no experience in the pastorate had been appointed a district superintendent at his first annual field conference. Privilege was (also) seen in the material possessions and salary.[56] Houghton attributed this to "the presupposition fashioned in large measure by Englishmen in the service of the British Raj, that their Indian workers were an inferior order of beings, not fit for positions of trust and responsibility."[57] The display of a sense of superiority on the part of the missionaries strengthened the belief of Hindus that Christianity was the religious side of the propagation of colonial power. Houghton summarised the attitudes of some of these missionaries as "officialism", with a sense of a master to his employee; a spirit of "masterfulness" with a relationship of superior to inferior and; some missionaries were more "self-seeking" than their calling allowed for.[58] Richard comments, "missionary history in India is inextricably tied to colonialism, a stigma that mars the work of Christ to this day".[59] Winslow, who struggled with superiority and identification said, "I must become an Indian to the Indians."[60] Because of his right attitude he was a tremendous blessing. His Indian colleagues accepted him because of his humility and identification with his Indian counterparts.[61]

Treating locals as less mature or less than equal still occurs among the Indian missionaries. Ralph Winter advises four stages of a missionary – the pioneer, the parent, the partner and the participation stage.[62] Present missionaries must practise all these four stages for the Church to grow.

Misunderstood Missionaries

In spite of all the contributions of missionaries to Indian communities, they were still misunderstood.[63] This showed particularly in the way they were suspected regarding their social service.

As early as 1813 Gordon Hall and his associates in Bombay gathered in five years 550 children and educated them. Government had not aroused itself to this need.[64] Samuel Fairbanks (1822–1898) who established himself in Vadala, Western India as an adviser for the farmers, solved so many disputed cases in the village that no court cases went from that village as they were solved wisely by the Missionary.[65] Social action is a Christian response to needs.

However, Waack, a missionary to Orissa, believed that when missionaries financially assisted needy Christians, even in small ways, it eventually became an obstacle.[66] Most missionaries helped people regardless of their various religious beliefs. Yet this is often misunderstood by people who accuse the missionaries of converting people with materialism.

Different Perspectives

Among recent secular journalists, in contrast to Khushwant Singh, Arun Shourie unfairly twisted the facts about missionaries in his book *Missionaries in India*.[67] Shourie associated all Europeans and American missionaries with the Colonial East India Company as its arms.[68] He misinterpreted missionaries' actions of good will and education as the consolidation of the British rule.[69] Vishal Mangalwadi has refuted this and wrote, "Shourie does not look for the objective facts ... he is not interpreting texts in their contexts. ... Rather, he *deconstructs* history and tries to uncover, the hidden lust for imperial power behind the missionary movement."[70]

Among some Hindus there were other priorities than freeing India from the Colonialists. Hedgewar – one of the chief inspirations behind the RSS – felt that liberating Hindus from Muslims was a greater priority than liberating India from the British. Gopal Krishna Agarkar, Bal Gangadhar Tilak's colleague, and Phule felt that reforming Hindu society should have priority over asking the British to quit India. Freedom would have come to India from the British as other British colonies without much of the Gandhian struggle.[71] The greater struggle of the British was to decide to whom to transfer India; the Maharajahs, the Brahmins, the Banias or to whom? Gandhi had a very difficult task holding the Freedom Movement together. If he had been able to keep them together the country would not have become India and Pakistan. Gandhi's non-violent movement first of all had to be applied to the people of India.

Were the Missionaries Bribing Colonialists?

Some missionaries who collaborated with the business-minded colonialists were called the "political Padri."[72] Given this stigma some people concluded that Christianity was foreign, or more precisely Western, and much more precisely British.[73] Devilal, the former Deputy Prime minister of India, said that all Christians should leave India.[74] Richard wrote, "missionaries were often accused of bribing Hindus to change religion, an accusation difficult to prove."[75] In this way missionaries were criticised for the good work they did. "Hindus considered that missionaries, united with the colonial Government, desired at any cost to make India Christian"[76] Some Indians held such misgivings about the missionaries.

According to Neill the word colonial itself was derogatory. Colonialism meant almost exclusively exploitation of weaker and defenceless peoples and its only results were destruction of what was good in ancient civilisations and the multiplication of measureless evils.[77]

Neill's useful definition does not fit well with the missionaries who sacrificed much and laboured hard in India and shared the Gospel of Christ.[78] The missionaries were not colonialists. Their self-sacrifice and genuineness can be viewed with admiration and gratitude.

Conclusion

Missionaries in their zeal to serve the people of India contributed much. However, at times their limitations were exaggerated to an extent that placed them on a level with the majority of the selfish colonialists. "To be fair on the missionaries, it cannot be said that they did not set out with sound policies in mind."[79] Most were clear about sharing of the Good News of Christ to the Indians. They had their human limitations, but they served with many sacrifices. The reason for this chapter is not to dwell on the failures of the foreign missionaries, but to thank God for their commitment to carry the Gospel in the midst of criticisms.

END NOTES

1 Isaiah 52:7; Romans 10:15.

2 Roger E. Hedlund, *Evangelisation and Church Growth* (Madras: CGRC, 1992), p. 217.

3 T. Stanley Soltau, *Missions at the Cross Roads* (Illinois: Van Campen Press, 1954), pp. 28–37.

4 Interview with Sunder Raj, IMA, Chennai, 30 May, 1997.

5 Singh, *India*, p. 75.

6 Ibid, p. 75.

7 Neill, *Call to Mission*, pp. 37–39.

8 Mason, *Wonder of Missions*, p. 71.

9 R. Pierce Beaver, *All Love Excelling* (Michigan: Eerdmans), 1968, p. 50.

10 Ibid, pp. 50–51.

11 Horace L. Fenton Jr., *Myths about Missions* (Illinois: IVP, 1973), pp. 11–12.

12 Ibid, p. 10.

13 Gerald Anderson, *Future of the Christian World Missions,*

William Danker (Ed.), (Grand Rapids: Eerdmans 1971), p. 139.

14 Jones, *The Christ of the Indian Road*, p. 16.

15 Singh, *India*, p. 76.

16 Neill, *Builders*, p. 63.

17 Ibid, pp. 63–64.

18 Winslow, *The Eyelids of the Dawn*, p. 77.

19 *Prarthana Samaj* means a society of prayer.

20 Stephen Neill, *The Christian Church in India and Pakistan* (Michigan: Eerdmans Publishing Company, 1970), p. 121. Quoted from the original translation by O. Wolff, *Christus Under den Hindus – Christus der Asiat*, pp. 62–67.

21 Jones, *Krishna or Christ*, p. 296.

22 Paul, *The Cross Over India*, p. 106.

23 Rupert E. Davis, *Methodism* (Middlesex: Penguin, 1963),

p. 171.

24 Singh, *India*, p. 72.

25 Lewis, *William Goudie*, p. 48.

26 John Murdoch, *Indian Missionary Manual: Hints to Young Missionaries in India* (London: Seelay, Jackson, & Halliday, 1870 2nd edition), p. 298. Quoted Graham Houghton, *The Impoverishment of Dependency* (Madras: CLS 1983), pp. 30–31.

27 Houghton, *Dependency*, p. 163.

28 Lewis, *William Goudie*, p. 48.

29 Houghton, *Dependency*, p. 246.

30 Stephen Neill, *A History of Christian Missions* (London: Penguin Books, 1990), p. 220.

31 Lesslie Newbigin, *The Good Shepherd* (Madras: CLS, 1974), p. 86.

32 Richard, *Christ-Bhakti*, pp. 56–57. Quoted from *The Harvest Field*, Vol. 39, No. 6, June (1918) 236–237.

33 Houghton, *Dependency*, p. 247.

34 Subash Samuel, Pastor of the local Church in Katihar. Personal Interview at Lucknow, UP, June 1994.

35 Brojendra Nath Banerjee, *Struggle for Justice to Dalit Christians* (New Delhi: New Age International (P) Ltd., 1997), pp. 1, 16. 'Dalit' in Sanskrit means 'trampled upon' and refers to low caste, officially Scheduled Castes, once 'untouchables'.

36 Ambrose Pinto S. J., *Dalit Christians. A Socio-Economic Survey* (Bangalore: Ashirvad, 1992), p. 29.

37 John Webster, *From Indian Church to Indian Theology*

38 Banerjee, *Justice to Dalit Christians*, p. 66.

39 Charles Hope Gill, "The strategic Value of Mass Movements in India," *The East and the West*, XIII, January (1915) 42–43. Quoted in Webster, *Indian Theology*, p. 23.

40 Frederick and Margaret Stock, *People Movements in the Punjab*, (Bombay: Gospel Literature Service, 1978), p. 22.

41 Houghton, *Dependency*, p. 106.

42 Winslow, *The Eyelids of the Dawn*, back cover page.

43 JC Winslow, *Narayan Vaman Tilak* (Pune: Word of Life Publications, 1996 [third edition]), p. 49.

44 Stock, *Punjab*, p. 22.

45 Ibid, p. 22.

46 Ibid, p. 23.

47 Houghton, *Dependency*, p. 247.

48 Suresh S., former Pastor of the AOG Church at Bettiah, Bihar. Interview at Kurukshetra, Haryana, June 1994.

49 SS Bhargava, Interview at Gorakhpur, June 1994.

50 Phil Parshall, "God's Communicator in the 80's". Winter, Hawthorne et al (Eds.), *World Christian Movement*, p. 478.

51 J. Waskom Pickett, *Christ's Way to India's Heart* (Lucknow: Lucknow Publishing House, 1938), pp. 14–15.

52 Ibid, p. 15. Cited in the Missionary Register, London, July 1813.

53 Ralph E. Dodge, *The Unpopular Missionary* (New Jersey: Fleming H. Revell Company, 1960), p. 28.

(Madras: Dalit Liberation Education Trust, 1992), p. 7.

54 Richard, *Christ-Bhakti*, p. 12.

55 Ibid, p. 19.

56 Ibid, pp. 24–25.

57 Houghton, *Dependency*, p. 246.

58 Ibid, pp. 220–221.

59 Ibid, p. 12.

60 Winslow, *The Eyelids of the Dawn*, pp. 74–75.

61 Ibid, p. 74.

62 Ralph D. Winter, "The Long Look: Eras of Missions History," in Ralph Winter, Steve Hawthorne et al (Eds.), *Perspectives on the World Christian Movement—A Reader*, (California: William Carey library, 1981) pp 170–171.

63 Otto Waack, *Church and Mission in India* (Delhi: ISPCK, 1997), pp. 415–416.

64 Alden H. Clarke, "Should Mission Carry on Social Work?" in Fennell Turner and Frank Sanders (Eds.), *The Foreign Missions Convention at Washington 1925* (New York: Fleming H. Revell, 1925), p. 138.

65 Ibid, p. 139.

66 Waack, *Church and Mission*, pp. 416–417.

67 Arun Shourie, *Missionaries in India* (New Delhi: ASA Publications, 1994).

68 Ibid, pp. 57–58.

69 Ibid, pp. 58–60.

70 Vishal Mangalwadi, *Missionary Conspiracy: Letters to a Postmodern Hindu*, (Mussoorie: Nivedit Books, 1996), p. 16.

71 Ibid, p. 214.

72 [n.a.], "Missionaries in India: Focus on Madhya Pradesh", in [n.a.], *Christianity in India*, (Madras: Vivekananda Kendra Prakashan, 1979), p. 182. Excepts from "Report of the Christian Missionary Activities Enquiry Committee, Madhya Pradesh". Published by All India Arya (Hindu) Dharma Sewa Sangh, PO Sewa Sanga, Sabzi Mandi, Delhi.

73 Neill, *Colonialism*, p. 98.

74 Graham Houghton, asked concerning Devilal in a Lecture in 1995. Should a statement of this nature be pronounced by responsible Minister like Devi Lal? Would this kind of comment bring unity to the nation? Who, in reality, are the nation builders in this country?

75 Richard, *Narayan Vaman Tilak*, p. 64.

76 Ibid, p. 67.

77 Neill, *Colonialism and Christian Missions*, p. 11.

78 Firth, *Indian Church History*, pp. 143–144.

79 Houghton, *Dependency*, p. 246.

3

Challenges of a Nation in Transition

What are the major challenges facing churches and missions reaching India? Should Christians despair?

In 1997 observer Aneja commented, "In this golden jubilee year, one wonders what we are more hurt and angry about—the two hundred years of colonial rule or fifty years of independent India's misrule?"[1]

Historically "India" was never a single nation but many kingdoms which were put together after Independence. Salman Rushdie calls it, "a dream that everyone agreed to dream. And now I think there actually is a country called India."[2] Both Indians and foreigners have difficulty understanding India. Some carry stereotyped ideas of sensationally televised images, with poverty, illiteracy, snakes and the rural scenes.

Modern India has changed. Its people, culture and economy cover opposite extremes. Shashak Tripathi says, "Enough has been said about the glorious past of India. What the world needs to be told is what India has by the way of resources and where it will stand internationally in the coming years."[3] India is economically moving ahead, and despite the drawback of its large population, functions somewhat miraculously as the largest democracy in the world.

Massive Population Growth

The population of 400 million at Independence doubled by 1987. Now the estimate is 950 million. The Government struggles with this enormous growth. While we have no precise figure of the percentage of Christians, estimates range from 2.6 percent to four.[4] However, the comparison in the table overleaf shows a significant proportionate decline.

In the ten years since 1987 the percentage of Christians decreased in twenty-two areas though the actual number is increasing. People are becoming Christians at a slower pace than the population growth. The way the population is growing out of control calls for innovative and varied strategies to present Christ, and increases the challenge to missionaries and mission leaders.

Comparative Christian Populations by Decades[5]			
AREA	1971	1981	1991
India	2.59 %	2.45 %	2.32 %
Andhra Pradesh	4.19 %	2.68 %	1.83 %
Arunachal Pradesh	0.79 %	4.32 %	10.29 %
Assam	4.46 %		3.32 %
Bihar	1.17 %	1.06 %	0.98 %
Goa		31.35 %	29.86 %
Gujarat	0.41 %	0.39 %	0.44 %
Haryana	0.10 %	0.09 %	0.01 %
Himachal Pradesh	0.10 %	0.09 %	0.09 %
Jammu Kashmir	0.16 %	0.14 %	
Karnataka	2.09 %	2.08 %	1.19 %
Kerala	21.05 %	20.56 %	19.32 %
Madhya Pradesh	0.61 %	0.68 %	0.65 %
Maharastra	1.42 %	1.27 %	1.12 %
Manipur		29.68 %	34.11 %
Meghalaya	46.98 %	52.62 %	64.58 %
Mizoram	24.19 %	83.81 %	85.73 %
Nagaland	66.76 %	80.21 %	87.47 %
Orissa	1.73 %	1.82 %	2.10 %
Punjab	1.20 %	1.10 %	1.11 %
Rajasthan	0.12 %	0.12 %	0.11 %
Sikkim	0.79 %	2.22 %	3.30 %
Tamil Nadu	5.75 %	5.78 %	5.69 %
Tripura	1.01 %	1.21 %	1.68 %
Uttar Pradesh	0.15 %	0.15 %	0.14 %
Delhi	1.08 %	0.99 %	0.88 %
Andaman & Nicobar	26.35 %	25.58 %	23.95 %
Chandigarh	0.97 %	0.99 %	0.78 %
Dader & Nagar Haveli		1.95 %	1.51 %
Daman & Diu		2.97 %	2.86 %

Women

At the 1991 census, India had 437,597,929 males and 406,332,932 females.[6] India is one of the few countries in the world where males outnumber the females. That gap is increasing, and demonstrates the oppression of women.

Only with a renewed mind will women be treated as equally created by God. Without it, gender violence grows and goes unpunished. There are over 5,000 dowry deaths each year. In spite of all the news of the betterment of women, the most vulnerable person in society is a girl child forsaken in the streets. She gets misused more than any one else. She needs immediate protection, care and rehabilitation, yet there is too little public awareness of this.

IK Gujral, Prime-Minister in 1997, announced an annual rupees five-hundred as an incentive to girl children for their education. This is a welcome move.[7] Journalist Asha Krishnaswamy wrote, "The status of women should have been better in the last five decades. I have come across brilliant women but they lack the freedom to blossom themselves as individuals."[8]

In spite of the changing status for women, it is still difficult for men to evangelise women. Yet the majority of the mission workers are men.[9]

The Poor

By some definitions thirty-five percent of the people of India live below the poverty line. This includes all the Scheduled Castes who increase 6.6 million a year. Although poverty is connected to structural oppression, ignorance and superstition, it is exacerbated by child labour. The result is a perpetual illiteracy. Poor parents complain they are unable to send their children to school and children end up in odd jobs. Society loses much. A study on child labour reported that Child labour reduces productivity.[10] As an example: in Jaipur, Rajasthan, the gem polishing trade employs 14,000 children.[11] We need to know more about the cause and cure of poverty.

Government and charity organisations have recently attempted education and transformation for these children. In a bridge-study for children who worked in a quarry, they studied to appear in Government examinations in Standard five, eight and ten. After this the students would be admitted to Government

Schools for higher studies.[12] Such model ventures will help in the future to alleviate the illiteracy problems and the poor.

Christian churches, missions, and local organisations have many programmes to help needy children in the slums of Bombay, Bhopal, Hyderabad, and many other cities. Out of nearly 100 missions with IMA, fifty-five reported that they have social activities including ministries to rehabilitate and transform the lives and prospects of disadvantaged children.[13]

Cities

Almost thirty percent of India's population, 300 million, live in cities. Six mega-cities have more than eight million people, and 303 cities have more than 100,000 people. Millions of rural people have moved to urban areas in search of better jobs, income and education, despite adverse living conditions for these new migrants. Twenty-three cities have over a million people, and Bangalore has the reputation of the fastest growing city in Asia. Not all these over populated cities cope with the infrastructure and pollution control needs. To improve local transport, the Government has approved Mass Rapid-Transit Systems (MRTS) and underground metro train services in Delhi, Bangalore, Mumbai, Hyderabad, Madras and Jaipur and expansion in Calcutta.[14] Congestion and system failure are compounded by corruption in government and local bodies allowing public funds to be siphoned off from development projects.

We need to focus more deliberately on urban poor and middle classes to reach them with the Gospel. Some work is done among the poor, but very little among the powerful middle class consumers.

Alyque Padamsee, one of the country's leading marketers and mass media experts, comments: "a middle class of 250 million people wants to go shopping."[15] This magical number is almost four times larger than the population of UK, twice that of Japan, and equivalent to the entire population of USA. IK Gujral said, "Our economy has taken off, agriculture is growing fast, we have a strong middle-class, stronger than the whole of Europe put together, and a market which is larger than that of the whole Europe."[16]

The Urban worldview is shaped by where people live, whom they associate with and what they see, hear and say. Then by education.[17] Misra explains that Western education broke the intellectual monopoly of the Brahmans by opening the door to all classes.[18] Educational institutes and schools became a booming enterprise in the cities.

Worldview is also shaped by industrialisation, automation, modern technologies of efficiency and competitiveness.[19] Materialism and consumerism shape many lives. Mass media brainwash people for good and/or bad. Radio, television, cinema, newspapers and magazines have revolutionised the dreams they visualise. Internationalisation and globalisation have opened minds to new worlds and worldviews. New values blend with old beliefs, perceptions and lifestyles. Cities present a new class of people for whom missions in India are hardly prepared.

The Rich and Powerful

There is no known solid strategy exclusively for reaching the rich in India with the Gospel. Even middle class Indians are not targeted. The slogan of "win the winnable" took missions to the poor, to Dalits, tribals and the marginalised. This ethos was perhaps right. But we need also a new ethos to reach the rich and the middle class. As Houghton says, "the rich have their own gods of money, wealth, power and prestige. They try to be secular and only nominally religious."[20] Let this not be an excuse for neglecting them. Even a senior IAS officer may commit suicide because of a disturbed marital life."[21] The middle class and the rich need the Lord Jesus as much as any one else.

The Educated

India's literacy marched from 5.1 percent in 1901 to 52.21 percent in 1991[22] and with it a reading appetite. The newspaper industry illustrates this point. "At the end of 1991, the number of newspapers[23] stood at 30,214 compared to 28,491 in 1990, showing an increase of six percent during the year."[24] This is a challenge we have hardly faced. Little effort is made to place quality Christian literature in the hands of educated people. Most evangelical Christian books were translated from non-Indian writers. There is no Christian magazine in the general market. While the secular press has gone on haunting the public with astonishing and innovative literature, missions dilly-dally. Our few attempt to produce books for non-Christians are ineffectual. Many read Christian books with as much devotion as other religious books, but our books lack punch.

Several Bible Societies have tried hard to produce Scriptures and other print materials. So have many other organisations. India Every Home Crusade, Campus Crusade for Christ, Gospel For Asia, Scripture Gift Mission, Evangelical Literature Service, Operation Mobilisation, Gospel Literature Service, Masihi Sahitya Sanstha, Christian Literature Service and others distributed a considerable amount of evangelistic literature. This did influence peoples' thinking. OM pressed on regardless of the critical label "book sellers". Though it is difficult to measure the achievements, the above missions deserve commendation for their single-minded thrust in literature.

Christian bookshops, struggling to survive, have gone into stationery just to pay their rent and the meagre salaries of their workers. Regional language publications barely survive. The Hindi Masihi Sahitya Sanstha at Delhi has ceased to function.

Another problem, apart from producing appropriate literature, is marketing and distribution. A marketing strategy for Christian literature hardly exists. Some Christians feel present Christian literature is not worthy to be handed out, as the quality, content and the appearance are unattractive.

Very little is done to encourage writers of evangelistic literature. Agencies like the Centre for Communication Skills (CCS) work hard to encourage Christian journalism,[25] conducting seminars to show how to get writing into the secular press. They even began a monthly amateur Christian writers' club to encourage, grow, share ideas and open doors. They say Christians should influence the secular press with Christian ethos instead of leaving it the domain of the agnostic, humanistic, impious and ungodly.[26] The few professional Christian journalists need to be encouraged and their skills tapped.

There can be no doubt of the need to target the reading, globalising, information hunting, educated mass. This is a challenge for missions myopically focused entirely on reaching tribals.

Illiteracy

Despite fifty years of reform, approximately fifty percent of Indians are illiterate. Thirty-five percent men and sixty-five percent women cannot read or write. Half of the two hundred million children do not attend school.[27] Amrik Singh in *Deccan Herald* said,

Various United Nation Agencies expressed deep concern over the prospect of India having half the illiterates of the world ... UP has one-sixth of India's population. In terms of illiteracy, it is one of the most backward states in the country. The rate of infant mortality is the highest in the country. Regarding illiteracy among the girls, it is better only than Rajasthan. In brief UP is one of the most backward states.[28]

The middle class can access education. Often the poor cannot. Paul J. Koola exclaims, "Illiteracy accounts for many a superstitious belief that makes man nothing more than two legged beast... Intellectual poverty is more dreadful than the economic poverty."[29]

Gospel Recording Association of India, radio programme agencies[30] and audio-visual agencies[31] serve well, especially to illiterates. Simple Scripture verses printed in poster form by Scripture Gift Mission proclaim the gospel. Almost every Catholic Church in the country proclaims the life of Jesus in picture form inside the church, helping people to remember, meditate on Christ and learn the story. Adult literacy classes have projected the Gospel to learners. However, taking the Gospel meaningfully to illiterates remains a challenge.

Extensive Geography – PIN CODE

Given India's vast geography, it has been officially divided into small sections called Postal Index Number code areas, each containing approximately 30,000 people. Out of 28,000 PIN codes, nearly 20,000 have not one resident pastor, evangelist, missionary or Christian Development Worker.[32] Placing Christian workers in these PIN Code areas[33] is a vital strategy, which can also be easily measured.

Gospel Echoing Missionary Society, Gospel For Asia, India Evangelistic Association, the Assemblies of God at Calcutta, and Karnataka Evangelical Fellowship are some missions which adopted PIN Code areas. GEMS has a goal of workers in 500 Pin Code areas of Bihar out of the 1500 total. So far they have placed workers in one hundred Pin Code areas.[34] Project North West 2000 AD, proposes to have churches in every Pin Code area in Punjab, Himachal Pradesh and Jammu and Kashmir by the year 2005.[35]

People Groups

In the same manner, Indian missions plan to reach the approximately 920 People Groups with populations over 10,000. At present only about 300 of these have any Christian witness and

congregation. The Indian Missions Association in collaboration
with Frontier Mission Centre and Church Growth Association of
India has brought out profiles of the people groups of India, most
of which are unreached.[36] IMA report said 204 People Groups with
over 50,000 population have no known Christian witnesses,[37] and
remain unreached.

Multiple Languages

India has 219 languages with more than 10,000 speakers. The
Bible is available to the people of only 46 of these languages. For 85
languages no scripture portions are available. The *Jesus* film is
available in only 47 languages of India.[38] Let mission planners
consider these facts.

To train Indian missionary translators, Indian Institute of
Cross-cultural Communication, IICCC, began in 1980 as an off-
shoot of IMA. IICCC reports that from 1980 to 1997 it trained 170
students, who have so far translated scripture portions in 34
languages. It has also, following the lead of NLCI[39], surveyed
further languages during the last three years.

Universalist Hinduism

Hinduism is arguably the most syncretistic religion in the
world. It is open to include any philosophy. In this sense it is a
tolerant religion.

However, as a reaction to minority rights, there are continuous
attempts to strengthen the powers of the majority Hindus. RSS has
been in the forefront in this.[40] Intolerant Hindu leaders attempt to
force their power by extremism, fanaticism and dogmatism. While
police watched inactively, fanatical Hindus demonstrated this by
forcefully demolishing the Babri Mosque at Ayodhya in December
1992. Eventually, forty-nine fanatics were charged in cases relating to the demolition of Babri Masjid,[41] but there is cynicism about
whether justice will be carried out.

With continued Hindu fanaticism the *Vishwa Hindu Parishad*, a
militant Hindu movement, drew an ambitious five-year plan to
revive the Ayodhya issue in Utter Pradesh.[42] Plans are afoot to
celebrate the 21st century as *"Hindu Shatabdi"*[43] and the VHP hopes
to construct a Ram Temple in Ayodhya. To further its plans of
Hindu revival, the VHP also launched a *"Jan Jagran"*[44] programme.[45]

Hinduism has many shades. Animistic Hinduism is followed

by the thirty percent of Indians classified as Other Backward Castes (OBC). Many subscribe to Ritualistic Hinduism. Then there is the Bakthi School concentrated on devotion with family deities and personal gods giving a sense of having a personalised relationship, of one to one. It has a shade of monotheism. Then there is philosophical Hinduism propagated by men like Dr. Radhakrishnan.

Of the above categories, we may say the Hindus who have been reached with the Gospel are from Animistic Hinduism, which was only thirty percent of the Indian population, the group attracted to the power encounter. Through power encounters many have submitted to Christ. These were the "winnables". The other seventy percent of the Indian Hindus are yet to be faced and brought to Christ.

Islam

By May twenty-third, 1981, 207 Dalit families, numbering around 1500 persons, embraced Islam at Meenakshipuram at Tamilnadu.[46] India's 140 million Muslims form one of the world's largest and most accessible Muslim communities.

Marginalised Dalits

In the Indian population, twenty percent are Dalits and eight percent belong to other scheduled castes. India has about 250 million Dalits. About seventy percent of the twenty-six million Christians are Dalits.[47] Henry Thiagaraj points out, "The Dalits have a very low literacy in India. For instance the Dalit women have only about eleven percent literacy whereas women from the other communities have about twenty percent literacy."[48]

Dalits were classified as Hindus. Yet many Dalits do not accept their classification as Hindus because of the treatment they encounter from the upper caste Hindus. Sunder Raj, quoting VT Rajashekar the foremost Dalit voice in India, says

KM Munshi made a constitutional fraud on 8 August 1947 and clubbed the entire Scheduled Backward Castes with the Hindus ... According to our Constitution our correct name is Scheduled Backward Castes because we are the Backward castes who were SCHEDULED (which simply means listed) by the President as for the command of Article 341. This is why came the name OTHER Backward Castes (OBC) for those who come under Article 340.[49]

The above situation was confirmed when Mr Ashok Singhal, the President of the Vishwa Hindu Parishad (VHP)[50], opposed the candidature of the Indian Vice-President KR Narayanan for presidency, saying that Narayanan was not a "true representative" of Dalits. According to Singhal,

He (KR Narayanan) has good connections with the Churches. We want the country's highest office to be represented by a person who represents the Hindu Culture. We are not opposing or supporting any one(!) We are merely placing facts before the people.[51]

This demonstrates prejudice against a Dalit and especially a man with some Christian connection. Singhal seemed to state that anyone could become a President of India except the minorities and the Dalits! The news agencies reported that Bal Raj Thackray, the Chief of Shiv Sena[52] also was not in favour of KR Narayanan as the President of India.[53]

The bias is perpetuated in many ways, often with violence. According to one estimate 750 Dalits are murdered each year in the inter-caste violence in India.

Henry Thiagaraj summed up the atrocities against Dalits, "Every hour two Dalits are assaulted. Every day three Dalit women are raped, two Dalits are murdered and two Dalit's houses are burnt in India."[54]

Akhilesh Mithal, in his column, wrote, "Discrimination based upon birth must be erased from the Hindu psyche. The SCs, STs and also women ... have to be nurtured, so that they regain self-respect. What are VHP/BJP/RSS doing about it?"[55]

Tribals

By far the majority of Indian missionaries work among the tribals who make up only eight percent of the population. Some people have criticised this. My own position is to agree with Devasagayam Ponraj, the author of several books on contextualisation and church planting among tribals, who said he was very unhappy with the criticism. He reacted strongly against the idea that people who work among the tribals could be shifted to reach non-tribals.[56] What the missionaries did among the tribals is very significant and they should continue their work, while, for the sake of non-tribals, the strategy should be to recruit and send more workers. It is inappropriate to shift existing workers among tribals. We need to challenge and channel more workers to others.[57]

Other Minorities

Apart from Christians, Dalits, tribals, and OBCs, there are several other minorities in India such as Jains, Parsees, Buddhists and Sikhs. We need to specifically study these minorities and learn how to communicate the gospel to them. We also need to disciple the sizeable number of nominal Christians who live in urban and semi-urban set-ups.

Politicians and Politics

During ten months from September 1996, there were four prime ministers in the nation. Utter Pradesh, with a population that far outstrips all other states, had President's rule long after the 1996 elections, because there was no majority party to form a government. Our politicians are in a rat race for power. "Kanshi Ram, chief of BSP - Bahujan Samaj Party, is interested only in power. Everything else is secondary,"[58] wrote Seema. Kanshi Ram is not un-typical. Each is trying to keep the other happy to maintain a power balance. PC Bhattacharjee, responding to Seema, said Kanshi Ram's political game was played at the cost of peace and harmony among the innocent, and largely illiterate, peace loving people.[59] This is our politicians' game - wheeling and dealing.

SS Bhandari, BJP Vice-President said, "To salvage our (BJP's) position in UP, we have to reduce the 'blue' colour of the administration and insert a shade of saffron (Hindu principles)".[60] The former Prime-Minister Deva Gowda blasted Laloo for making Bihar into the Jungle Raj.[61] To ensure that all would be returned to him when he was cleared of the charges, Laloo dramatically, installed his wife Rabri Devi as the Chief-Minister of Bihar.[62] She came straight from the kitchen to politics.[63]

Such situations create a deep-seated insecurity and instability, an environment that does not help in communicating the Gospel. Surrounded by political turmoil and *bandhs*,[64] Christians find it difficult to plan evangelism or befriend politicians.

Here is an example. Christians promoting the need for Dalit reservations to include Christians, approached Deva Gowda, the then Prime-minister. He was considering the bill to be brought in the Parliament for discussion and action. This would have given poor Dalit Christians reservation like any other Dalits who are economically backward. However, Gowda was forced to resign for political reasons, and the petition of Dalit Christians to be considered for reservation was shelved.[65]

However, politically, India has retained freedom of religion as a secular state with only occasional superficial restrictions.

When the Deva Gowda Government fell, journalist Tavleen Singh questioned, "We should ask Kesari, and the Congress party, if they have any idea of the damage the country's economy has suffered on account of their whims?"[66] She expressed a widely felt sense of setback. Indians wonder if their country is really progressing, or if the politicking is actually harmful?

P. Chidambaram, the then finance Minister, said in frustration, "The main obstacle to reforms is the political parties. The people are ten years ahead of the parties".[67] The general feeling is that the politicians play power games more than helping those who are really in need.

Do we in Missions and churches have any answers for the nation?

Superstitions and Primitive ideas

"A four year old girl, allegedly a victim of black magic, died at Elanthoor, in Kerala. Five people have been taken in to custody. Among those arrested were the child's father and the child's uncle."[68] "Two donkeys tied the knots and were married as a ceremony to appease the rain god as Bijapur did not have rain for a long time."[69] Ms. Renuka Chaudhary an educated Health Minister was dependent upon Mr. Sharma, a *Vaasthu* expert to advise on the direction of seating in her office. He wanted to check out the Prime Minister's office and residence to make doubly sure that Ms. Choudhary's tenure is safe and long.[70] A businessman, Mukherjee, makes money by bottling water from the river Ganga, marked holy water *Gangadhara*. He markets these even to the clients in the Gulf and USA.[71]

These examples show how far the country is steeped in superstitions, from the ordinary person right to the office of the Prime Minister. Such beliefs exist among all religious groups, including some Christians, depending on their people group and how much they have learned of the Bible. Breaking down these illogical habits is hard unless people know Jesus, the will of God and the freedom He brings to lives.

Difficulties of Cross-Cultural Living and Communication

A mission field is defined as any cultural group that does not have an established group of disciples. They will be reached only if someone from outside their culture is willing to sacrifice his own comfortable community to reach them with the Gospel of Christ.[72]

"600 million people (of India), though geographical neighbours to Christian populations, are nonetheless culturally distant and can only be reached by cross-cultural evangelism."[73] "An unreached people group is one within which there is no indigenous community of believing Christians able to evangelise this people group."[74] Edward Dayton defines, "an unreached people group is a group which is less than twenty percent practising Christian."[75] Patrick Johnstone believed that a society should have at least five percent Christians to reach their own people.[76] Some do not specify the percentage, but a viable Church in a society has a capacity to spread the Good News within their own community.[77] In Johnstone's words an unreached people are,

> An ethno-linguistic people among whom there is no viable indigenous community of believing Christians with adequate numbers and resources to evangelise their own people without outside (cross-cultural) assistance.[78]

Ponraj dramatically describes the magnitude of the task of reaching unreached people.

> The most stunning and awesome reality of the need for cross cultural missions is that even if Christianity flexed all its muscle, and shouted the Gospel to all within its sphere, still there would be silence among over two billion people (of the world). Why? Because of cultural distances and barriers[79] between the evangelising force and the people without Christ.[80]

Many communities in India, especially in North India, will never hear the Gospel unless some person enters cross-culturally among them. This is because there is no viable church among them which is able to permeate its own society with the Gospel of Christ. Cross-cultural missionaries have to enter new groups with the message of Christ.

Corruption and Evil

Sin and deterioration have always corrupted the human heart. Some argue that education, freedom, human dignity, equality, economic uplift and dialogue would bring out the best in human minds. They have merely shown its impotency. Here are some newspaper examples. A thirty-four year-old IAS officer, suspended by the DOPT[81], following charges of shoplifting in London a month ago."[82] Union Home Minister Inderjit Gupta sanctioned prosecution of the controversial 'godman' Chandraswamy for not reporting foreign contributions of more than Rupees three crores (Rs. 30,000,000) received by his Vishwa Dharmavtan Trust. He already has a dozen cases of FERA violations against him.[83] The Gowdas beat a Dalit young man to death just for a pot of toddy in Gudipadu, a village in AP. In the Government hospital for a bribe of Rs. 450, the lady doctor agreed to not do a post-mortem. The police also did not register the case easily.[84] Corrupt hearts need to be changed by the Gospel.

Coping with Tension

One must tread carefully through religious, geographical, philosophical and political tensions.

On the eve of Independence on August 15, 1947, Sardar Vallabai Patel impressed on the country, "our first task is to stabilise, consolidate, and strengthen ourselves. The rest (of the tasks) can have only secondary priority."[85] Although the nation has gone forward with many reforms and changes, it has struggled to stabilise. Political tensions and scams continuously rock the nation.

Mahatma Gandhi believed the British presence caused the communal trouble. He repeatedly said, "You will find communal disharmony gone when the British no longer rule us". He was deeply disappointed that his dream did not materialise.[86] Cosmetic rearrangements in the nation have not lessened tensions.

One of the tensions is being an Indian. Some like Vable, like to call all Indians "Hindus", but this has connotations.[87] Is being a Hindu equivalent to being an Indian or only to being a religious Hindu? Muslims, Christians and other minorities feel that a Hindu means a follower of Hinduism. Arya Samajees[88] disagree.

Bagawan[89] Rajneesh had a following of many elite and educated people. He drew many rich Indians and foreigners into his fold and his community in Pune. His death caused much confusion, yet there are still many followers. Eckart Floether, a German disciple and an ex-Sannyasin[90] said,

> People were injured, raped and suffered emotional problems in Rajneesh's encounter groups. He was a spiritual Hitler, a highly developed demonic figure.

His ultimate goal was to create a mindless man because only that man can reach the enlightenment.[91]

Commonly on Indian roads a sacred stone is replaced by a small temple, which is replaced by a sizeable structure. Often people do this to grab public land to establish a private income. At Tiruttani courageous highway personnel, facing stiff resistance and protest from political parties, demolished some structures like this.[92] Is this a form of communalism?

The mass media, knowingly or otherwise, often exacerbate communalism. Reporting is sometimes counter-productive. "One of the saddest changes in the Indian media in the last fifty years is its opening up to communal influences as never before."[93] There are numerous tensions within and between the states. In the North Eastern States the Naga-Kuki violence, drugs and AIDS do great damage. Inter-tribal animosity has strong historic roots.[94]

While the middle-class prospers, the poor are being trampled, and there is a wide disparity between these classes. Tension between the rich and the poor, between the haves and have-nots is enormous and growing.[95]

Vishal Mangalwadi writes,

India's present problems spring not from corrupt politicians, illiteracy, poverty, over population or a bad Constitution, but from the fact that as a nation we chose Secular Humanism instead of the Gospel, and now, having reached the dead end with that route, Post-modern India is opting for pre-modern Hinduism.[96]

The Harvest Force

These are the formidable challenges facing mission in India. Yet mission agencies press forward carrying the message of Christ. Some thought the 1970's moratorium on the entry of foreign missionaries signalled the end of proclamation of the Lord Jesus Christ. On the contrary, God raised up many Indian nationals to communicate Christ with similar or even greater enthusiasm. In the fifty years since Independence dozens of missions have sprung up.

Larry Pate classifies India as first among the top ten Two-Thirds World missionary-sending countries of the world.[97] The following chart of the numerical growth of Indian missionaries reinforces the point.

Indian Missionaries Twenty-five years (1972-1997) of Growth			
Year	Cross-Cultural Missionaries	Domestic or Local Missionaries[98]	Total
1972	543		543
1980	2,208		2,208
1983	3,369		3,369
1988	10,243		10,243
1994	12,000		12,000. [99]
1997	15,000	5,000	20,000. [100]

While pessimism may sometimes trouble the minds of Church and mission leaders, let us instead examine the good things God is doing.

It is reported that the number of Christian workers alone is nearly 50,000 to 60,000. About fifteen to twenty percent of these workers can understand English fairly well. In addition to this there is an increasing involvement of the lay persons who are either supporting or willing to support the cause of the Church in various ways. The population of this kind of committed lay persons may not be less than twice the population of the full time Christian workers. A large segment of these lay people belong to the middle class or upper middle class.[101]

Here we have a very considerable harvest force to evangelise this nation.

Conclusion

Tensions and dissatisfaction thrive in modern India. This is our backdrop. No wonder some Christians despair. This is our challenge—to present the Gospel to the people in India, as it now is, as we approach the turn of the century. Whether churches and missions are up to it or not will only be known in the future.

END NOTES

1 _____ "Letters," *India Today*. September 8, (1997) p. 9.

2 _____ "A Fantasy Called India," From a conversation with Salman Rushdie, quoted from the book *Midnight's Children*. *India Today*, August 18, (1997) 58.

3 Shashak Tripathi, *The Asian Age*. Sept. 27, (1997) 13.

4 Johnstone, *Operation World* (Carlisle: OM Books, 1993), p. 274.

5 [n.a.], *India People Prayer Diary* (Madras: Church Growth Association of India, 1996), pp. 1–62.

6 43,75,97,929 males and 40,63,32,932 females = 437.5 million males and 406.33 million females.

7 _____, Tamil Radio News at 7 AM, September, 12 (1997).

8 Asha Krishnaswamy, "Where we have Gone Wrong". *Deccan Herald*, August 13, (1997) 7.

9 More on women is found in Chapter Seven.

10 Editor, "Child Labour Reduces Productivity, Says Study", *The Indian Express* (Chennai, 1 July 1997), p. 3.

11 Editor, "Rajasthan Government to Conduct Survey", *Legal News and Views* (Vol. 11 No 7, July 1997), pp. 34–35.

12 Editor, "'Bridge Course' for Quarry Children", *The Indian Express* (Chennai, 1 June 1997), p. 5.

13 [n.a.], *Directory of Indian Missions* (Chennai: IMA, January 1996).

14 Shefali Rekhi, "MRTS Troubled Route," *India Today*, October 15, (1996), pp.132–133.

15 [n.a], "India's Neo-karma Generation", Excerpted from an article by Kevin Murphy in the *International Herald Tribune; Manorama Year Book 1995*, (Kottayam: Malayala Manorama, 1995), p. 547.

16 _____ "The Prophets of doom

have been proved wrong" *The Asian Age* August 15, (1997) 3.

17 Misra, *The Indian Middle Classes*, p. 5.

18 Ibid, p. 338.

19 Ibid, p. 6.

20 Graham Houghton, Discussion, SAIACS, October 1997.

21 _____, "Suicide by Top IFS Officer in Srinagar," *The Asian Age*. September 11, (1997) 1.

22 Sachdeva (Ed.)," Newspapers", *Competition 1995*, p. 712.

23 Dailies, tri/biweeklies, and other periodicals.

24 Sachdeva (Ed.), "Education", *Competition 1995*, p. 773.

25 Mrs and Mr Pamela and George Ninan, Centre for Communication Skills, 9, Ashoka Road, Ashville Apts., St. Thomas Town, Bangalore 560084.

26 Pamela Ninan, Writers workshop, Bangalore, March 1997.

27 _____ "Prayer Concerns," *OM Arpana Prayer letter*. August / September (1997).

28 Amrik Singh, "Reading Between Times", *Deccan Herald – Sunday Herald* (July 6, 1997), p. 5.

29 Paul J. Koola, *Population and Manipulation* (Bangalore: Asian Trading Corporation, 1979), p. 104.

30 FEBA, WV, Back to the Bible, FEBC and other Radios.

31 Campus Crusade for Christ with Jesus' film has done much. 90 teams show "Jesus" Movie across the nation. GIFTS with the dubbing and distributions of Christian videos has spread the Christian message. Many evangelistic agencies carried these films and videos and screened them across the nation. Many have mobile teams. Day Spring International, has bought the copy Right of the locally produced Telugu film on Jesus. The actor himself had become the promoter and is sympathetic and believed to have made a commitment to follow Christ. More is being done in the Indian TV with a serial on Saturday morning at 9 a.m. on the life of Christ. OM, GFA and other missions across India have had teams continuously showing movies of Christ. Several thousands of people have made commitment to Christ by watching them.

32 [n.a.], "Prayer Resources Based on Research done by IMA", *Indian Missions* (January–March 1997), p. 24.

33 *Indian Missions* (January–March 1997), p. 24. For further study refer to *Go into all ... series* of books published by India Missions Association.

34 James Kaiser, IMA Ministry Coordinator, reporting on his visit to GEMS in Bihar, Chennai, August 11, 1997.

35 Dr Alex P. Abraham, an unpublished paper. The plan was to come in operation by January 1, 1997.

36 *Indian Missions* (January – March 1997), p. 24.

37 IMA letter to the CEOs of member Missions, November 13, 1997.

38 *Indian Missions* (January–March 1997), p. 24.

39 NLCI – New Life Computers India. This agency in Bangalore trains translators in computers. They single-mindedly pursue and encourage people to get into translation of Scripture in the languages where it is not available.

40 CV Mathew, *Neo - Hinduism: A Missionary Religion* (Madras: CGRC, 1987), pp. 34–35. RSS has helped unite all the major Hindus forces. It is one of the most disciplined forces in India and a major political force. But its hatred, intolerance and aggressive militancy are oppressive and offensive in a secular state.

41 _____ "Advani, Kalyan, 47 others to be charged in Babri Masjid Case," *The Indian Express,* Chennai, p. 1.

42 Amita Verma, "VHP to revive Ayodhya issue", *The Asian Age,* (12 June 1997), p. 2.

43 *Hindu Shatabdi* celebrations – The century of Hindu celebrations.

44 *Jan Jagran*—The awakening of people.

45 Verma, "VHP to revive Ayodhya issue," *The Asian Age,* (12 June 1997), p. 2.

46 Mumtaz Ali Khan, *Mass Conversion of Meenakshipuram* (Madras: CLS, 1983), p. 43.

47 Editor, "Around the World," *Friends Focus* (April 1997), p. 48.

48 1981 statistics. Henry Thiagaraj [the managing Trustee of Dalit Liberation Education Trust and the Convenor of Human Rights Education Movement of India], an open letter dated 9 June 1997, to all concerned after he presented the paper at the UN, Geneva. "Statement of the Dalit Liberation Education Trust in the Working Group on Minorities of the United Nations Human Rights Commission: Geneva," Paper Presented in the UN Working Group on Minorities—Third Session, (26–30 May 1997).

49 Ebenezer Sunder Raj, *Reservation Or Dalit Christians! Why?* (New Delhi: National Committee for SC Christians, November 1995), p. 2.

50 *Vishwa Hindu Parishad*—This means Hindu World Federation. This is a militant Hindu movement.

51 Correspondent, "VHP Opposes Narayanan's Candidature," *The Asian Age* (Bangalore, 22 June 1997), p. 2.

52 Shiv Sena is another militant Hindu Party. Leader Bal Thackray is known for caustic talks offensive to minorities.

53 Correspondent, "VHP Opposes Narayanan's Candidature," *The Asian Age* (Bangalore, 22 June 1997), p. 2.

54 Thiagaraj, "Dalit Liberation Education. Paper to UN Working Group on Minorities, (26 – 30 May 1997), p. 2.

55 Akhilesh Mithal, "How Gandhi Unveiled the Power of Indian Women," *The Asian Age,* October 1 (1997) 24.

56 S. Devasagayam Ponraj, Personal Interview while visiting SAIACS to lecture, Bangalore, October 1996.

57 Ponraj, Interview, SAIACS, Bangalore, October 1996.

58 Seema Mustafa, "The UP drama: Power is the central theme," *The Asian Age*, September 20 (1997) 12.

59 PC Bhattacharjee, "The UP Scene: Power takes Precedence Over Peace," *The Asian Age*, October 1, (1997) 12.

60 Bhandari SS, BJP Vice-President. "Thus Spake ..." *Deccan Herald*. September 28, (1997) 20.

61 Special Correspondent, "Gowda Blasts Laloo for Bihar Jungle Raj", *The Asian Age*. August, 4 (1997) 1.

62 Swapan Das Gupta, Farzand Ahmed, Javed M. Ansari and Sanjay Kumar Jha, "Laloo's Last Laugh," *India Today*, August 4, (1997) 30–36.

63 Farzand Ahmed and Ashok Malik, "Serving Her Lord", *India Today*, August 4, (1997) 31–32.

64 *Bandhs*—Closing down of all shops and institutions called by the opposition parties. When this happens frequently, it affects the morale of the people and causes confusion in industry and loss of revenue due to non-productivity.

65 Sunder Raj, IMA, Interview, Chennai. April, 1997.

66 Tavleen Singh, " There is Nothing Wrong with the Lust for Power," *Indian Express*, April 13, (1997) 8.

67 P. Chidambaram, Finance Minister, "Thus Spake ..." *Deccan Herald*, September 28, (1997) 20.

68 _____ "Girl Dies of Black Magic," *The Asian Age*, August 24, (1997) 3.

69 Veeroo Hosmath, "Donkeys tie the knots to bring rains," *The Asian Age*, September 20, (1997) 1.

70 Special Correspondent, "Renuka's *vaastu* expert makes seat adjustment," *The Asian Age* (June 12, 1997), p. 3.

71 Haima Sukhu, "Holy River's Waters will be Exported," *The Asian Age* (Bangalore June 21, 1997), p. 3.

72 KP Yohannan, *Revolution in World Missions God's Third Wave* (Altamonte Springs, Florida: Creation House, 1986), p. 157.

73 S. Devasagayam Ponraj, "The Relevance of Cross-Cultural Mission In India." [n.a.], *Inheriting God's Perspective* (Bangalore: Mission Frontiers, 1996), p. 62.

74 Wayne Gregory, '"Nations" and "Countries"', [n.a.], *Inheriting God's Perspective* (Bangalore: Mission Frontiers, 1996), p. 58.

75 Dayton, "To Reach Unreached," *Perspectives*, p. 587.

76 Patrick Johnstone, Lectures on the ship M.V. Logos, Papua New Guinea, July—August 1979.

77 Dayton, "Reach the Unreached," *Perspectives*, p. 587.

78 Johnstone, *Operation World*, p. 655.

79 Cultural distances and barriers such as languages, cultures, castes and other.

80 Ponraj, "Cross-Cultural Mission," *God's Perspectives*, p. 64.

81 DOPT—Department of Person-

nel and Training.

82 Editor, "IAS Officer Suspended for Shoplifting", *Legal News and Views* (July 1997), p. 3.

83 _____, "Godman's Friday Turns Foe," *The Asian Age*, September 29 (1997) 13.

84 Maurice and Theresa, "Cold-Blooded Murder of Dalit Youth," *Integral Liberation*, Vol.1 No. 2. June (1997) 105, 106, 111.

85 LC Jain "On Being Fifty and Free be Glad and Make it Good," *Deccan Herald*, Bangalore, August 15, (1997) 8.

86 Editor, "A Society Temporarily gone Mad," *The Hindu*, September 12, (1997) 11.

87 D. Vable, *The Arya Samaj; Hindu without Hinduism*, (Delhi: Vikas Publishing House PVT. Ltd, 1983), pp. x–xi.

88 Dayanand Saraswati founded Arya Samaj around 1870. He opposed the caste system, idolatry and some superstitions. The popularity of Arya Samaj grew mainly because of its social reforms, educational and national as well as social welfare activities. Dayanand met Christian missionaries in 1866 and Keshav Chandra Sen in 1872 and was influenced in his thinking, but did not follow Christ. His thoughts gave birth to Hindu militant groups such as Rastriya Swayam Sevak (men), Sevaki (women) / RSS, Jana Sangh, Vishwa Hindu Parishad / VHP and Bajrang Dal. Arya Samaj started 3 other purification movements. They are (a) Reclaiming and reconverting people converted to Christianity and Islam. (b) Giving sacred thread to untouchables to give them same status as themselves. (c) National education with Sanskrit and Vedic emphasis.
Source:
Vable, *The Arya Samaj*, Introduction pages.
Zachariah, Alayamma. *Modern Religious and Secular Movements* (Bangalore: Theological Book Trust. 1990).
K. Rajendran, "The Challenges of Arya Samaj and Christian Response," SAIACS, Bangalore October 1995. Unpublished paper.

89 Bagawan—god.

90 Sannyasin—a female Sage.

91 Zachariah, *Modern Religions*, p. 96.

92 _____"Unauthorised shops and encroachments removed," The Indian Express, Chennai, August 11, (1997) 4.

93 G. S. Bhargava, "Blue Pencil," *Deccan Herald*, September 28, (1997) 20.

94 _____ "Prayer Concerns," *OM Arpana Prayer letter*, August / September (1997). Quoted from Prayer Fellowship International.

95 Asha Krishnaswamy, "Where we have Gone Wrong," *Deccan Herald*, August 13, (1997) 7.

96 Richard and Vishal Mangalwadi, "A Review Dialogue," *To All Men All Things*, (Erode: Vol. 7 No. 1, April 1997), p. 6.

97 Pate, "Two-Thirds World Missions," Taylor (Ed.),

Missionary Training, p. 32.

98 Ebenezer Sunder Raj, of IMA classifies Indian missionaries as cross-cultural and local missionaries, personal interview, Chennai, 15 June 1997.

99 S.Vasantharaj Albert, *A Portrait of India III* (Madras: Church Growth Association of India. 1995), p. 36.

100 Sunder Raj, Interview, Chennai, 16 June 1997. According to him, this 20,000 include 5,000 missionaries cross-culturally doing E2 and E3 evangelism, working through the churches. This is a low and an approximate figure. All the other missionaries work with missions.

101 Vasantharaj Albert, "Editorial," *India Church Growth Quarterly*, (Vol. 3 No 2, July – September 1996), p. 2.

4

Modern Indian Missions and their Decisions

By 1997 the Indian Missions Association (IMA) had one hundred affiliated missions.[1] Outside of IMA there were scores of other mission agencies including several denominational agencies.[2] Patrick Johnstone quoted 198 mission agencies in India in 1993.[3] Gnanadasan, a Minister of an ECI church listed 300 mission organisations in 1992.[4] The differences may depend on definition.

Before Independence, the indigenous Marthoma Church of Kerala formed Marthoma Evangelistic Association in 1888 and sent Malayalee missionaries out to several parts of India and established Christian Ashrams, through indigenous funds. It was the first evangelistic association initiated by Asians. Then the Indian Missionary Society (IMS)[5], and the National Missionary Society (NMS) were established successively in 1903 and 1905. However, there was little national mission activity apart from these three missions prior to Independence.

Indian Missions Under Way

Independence and the departure of many foreign missionaries forced Indians to consider mission endeavour seriously. They no longer felt dominated by foreign missionaries.[6] This was good, because it forced them to mature when fellow Indians found it difficult to follow Indian leaders.[7]

Initially Indian Christian leaders carried on with some difficulty from foreign missionaries. They struggled and made mistakes, especially in leadership, learning as they went. But in time Indian missions and leaders emerged and forged a healthy partnership with former Western missionaries. Mutual trust grew, as people could see the Lord start to work through new leaders.

New missions blossomed with fresh visions and strategies, each with a distinctive nature depending upon the burden and the areas where it wanted to work. Indigenous mission endeavour and consciousness grew. Sam Lazarus writes positively, "the last two decades, namely the 70's and 80's, have witnessed an unprecedented growth in the area of mission work and cross cultural evangelism resulting in 'mushrooming of Missions'."[8] On the negative side, with a proliferation of new missions, the churches are confused about the genuineness of missions not knowing which to support.[9]

The Indian Church had to grapple and come up with its own answers which worked in its categories. Many denominational churches which had lost their identity had to re-group under a common banner.[10] Ecumenical thinking established a new Church identity. Until Independence, there were only denominational churches established by different missions. Now the Church wanted a single identity. Thus came about the Church of South India and the Church of North India. Their slogan was, "Unity for Witness,"[11] though priority was eventually given to unity rather than witness. Some evangelicals within these felt there was a "witness-less unity," which in time prompted them to strengthen denominational Indian missions such as the Marthoma Mission, IMS and NMS.

Then new denominational missions came into being such as the Nagaland Missionary Movement, the Zoram Evangelical Fellowship, the Presbyterian Synod of Mizoram[12] and others including the forty-five Pentecostal missions.[13] (Most North East Missions do not extend to mainland India.) These denominational missions reported directly to Bishops and Presidents. PT Abraham, an active leader of the Sharon Pentecostal Fellowship says,

> The Pentecostal-Charismatic Mission Agencies emerged largely in the decades of 1970 and 1980. In the decade 1970, twenty-one, and in the decade of 1980 another twenty-four more agencies were started. In 1988 there were 3,661 missionaries working with PCM agencies.[14]

Following this the "non-denominational or "inter-denominational" and "indigenous" "faith" missions grew. They did not report to Bishops but to their leaders and the supporting constituency. Some of the best known of these are FMPB (1962), IEM (1965), CGMM, GEMS (1970). There are many others. They were more independent and moved to the most needy areas.

Non-classical Missions with roots in the West also found a responding chord which enabled them to continue in India – the Union of Evangelical Students of India, Scripture Union, Global Outreach, Youth for Christ, Far East Broadcasting Association, Gospel Recording Association, Operation Mobilisation, India Every Home Crusade, Youth With A Mission, and Every Creature Crusade. These had not identified with the classical Missions and were almost a parallel-force to the traditional Missions. While the traditional Western missionaries were returning to their own countries, some remained here. In these semi-Western and Indian missions, the Western missionaries have had different roles from those played by pre-independence missionaries. They became coaches, teachers, colleagues and facilitators. They ceased to run missions by themselves.

Without the continued partnership of non-traditional missions, it would have been difficult to enlist and develop a force of Indian missionaries. The above missions gave vision and training to the young people who eventually became missionaries with Indian missions.[15] Typical of this is Operation Mobilisation India which has trained nearly 10,000 young people in grassroots evangelism over the past thirty-five years.[16] Most of these moved on to other missions as evangelists, church planters, and mission leaders, and many in secular fields establish themselves as witnesses for Christ. OM leaders feel fulfilled with graduates serving across the nation in Missions and in other capacities.[17]

Every Creature Crusade – ECC has forty mission teams of church planters across India. Much like OM, they developed evangelism strategies on the job. Houghton describes these teams as an open air seminary for three years, in the way the Lord Jesus ministered with His disciples.[18]

South Asian Campus Crusade for Christ (CCC) has nearly one hundred teams across the nation continuously projecting the *Jesus* film.[19] Day Spring International extensively uses a *Jesus* film produced by an Indian secular film producer.[20]

Som Thomas is a computer software engineer with TATA. Ravi Antine is a post graduate lecturer in an engineering college. In Bangalore both acknowledge, like thousands of others, that UESI greatly influenced their lives and they are still steadily linked with the local UESI. Both Som and Ravi felt that God has used them as witnesses in their field of work.[21] Indeed, the non-traditional missions have been a great influence in the lives of the people.

All the above categories in missions encouraged growth in Indian leadership for missions. Amidst trial and error significant evangelism has been and is achieved.

The AD 2000 and Beyond Movement highlighted the following as the achievements in North India in the last twenty-five years.

The Indian Evangelical Team has planted 700 congregations, The Indian Evangelical Mission over 400

congregations, Friends Missionary Prayer Band 400,
The Evangelical Church of India 400, Bible Centred
Ministries 312 congregations and 1500 preaching
centres, The Rajasthan Bible Institute more than 600
churches and prayer groups, Gospel for Asia 750
churches, Philadelphia Fellowship Churches 550
congregations, Vishwa Vani eighty churches ... . In
Bihar ... Maltos and Santhalis have experienced 34,000
baptisms in the last ten years, worshipping in 375
churches ... . In the last four to five years more than
6,000 Santhalis have been baptised and gathered in 116
worshipping groups.[22]

The New Life Churches established by Pastor Joseph in the
early 1980s in Bombay reported phenomenal growth. Since the
ministry started 2200 churches have been planted,[23] 3000 cell
groups have come into being and 2500 missionaries have been sent
to minister in different cities.[24] As a result of a blitz, door-to-door
programme called Love Bombay in 1992, 1,700 New Life churches
came into being in the past five years. Forty percent of the converts
are from the slums and sixty percent of believers are from the
middle and upper middle classes of society in Bombay city. With
five thousand New Life Churches in India, it is considered the
tenth largest denomination in the world.[25]

Missions grew and had a ripple effect in passing the vision.
When the FMPB missionaries were in the Dang district of Gujarat,
the churches in that area were moved to form the Gujarat Missionary movement in 1984. The Methodist Conference acknowledged
that FMPB had inspired their missionary movement in 1982.[26]

Fifty years ago according to Earl Cressy, the traditional understanding of the mission was to correspond with the three cultural
levels of the populations, namely the primitives, the peasant
villagers, and those on the urban level who are the carriers of the
four great non-Christian cultures,[27] Hinduism, Buddhism, Confu-
cianism and Islam, which needed distinctive mission strategy.[28]
This clearly defined the kind of mindset and the thinking in
missions till the mid-Twentieth century. As the missionaries
started penetrating to the heartland of people and religions, they
found that there were even more distinctive features among the
people they served. Then came the recognition of divisions of
people groups, language groups and ethnic groups. It also dawned
on the missionaries and the mission strategists that each group had

needed distinct strategies, bridges, tools, approaches and specifically trained workers. As this awareness dawned, trainers slowly
adapted in institutions and missions. Although there was general
theological training, few received on-the-job training to cope with
the special divisions of people to whom the Gospel was carried.

Despite the above information, Indian missions made little use
of statistics for decisions about their direction and priorities.

With inadequate research in the past fifty years in the National
FORUM of Evangelism and Missions,[29] there was no authenticated
data with which to plan future directions for missionaries. They
needed national answers on:

+ The number of church congregations;
+ The number of, and the effect on the people who listened to the
  Christian radio programmes;
+ The quantity and the influence of literature distributed;
+ The number of colleges which have Christian witness;
+ The number of mission workers with agencies and with
  Churches;
+ The number of local and cross-cultural workers across the
  nation by districts;
+ The number of workers among the Muslims, poor, villages and
  other particular groups;
+ The number of non-Christians doing Bible correspondence
  courses;
+ The number of people who have access to the whole or portions
  of the Bible;[30]
+ The status of the churches mobilised toward evangelism;
+ The number of people groups, colonies and villages covered by
  prayer;
+ The number of Indian missionaries sent overseas;
+ The number and style of partnerships between missions and
  churches;
+ The number of Tent-makers;
+ The status of ministry among the children and the youth; and,
+ The number of youths and others mobilised in evangelism.[31]

As a result of the dialogue between the National Forum for
Evangelism and Missions, the National Christian Council (NCCI)
and the evangelical mission bodies held a Joint Mission Consultation at Bangalore from twentieth to twenty-second of January,
1998. Here the mainline churches agreed to consider supporting
the member missions of IMA as they had difficulty identifying

with the mushrooming missions looking for funds and personnel from the main-line churches. This achievement is a milestone in the history of missions with evangelicals and ecumenicals joining hands to think mission corporately.[32]

Present Directions and Trends

In Missions there was at times ambiguity in terms, meanings, philosophy, personality, direction and focus. We need clarity and definition for Missions to go forward.

Ambiguity: Concepts and Missionary Actions.

Roberta Winter noted a classic example of how confusion in theology kept Christians from being involved in evangelism. A little after three hundred AD., Emperor Constantine converted to Christianity and liberated the Christians from persecution. But

The believers discovered a new problem. They found that they differed in theology and sought to clarify what was correct. Their argumentation replaced evangelisation, so no one was sent to tribal peoples beyond their borders, except for the heretics who were driven out of the Empire.[33]

The theology and the Biblical basis of mission determine the direction of mission work. Apart from the spiritual opposition from the evil unseen powers[34], differences over interpreting terms and meanings have caused havoc in Missions.

To understand the disagreements Peter E. Gillquist used an unusual fiction about the beginning of the world's first two denominations.

Two blind men healed of Jesus were sharing notes. One said that he was sitting on the road to Jericho and shouted to Jesus to heal him. Jesus came to him and healed him. But the other started arguing that it was not possible to have happened that way because Jesus needed mud to heal the blind. In his case, Jesus first spat in His hands and took some mud mixed it and applied it on the blind man's eyes and then he asked him to go to a pool and wash the mud. So folks, this is how these world's first two denominations started. The "Mudites" and the "Anti-Mudites".[35]

Similar to the story of "Mudites" and "Anti-Mudites" there came many misunderstandings which caused unnecessary divisions among Christians. Divisions arose on methods of work, the people to be reached, the initiatives and areas for new work,[36] accountability structure,[37] the direction,[38] the church government, the strategy, the cooperation and the understanding of the basis of mission. These caused much confusion.

There were confusions about evangelism, evangelisation and mission.[39] David Samuel who attended a seminar on Nation Building by the Christians at Bangalore said that there was much confusion on deciding the meaning of "Nation".[40] Kingsley Arunothaya Kumar and R. Billy shockingly pointed out that the great Basel Mission of Switzerland has recently decided to stop preaching the Gospel of repentance, but to tell a Muslim to be a good Muslim.[41] According to CT Kurian who was a Professor of Economics at Madras Christian College, mission meant initiating (social) changes in society at various levels.[42] "The concept of humanisation as the goal of mission has also influenced many Indian church leaders."[43] PM Thomas, the CEO of KEF writes of confusion in the terms "Church" and "Missions".

It is unfortunate that the term "Church" is used for only a few old denominations. When the ministry starts in a virgin area it is a mission; but when there are two converts it is a church because that is the quorum Jesus taught. Almost all "Churches" or denominations had a small beginning as a Mission. I suppose here the "Church" means, "big (mainline) church" and "Mission" means small church. Or else, if the church is a missionary church they can be called "big mission" or call it "small mission." And if the Mission has lost it's missionary vision, the terms "Dead mission" or "Dead church" can be used.[44]

Gopal Hembrom, a missionary and a church planter at Patna, Bihar said, a missionary is "a sent" person to do a particular job for someone else. This meant that if a sending body wanted something, the missionary had to fulfil the wishes of his sending body to whom he was financially responsible. Thus the sending body kept a hold on the missionary.[45]

In North America, when the Laymen's Missionary Movement was active in the 1850's, they were unwilling to generalise "missions" to include home missions. This led to conflict and non-involvement of some denominations.[46] This was perhaps why Ralph Winter described different mission activities in different terms so as to avoid confusion. He called 'cross-cultural mission to a people or area where there was no viable church', "frontier mission". But if a missionary went cross-culturally to serve an existing church, he was called a "regular missionary." There were also other terms such as E1, E2, and E3 evangelisms, denoting types of mission work.[47]

Much was discussed on holistic mission and holistic evangelism. Mission and evangelism were considered different. Wagner said there were many terms for evangelism such as M1, M2, and M3[48] which were the same as E1, E2, and E3[49]. These were connected to sending missionaries from culture to culture as in Jerusalem, Judea, Samaria and the uttermost parts of the world.[50] N1, N2, and N3[51] representing the Christian nurture. S1, S2, and S3[52] representing Christian service. Service was neither evangelism nor nurture. It focused on the cultural mandate which is "looking after God's creation". Service does not save sinners, but evangelism does.[53] George Verwer mentioned that the term missionary was at times defined in completely different ways.[54]

Philosophical confusion reflected adversely on Missions. There were differences in focus and strategy. Evangelism and church planting were done in different ways that drove missions apart, depending upon the leaders' and the followers' preferences. Confusion caused unnecessary criticisms. Patrick Joshua said in a conference, "An organisation should have an evangelical element. It should have a 'soul' which is ethos and values. It should cope with ethnic identity. Systems and structure are only the secondary issues."[55]

To tackle this confusion of terms, OM put out a booklet, *OM's Book of Standard Definitions*,[56] defining words and concepts regularly used. Often words and concepts have different meanings to a listener depending upon their experience and background. We need a standard mission vocabulary for Christians and theologians to use.

Personality conflicts in missions come about because of individual temperaments, spiritual views, ethos, upbringing, vision and drive. Eventually, the strongest leader emerges as the authority figure and sets directions for the mission. A powerful leader leads his people in the direction where *he* wants to go. A powerful personality might have either the spiritual authority or money power or even muscle power.

When the power is misused, it could spiritually have adverse effects on the mission. This has become a power game in many missions, where the leader governs his team through power of personality, rejects criticisms and uses manipulative politics. Vision, direction and focus become hazy. This at times breeds insecurity, counter attacks, politicking, fractured groups, mistrust and selfishness. Efforts at partnership are hindered because solvable issues are often left unsolved. Some situations still lack clarity.

Analysis of Mission Thrust

In 1995, eighty-six member missions of India Missions Association had nearly 12,000 missionaries across India. The table on the following page indicates their main emphases.[57]

Quite obviously the vision and ethos of missions varies enormously. Evangelism was stressed by fifty-five agencies. Church planting by fifty-four; Social and community development work by fifty-five agencies. Evangelism and social concerns are clearly important throughout the missions of IMA. Interestingly, Joshi Jayaprakash in his survey of missions in 1987, said that 57.17 percent of the missionaries were involved in church planting and only 7.17 percent were doing development work. 1.25 percent were in translation work and 11.49 percent in other ministries! 20.99 percent were not clear on what they were doing.[59] Now, after ten years, approximately fifty percent of the missionaries are in evangelism and church planting and almost the same percentage in social concerns. The reasons are not clear, but it could be the influence of Liberation Theology and also a concern to help the poor and the needy.

For many of these missions, social concerns are as crucial as preaching the Gospel. Most social missions saw their work not just as camouflage to survive in society, but as a demonstration of Christian love and concern for the people. At times they get carried away with social concerns and neglect the spiritual uplift of a community, losing the focus of bringing people to Christ and adding them to the Church.

Some missions appeared to lose direction, missing the larger spiritual challenge due to special sentiment for the poor and the tribals, focusing on micro issues, the control of finances and strategies by external (foreign) persons or boards, lack of planning and a lack of directive leadership to work and workers.

Main Emphases of Indian Missions[58]		
Emphasis	Evangelism Oriented Missions	Social ministry Oriented Missions
Evangelism	55	
Church Planting		54
Social & Community Development work		34
Orphanages and Children Homes		21
Missionary Training	21	
School and Education		17
Christian Literature Distribution		16
Seekers Rally & Follow-up	13	
Medical Work		12
Tribal Evangelism	11	
Bible Schools & Colleges	11	
Youth & Student Work	7	
Film Ministry	7	
Rehabilitation & Counselling		7
Adult Literacy		7
Bible Translation	6	
Child Evangelism	5	
Christian Book Publishing	4	
Slum Work	4	4
Audio/Video	4	
Evangelism to Muslims	3	
Vocational Training		3
Research and Information	3	
Radio	3	
Prayer Network	3	
Revival	3	
Evangelism to the Handicapped	3	
Mission Consultations	2	
Tent Makers	1	
Sponsoring Missionaries	1	
Women's Work	1(Specified)	Unspecified
Prison Camps	1	
Medical Fellowship	1	
Gospel in Discs	1	
Leprosy eradication	1	
Total	175	175

Neglect of the Muslim Population.

At the same time as the high emphasis on Tribals, Muslims are neglected. Judged by the size of the Muslim population in India, at least fourteen percent of the missionary force should be working among the 140 million Muslims. In actuality a very negligible number of people work among them and no great attempts have been made to strengthen this force.

Among the nearly one hundred member missions of IMA, only two agencies have had anything exclusively to do with Muslims. Two or three agencies have not specified their actual focus of work among the Muslims, but have teams working among them.[60] Kashmir Evangelical Fellowship (KEF), Youth With A Mission (YWAM), Indian Evangelical Missions (IEM), Friends Missionary Prayer Band (FMPB), India Every Home Crusade (IEHC), Fellowship for Neighbours India (FFNI), Al Bashir, Bishara, Operation Mobilisation (OM) and a few others were attempting to reach out to these people.[61]

Apart from IMA associated agencies, three or four groups work especially among Muslims. Their work is sparse and totally on their own with very little guidance and accountability. Their reason, they report, is that the mainstream missions and churches did not understand work among the Muslims nor were they burdened to work among them.[62] There were other mission agencies working generally among the Muslims but with very little effect, concentration or results in terms of people coming to Christ.

Many agencies and churches did not even recognise the different sectors of Muslim society, which has many divisions, especially *Shia* and *Sunni*. *Shia* teaching, with many spiritual leaders, is popular, mixed with all kinds of beliefs and is syncretistic in nature. *Sunnis* have no spiritual leader except Muhammad himself.[63] The number of divisions in Islam is mind boggling even in one city.

> Bombay's Muslims form a complex mosaic. One and a
> half million people are divided into several groups
> based on a variety of factors, such as religious sect,
> region of origin, migration, socio-economic status and
> occupation.[64] ... Taxonomy of Bombay Muslims.[65]

Planning one general strategy to help these groups to know Christ will not yield results. Mission agencies said Muslims were too hard to reach and were not responsive to the Gospel. This attitude bypasses the Muslims to "win the winnables."

A Christian worker in a major agency said that he has never had a Muslim friend and did not even know what they believed and how to approach them. He felt that Muslims were hard to talk to about Christ. Similarly a woman, a second generation Christian and a worker in a major Christian ministry, has had no Muslim friends. Her only contact was when a Muslim in a shop commented to her that Christians and Muslims worship the same God. She agreed but was not able to carry on talking about any other issues as she was not knowledgeable and comfortable to discuss anything, because the shop keepers were Muslims. She felt lost. Like these two, many Christians, and even Christian workers, have no social contacts with Muslims and are unable to share Christ (*Isa*). They say it is too hard and so have not tried. If Christians continue this way, Muslims will remain unreached.

According to Abubakker of FFNI, there is much common ground between Muslims and Christians. The Muslims are culturally distinct people and not closed to the Gospel. They are closer to Christians in terms of some teachings and also by the experience of being a minority group. He feels Christians could very easily befriend them and share their faith. Abubakker is willing to help Missions by conducting seminars to equip Christians to share Christ to Muslims. In the midst of his own outreach, his goal is to connect and bridge missionary-thinking that will make it possible for them to reach Muslims.[66]

One popular mission almost lost confidence in other missions and churches. It bypassed the churches and did what it felt was right. This mission recruited its own people and trained them to reach Muslims as contextually as possible. They have more success in winning Muslims to Christ than others. People come to Christ in small numbers and grow in the faith. They hold worship services similar to the new believers' previous background.

It is hard to bring together those who work among Muslims to plan strategies because of their allegiance to donors, the fear of exposing the donors to others, minor differences in the ethos of their approach and also personality struggles. Attempts to bring FFNI and OM and Al Bashir together have not worked, as there were differences in approach and trust. It needs someone with a common bond and vision to bridge the different approaches.

Muslim evangelism needs creative approaches. PV Kurian and the teams in North India have adopted a very contextualised method which has borne fruit. Kurian says there are many challenges, such as finding workers willing for such a specialised ministry that takes time and effort and does not have the glories of hundreds of people coming to Christ.[67] As part of the creative effort to reach the Muslims, a new English New Testament is being published for Muslim readership.

Missionaries are nearing completion of an English-language New Testament for Muslims. The volume uses familiar names such as Ibrahim for Abraham and Yakub for Jacob. It will have a culturally appropriate cover and illustrations. An estimated five to twenty-five percent of Muslims worldwide speak English.[68]

Similar attempts have been made in Urdu and Hindi and other languages, but this is one of the first attempts to make an English Bible to fill the need.

Abubakker suggested the following to reach Muslims: Influence pastors and key leaders in the Church; organise seminars to bring an awareness of Muslims as unreached people; use Christmas and other celebrations as a means to entry and reaching out to them.[69]

When Muslims come to Christ, they should not be forced to come to church if they are not comfortable, at least for a time. Their names should not be changed. They should be accepted even if they are not baptised and should even be allowed to worship Christ five times in the mosques according to their custom, to start with. Eventually, they have to be strengthened in their faith and other Christians have to stand with them in the times of need as they slowly proclaim their faith in Christ. Muslims come into individualistic Christian communities from a close-knit community. Thus it takes time for Muslims to understand Christianity and vis-à-vis. It is strongly advised that neither Mohammed nor Muslim customs should be criticised even when they become the sympathizers of the Gospel. Those who try to penetrate this community should give up eating pork.[70]

Few missions have set their minds on reaching Muslims with the Gospel, nor are they aware of others who are working among them. Because they have not worked among the Muslims, they did not encourage workers like Abubakker, PV Kurian, Edison Christian (Al Bashir) and others. The need is not only to reach the Muslims with the Gospel, but also to acknowledge the workers, encourage, train, stand with them and send more Christian workers to reach out into the neighbourhood of Muslims with the Gospel. Because churches and missions are indifferent to Muslims, workers among Muslims feel let down by not having the support of the churches and missions. They easily feel demoralised. However, a few carry on working. Abubakker says that when he arranged seminars to train workers for Muslims, no mission groups were interested in sending any workers. He believes that at least in Bible seminaries the teaching of comparative religions should aim at penetration of the Muslim community with the Gospel and at the leading of at least one or two Muslims to Christ.[71]

Wherever the fault lies, the right direction has not been yet set to reach out to Muslims.

Neglect of City Middle and Upper Middle Class People

To quote Jayaprakash, "The tribals should be won to Christ. The rural populations are vast and require multiplied evangelistic efforts. But we dare not neglect the cities with their complexities and challenging needs."[72] We need to examine the following issues.

Firstly, the quality of people who would work among them. They cannot be novices who just have a BD from a seminary and no experience. The task needs men and women who can intelligently and clearly communicate the Gospel to the well-educated and gifted Middle Class. They must be trained well, people of good self-image, confident, well-educated with a good understanding of the society they have to penetrate.

Secondly, their pay scales must be revised and not always kept on a par with tribal workers. Even a well-known Christian leader thought that Rs. 3000 was enough for an educated single person and Rs. 5000 for a couple. On this it would be impossible to live and maintain a middle-class lifestyle. "(The missionary) needs to identify with the people among whom he works. This may affect the lifestyle of the missionary ... . Too much suffering will affect his performance and result in frustration."[73] Roy T. Daniel who researched the subject said, "Today the necessary lifestyle would cost Rs. 4000 to 6000 in large cities, and Rs. 6,000 to 10,000 in cosmopolitan cities and commercial townships."[74] This should be apart from house rent.

Should the missionaries only identify with the lowest level of society? Som Thomas, a computer software engineer, committed to

Christ and active in his local church and in UESI, claimed he
honestly could not survive on the salary paid for the missionaries.
Both he and his wife have to work to survive in a city.[75] In other
words, he would not survive as a missionary to middle class and
upper middle class people.

It is not enough for the missionary to meet middle class people.
Middle class people have to feel comfortable when visiting the
missionary and allow their children to play with the children of
the missionary without looking down on them. For the sake of
both the children and the outreach, we must be realistic about
urban missionary salaries, unless we want mission work to continue to be synonymous only with tribal work.

Some argue that, since some donors to mission live in the same
monthly income as the lowest paid missionaries, missions should
not pay more salary than a donor's salary.[76] This is not a logical
argument. Circumstances in the cities are very different. One
mission leader argued that the middle-class churches in the cities
should be reaching out to the middle class.[77] But this is not happening. Most outreach by middle class city church members is to
slums and to nominal Christians. Very few churches in the cities
target the business class, the executives and the middle class
"Yuppy" Indians except in minimal numbers by groups like the
New Life Fellowship in Bombay. As long as this mindset exists,
middle class Indians will remain unchallenged. "The challenge is
immense, and can no longer be ignored."[78] Many town churches
are too preoccupied with the struggle for survival to reach out to
the middle class.

Neglect of the Handicapped

Let's look first at the blind.
According to 1981 census, there were nine million
visually handicapped people in India. Every seventh
Indian was a blind person. "A person is blind, if his
visual acuity is 20/200". It simply means that what he
sees with difficulty at distance of twenty feet can be seen
clearly from a distance of 200 feet by the normal eyes.[79]
Alfred George, the Director of the Christian Foundation for the
Blind is perhaps the only blind person to have got a Bachelor of
Theology degree from the Serampore College. Christian Foundation for the Blind produces literature for the blind and work
among the blind women. They get a forty percent subsidy from the

government and the rest through donations. They also use Braille literature printed by Scripture Gift Mission (SGM). There are other initiatives, but too little is done for the handicapped.

Chinnasamy Sekar, the Director of Living Light limited himself to work among people with all handicaps, feeling with his wife that God wanted them to serve these people. They have led many to Christ. Sekar reasons that there are very few churches in Bangalore which receive and accommodate handicapped people. He runs a hostel for the blind and personally looks after them and feeds them for a small cost. He feels that running a hostel and feeding the blind keeps him close to reality, avoiding theory. He contacts Government and Christian agencies to help them and find jobs for them. He often conducts seminars to which he invites other Christians and government dignitaries to highlight the plight of the handicapped. One of the men he serves is totally bedridden and is moved around in a push cart by others. He believes that for the handicapped starting automatic laundry and other cottage industries could help them to be rehabilitated. His depth of feeling has brought many handicapped people to his church. He asks churches to do more for the handicapped, and help them be in the main regular churches as normal members.[80]

Prabhu Rayan, the Director of India Fellowship for Visually Handicapped (IFVH) feels that two main hindrances for this ministry are the ignorance and attitude of Christians. He suggested that in the future every church and mission could plan to work among the Blind and also integrate them into church life.[81]

Sue Stillman, from the *Nambikkai* Foundation, working among the deaf said that it took a lot of patience, perseverance, love and encouragement to reach out to the deaf. To communicate the Gospel all types of tools and methods have to be employed. It would be better to train Christians who are deaf themselves so they can share Christ with others. She says the deaf have a very low self-image.[82] Sekar said this is true of most handicapped people and so he spends much time counselling and encouraging them.[83] A special effort must be attempted to work among the handicapped.

The Tribal Emphasis

The concentration of Christian work among the tribals is very high. According to Vasantharaj Albert,

Most of the Church planting efforts – nearly eighty

percent – of the indigenous missions is directed to the tribals who constitute only eight percent of the Indian population. The need is to direct more resources to the evangelisation of the caste groups.[84]

The ethos of many missions is, "win the winnable" while we can.[85] This might have been a good ethos and positive in the sense that while the people are responsive, mission has to be accomplished. According to McGavran, people groups were receptive only at a certain period of their history. It is important to identify those times and then sow the seed of the Gospel.[86] But missions in India have neglected other people by just concentrating their work among the tribals.

> The growth of Christian population has slowed down in the last fifteen years... (Growth) is mostly among the tribal population, ... (where) we may be keeping fifty missionaries when only five are needed,... The growth of Christians among the scheduled castes has slowed down ... in some places stopped.[87]

Ponraj was unhappy when people suggested we should now ignore tribals and divert missionaries to other work. He was in favour of missions meeting the needs of other people, but not at the cost of decreasing the effort to win the reachable tribal.[88]

Dr. Devadason, the field Director of FMPB said work among Muslims and others is good but let the missions focus on winning the eight percent of the tribals which will catapult the percentage in favour of the Christians in the Indian population. Once that is done the percentage of Christians would be more than the present minority of India and would have a voice in the nation.[89] A similar view is held by many Indian Christian leaders who send their workers among the tribals.[90] Graham Houghton wondered if this was a sound argument.[91]

Joseph D'Souza of OM India said that this emphasis of reaching the tribals will not change in the coming decades as the direction is already been set by many of the Indian missions. The goal of major missions like FMPB, IEM and others is tribal-oriented. At this juncture to change direction would be hard even if some of them want to change.[92]

This is not a new revelation. This was pronounced ten years back by Jayaprakash. He said, "The missionary task is to bring all peoples to faith and obedience. Christian missionary work in India is in danger of becoming synonymous with tribal work."[93] However, in the last ten years not many seem to have taken notice of this comment. If they have, there could have been a change of direction and today the missions' strategy would be to reach more than the tribals in this nation. Nevertheless, the major drive in Indian missions is to the tribals. Roger Hedlund rightly observed that, "Tribal communities—the primary target of the Indian missionary effort—are regarded as 'uncivilised', while India's majority population is largely ignored by the Indian Mission Agencies."[94]

This is a matter of will to change. When a mission leader felt that the tribals were the ones to be reached then they drove their mission in that direction, even to the point of neglecting others. Changing would take energy, manpower, drive, leadership, a will to change, and explanation to the missionary and the supporting constituency. D'Souza is perhaps right. Nothing much will change in the next decade![95]

Ramanathan, a BD graduate from UBS, who for a while headed the IMA Research department, said another reason for the tribal thrust is that many missionaries are more equipped to reach the tribals and the poor in the slums than meeting middle class city people or any other castes in India. Very few missionaries could function meaningfully in eye-to-eye interaction with the urban elite and the intellectual middle class.[96]

DB Hrudaya, the Director of Orissa Follow-up Ministries confirmed the above view in a report on OFM's 100 missionaries concentrated work among ten people groups of Orissa. Out of his work among ten people groups nine of them are tribals. When asked why he concentrated work among these tribal groups, Hrudaya answered that his workers came from these same tribes, they were receptive and it was not expensive to work among these peoples. These three reasons led Orissa Follow-up to work among these ten groups. In fact in Orissa only twenty-four percent of the people are in the category of Scheduled Castes (SC) and Scheduled Tribes (ST). The rest of the seventy-six percent were not ST and SC people. Because the workers were not from these seventy-six percent peoples of Orissa, and because it was cheaper to work among the tribals, the mission chose to work among them. Of course, the people were responsive.[97] This is just one example of how missions work among the people groups. Most missions follow a similar reasoning.

It is also mentally easier to work among the tribals than to

work among the educated, to whom the Gospel has to be explained intellectually as well as just presenting it as a faith. The
tribals appreciate the presence of the missionaries, as they are
uplifted in their lives through the endeavours of the missionaries.
With spiritual enlightenment comes renaissance and often social
change.

Missionaries are also more challenged to go to the tribals as
they feel concern for their hopelessness, oppression and poverty.
They feel a sense of service to God, since bringing justice to the
poor and the tribals brings social uplift to their lives. But by only
reaching the tribals with the Gospel, do Christians punish the rich
and the privileged for being the oppressors?

To bring change in the all-consuming outreach to tribals and
also to sensitize Christians to other people, it is better that street
children be adopted and cared for rather than orphanages be
established only for tribal children.[98]

Homogenous Unit Principle (HUP) focus

Rev. G. Raja Bahadur voices the HUP principle.
We in the Evangelical Church in India (ECI) take
seriously the missiological advice of Dr. Donald
McGavran, the father of Church growth movement,
win the winnable when they are responsive. ECI
churches are hotly harvest conscious. We attend as
quickly as possible to any Macedonian call either from
a far off place or from a close quarter. We lose no time
(in reaching them) ... ECI always goes to the poor and
our slum churches will bear testimony to this. As our
Bishop (Ezra Sargunam) says to his ECI pastors, 'we
will continue to go to the poor till we make every one
of them rich in Christ' [99]
Vasantharaj explains the need for goals:
Long term ministry was surprisingly absent. The Church
suffers from the lack of visions regarding reaching the
people groups. Mission agencies may have vision for
many worthy things. But it is very common to see the
evangelistic agencies active in their ministries without
goals to reach specific people groups.[100]
Ponraj points out the following advantages of working
through people group movements. They become strong and stable.
When they become Christians, they are not socially dislocated.

This produces indigenous churches. It helps them to overcome social resistance to the Gospel because when a significant number of people came to Christ there is less opposition and persecution. Their own homogenous fellowship sustains them. It helps them to grow rapidly.[101] FMPB reported that out of 75,000 Maltos in Bihar about half of them came to Christ in a short span of time.[102]

To encourage a people movement Ponraj suggested that one must believe that it comes from God. One must survey to determine the responsiveness of the people, encourage group decisions, baptising families rather than individuals, plan nurture programmes before and after baptism to help them in life-long discipleship. Bringing people to Christ with little social and cultural dislocation helps them to become a mission-minded church from day one.[103]

Evangelism along people group lines appears to be the New Testament model. But one may also oppose it for dividing people on caste and culture lines and perpetuating *Varnashrama Dharma*, the elitist Hindu idea of caste. People also tend to stick together as castes even after they become Christians for several generations, which is, of course inconsistent with the picture of the Church as one body, brothers and sisters in Christ.

Peter Wagner took a middle road saying,

The Homogeneous Unit Principle, though it is a penultimate not an ultimate, characteristic of the kingdom of God, does provide a useful tool not only for the effective implementation of the evangelistic mandate, but also for helping people of differing human groups to live together in greater love and harmony.[104]

This HUP concept is still argued vehemently in Churches and missions with points for and against it. Churches still divide by castes, especially in the South. Even the Brethren and Pentecostal denominations, while giving lip service to oneness in Christ, are widely divided in the Church, both in Kerala and in Tamil Nadu. The test comes if, when Holy Communion is served in the same cup, people find it difficult to accept. Another far-reaching test comes in arranging marriages. Watch the reaction if Pulayans or their children aim to marry people of so-called high caste. Caste and shades of colour are still shamefully and dishonourably practised, and marriage partners chosen as though buying the best cattle in the world.

Let each person examine himself or herself before God, and get on with winning people to Christ in whichever way is comfortable for that person. A method that works in one place might not work in another situation.

Church Growth Research Centre, in spite of resistance from some missions, endeavours to get missions to focus on winning people group by group, as some groups do feel comfortable that way. Vasantha Raj, the Director of CGRC trains people for planting Churches by people groups.

Locating People by Geographic, Ethnic and Linguistic Groups.

IMA identifies and presents its research in these categories, encouraging missions to choose where to work. IMA lists least-reached language groups, ethnic groups and geographical—PIN Code—groups, compiling the research in books. An IMA letter to mission leaders, refering to 204 people groups each with over 50,000 population, read,

> If you send your missionaries/evangelists to work among one of these TOTALLY UNREACHED people groups, IMA will be able to assist with Rs. 1000–3000 per month for a single person and more for a couple. If you send a missionary/evangelist to a TOTALLY UNREACHED PIN code area, IMA may be able to assist with Rs. 1000 per month. IMA will give information and guidance as to where to go.[105]

Mission leaders should consider a right approach for the right reasons, instead of working only among people where the results are sensational and get most attention.

Using PIN Code is a flexible innovation targeting a geographically limited area. Although, pioneering Protestant missionaries operated by religion and geography, breaking to PIN Code is a mixture between reaching people by ethnic people groups (HUP), and by religious groupings. The PIN Code helps missions to identify at least the physical proximity of churches and thus the reached and unreached areas. The PIN Code approach can be used also by some mission agencies that are philosophically opposed to reaching people by ethnic people groups (i.e. the HUP approach). Whatever the means, peoples *have* to be reached.

Conclusion

God has raised up many missions through which a host of missionaries have been sent forth but much more remains yet to be done.

We need sharper analysis to avoid confusion, training in Bible seminaries, in mission stations, among missionaries and in local churches. We need pastors trained to help congregations to understand missions.

Missions must pause and consider strategy before action, planning anew to avoid outdated methods. In the light of the new information available, the heads of the missions have to decide on their direction while appreciating other missions, complementing each other both in tools and approaches. To reach people with Christ adequately, we should use all methods to target people—PIN Code, language and people group—each mission using a method with which it is comfortable.

Clearly our missions have neglected Muslim communities. Even though the Muslims are more open in India than in any other country in the world, missions have dragged their feet, failing to grasp the opportunity to work among them.

Clearly also, missions are reluctant to divert attention from reaching tribals. Let us recruit fresh well-trained men and women to answer the challenges of presenting Christ and changing lives.

We have also neglected the urban middle class and must make conscious efforts in recruiting, training, and resourcing the right people to remedy this situation. Missions have hardly made a dent for Christ in the cities.

In all these areas we have much to learn and do.

END NOTES

1 IMA, Chennai, July 1997.
2 L. Joshi Jayaprakash, *Evaluation of Indigenous Missions in India (Madras: CGRC, 1987), pp. 22–68.*
3 Johnstone, *Operation World*, p. 276.
4 A. Gnanadasan, *Mission Mandate*, pp. 461–492. This list is quoted from Larry D. Pate, *Every*

People Directory, (1998).
5 In February 1903, Bishop Vedanayagam Samuel Azariah helped to form the Indian Missionary Society of Tirunelveli, a land mark in church and mission planting. J. Edwin Orr, *Evangelical Awakenings in Southern Asia*

(Minneapolis: Bethany Fellowship, 1975), p. 127.

6 Houghton, *Dependency*, pp. 216–218.

7 Ibid, pp. 23–24.

8 Sam Lazarus, "Preface," Sam Lazarus [Ed.], *Proclaiming Christ* (Madras: CGAI, 1992), p. iii.

9 Findings in Church-Mission consultation, held at ECC, Whitefield, Bangalore, January 20–22, 1998.

10 Paul, *The Cross Over India*, p. 100.

11 Sunder Raj's Lecture during the MISSION CONGRESS conducted by National Council of Churches in India, Bangalore, August 14–16, 1997.

12 The Presbyterian Synod of Mizoram has approximately 600 missionaries.

13 PT Abraham, "Pentecostal-Charismatic Missionary Outreach," in Lazarus [Ed.], *Proclaiming Christ*, p. 101.

14 Ibid.

15 Discussion and Interview with Mr. Ebenezer Sunder Raj, India Missions Association, Chennai, 15 July, 1997.

16 *OM India and You*, an Introduction brochure of OM India.

17 T. Divakaran, Associate Director, Operation Mobilisation, personal interview, Secunderabad, 17 April, 1997.

18 Houghton, SAIACS, Chapel Service, Bangalore, October 16, 1996.

19 George Ninan, CCC. Personal Interview, March 1997.

20 Day Spring International uses this *Jesus* movie *Karunamayadu* (The Ocean of Grace) originally produced by the secular cinema in Telugu. Now that has been dubbed in Tamil (*Karuna Murthi*) and Hindi (*Daya Sagar*). *Daya Sagar* showed in the main Doordarshan Indian TV network on Saturdays at 9.00 a.m.

21 Som Thomas and Ravi Antine, personal interviews, Bangalore, March 2, 1997.

22 [n.a], *To the Uttermost Part The Call to North India* (Colorado: AD 2000 and Beyond & Joshua Project 2000, 1997), p. 8.

23 These churches are very small, mostly meet in homes and are not to be compared with huge denominational churches.

24 [n.a.], *New Life Fellowship Changing Destinies of the World*, (Bombay: New Life Fellowship, 1997), p. 7.

25 Jacob Sernao, One of the leaders of the New Life Churches of Bombay, interview at Nagpur, April, 15, 1997.

26 Editor, "FMPB's Contribution to the Church in Gujarat," *Friends Focus*, April (1997) p. 42.

27 Primitive peoples were the lowest level. Peasant villagers were organised with village social organisation and peasant village psychology and religion. The primitive and the peasant village culture levels have received greater emphasis from the Christian movement.

28 Cressy, *Cultures of East Asia*, pp. 43–44.

29 National FORUM of Missions, Nagpur, April 16–18, 1997.

30 Further information of un-reached people and languages refer IMA books *The languages of India, The people groups of India* and other.

31 Most groups responsible for measuring different areas have accepted except the social concern survey. Some struggle with finances to do the survey and some do not have the team, the infrastructure to do the job. However, the efforts are under way. For more details on FORUM refer also to p. 89.

32 Church-Mission Consultation jointly organised by IMA and NCCI at ECC Whitefield, Bangalore, January 20–23, 1998.

33 Roberta Winter, "The Kingdom Strikes Back," Budelman, Ralph (Ed.), *Inheriting God's Perspective*, (Bangalore: Mission Frontiers, 1996), pp. 30–31.

34 Ephesians 6: 10–12. Finally, my brethren, be strong in the Lord and in the power of His might. Put on the whole armour of God, that you may be able to stand against the wiles of the devil.

35 Peter E. Gillquist, *Let's Quit Fighting about the Holy Spirit*, (London: Lakeland, 1971) pp. 86–87.

36 Some never bothered about bringing people to Christ, reasoning that God has already chosen the ones who supposed to come to Him anyway.

37 Accountability structure has to do with answering to the Church or Mission Some claimed that the missions should spring out only from and through a church (which often did nothing till a mission Agency came into being in that area). When a mission re-cruited people and appealed for money, some churches objected and claimed missions should originate from the Church as seen in the Acts 13. This caused strife on where missions should originate. The discussion between church and para-church, each trying to establish their authority, is still with us.

38 The concept of "Win the Winnable" came from the understanding that God has selected these winnable for the kingdom, and because mass conversion added more people.
The Gospel to the poor aimed at bringing justice to the poor. They, however responded to Christ for both spiritual and other reasons such as a human dignity, freedom from caste system and other.
The holistic and the social service emphasis came from the theological understanding that Jesus was interested in redeeming the whole man and not just his soul. Many mis-sions not only proclaimed the Gospel and made disciples but also uplifted the poor and provided the human dignity through Christ. For some Christians, uplifting the poor and bringing justice has been

more important, even if a person eventually may not follow Christ. Some believed that the concept of love your neighbour is uplifting the neighbour without the a slightest notion of sharing the Gospel to them. Then, pluralistic thinking [more than one way to reach God] also made Christians complacent in sharing their faith.

39 Discussions in EC, Operation Mobilisation, 1993.

40 Dr David Samuel, Director TAFTEE, Interview, Bangalore, IEM Campus during IMA Training Committee, September 6, 1997.

41 Kingsley Arunothaya Kumar and R. Billy, "'Evangelical Mission Thought and Practice'—Could it be more Indian?" Siga Arles & I. Ben Wati (Eds.), *Pilgrimage 2100*, (Bangalore: Centre for Contemporary Christianity, 1995), p. 68.

42 CT Kurian. *Mission and Proclamation*, (Madras: CLS, 1981), pp. 42–46.

43 Harris, "The Theological Pilgrimage," p. 73.

44 PM Thomas, "Some Thoughts on Churches and Missions," unpublished paper, 1997.

45 Gopal Hembrom, interview while he visited, Bangalore, September 14, 1997.

46 [n.a], "The Awakening of Student and Laymen A Call for A Mission Renewal Movement," Ralph Budelman [Ed.], *Inheriting God's Perspective*, p. 50.

47 Winter, "The Task Remaining," from Winter, Hawthorne et al (Eds.), *Perspectives*, pp. 312–326.

48 M1, M2, and M3—Mission 1, 2, 3.

49 E1, E2, and E3—Evangelism 1, 2, 3.

50 Acts 1:8.

51 N1, N2, and N3—Christian Nurture 1, 2, 3. Ephesians 4:13–14.

52 S1, S2, and S3—Service 1, 2, 3.

53 Peter Wagner, *Church Growth and the Whole Gospel*, (Kent: Marc Europe, 1987), p 92.

54 George Verwer, "Acts 13—Breakthrough 2000," message on audio tape, Manchester: *Things that Matter*, J 963, June 16, 1996.

55 Reported by David Samuel, Bangalore, Sept., 6, 1997.

56 Refer to Appendix 1 for *OM's Book of Standard Definitions* (Carlisle: OM International, June 1994).

57 [n.a.], *Indian Missions*, (Chennai: IMA, January 1996).

58 [n.a.], *Directory of Indian Missions*.

59 Jayaprakash, *Missions of India*, p. 20b.

60 Fellowship for Neighbours India, (FFNI), Al Bashir are the only two agencies listed in the *Directory of Indian Missions*. Youth With a Missions and Operation Mobilisation is not listed in the book. However, they all are involved in a mini scale compared to the Muslim population of India. Refer to *Directory of Indian Missions*.

61 Sunder Raj, IMA, Interview, Chennai, 30 July 1997.

62 Abubakker, FFNI, Interview, Vellore, 31 August 1996.

63 [n.a.] *Reaching Bombay's Muslims*, Introduction p. viii.

64 Ibid, p. 1.

65 Ibid.

66 Abubakker, FFNI, Interview, Vellore, 31 August 1996.

67 Kurian from North India. Interview, Bangalore, April 28, 1997.

68 Editor, News, *Pulse*, September 6, 1996.

69 Abubakker, interview, FFNI, Vellore, 31 August 1996.

70 Ibid.

71 Ibid.

72 Jayaprakash, *Missions of India*, p. 21.

73 Ibid, p. 21.

74 Roy T. Daniel, "Missionary's Cost Index," *Insight India—Assembly Testimony Journal*, April–June (1997) 8.

75 Som Thomas, personal interview, Bangalore, June 1997.

76 Vijayan, an independent worker who has a few evangelists working with him and paid very little, interview while visiting Bangalore, July 1996.

77 Discussion, name withheld, Bangalore, February 2, 1998.

78 Marcia M., interview, Bangalore, December 3, 1997.

79 RZ Prabhu Rayan, "Ministry Among the Visually Handicapped People," *Changing World* (Madras: UESI, 1990), pp. 28–32.

80 C. Sekar, interview, Bangalore, March 12, 1997.

81 Prabhu Rayan, *Changing World*, p. 30.

82 Sue Stillman, "Ministry to the Handicapped (Deaf)" in *Changing World*, pp. 33–38.

83 C. Sekar, interview, Bangalore, March 12, 1997.

84 Vasantharaj Albert, "Joshua Project People List An Indian Analysis", *ICGQ*, (Vol. 3 No 2, July–Sept. 1996), p. 3.

85 Vasantharaj Albert. "A Report on the Status of Evangelisation of India An Over View," *Second National Consultation on Evangelism, Hyderabad, September 1996*. (Chennai: India Missions Association, 1996), p. 14.

86 D McGavran, "Try These Seven Steps for Planting Churches". *Global Church Growth Bulletin*, May/June, 1981, p. 35.

87 Vasantharaj, "India An Over View," p. 14.

88 SD Ponraj, interview at SAIACS, Bangalore, November 1996.

89 Dr Devadasan, Field Director of FMPB, lecture at the Mission Conference, for the students of Bangarapet Bible College, November 12–15, 1992.

90 Interaction with several Indian Mission Leaders.

91 Houghton, SAIACS, Bangalore November 1997.

92 Joseph D'Souza, interview, Hyderabad OM Campus, April 15, 1997.

93 Jayaprakash, *Missions of India*, p. 6.

94 Hedlund, *Evangelisation and Church Growth*, p. 251.

95 D'Souza, interview, Hyderabad, April 15, 1997.

96 Ramanathan, IMA Research Coordinator, personal interview, Chennai, 30 July 1997.

97 Hrudaya, OFU, interview, Chennai, July 31, 1997.

98 Sunder Raj, interview, Chennai, July 28, 1997.

99 G. Raja Bahadur, "Opportunities and responsibility for the Indian Church to Evangelise with Special Reference to ECI," a paper submitted for IMA / NCE at Hyderabad, September 25–29, 1996.

100 Vasantharaj Albert, "Editorial," *India Church Growth Quarterly*, (Vol. 3 No 2, July–Sept. 1996), p. 2.

101 Ponraj, *Church Growth Studies*, p. 16.

102 Patrick Joshua, at SAIACS Chapel, Bangalore 1996.

103 Ponraj, *Church Growth Studies*, pp. 22–23.

104 Wagner, *Church Growth*, p. 181.

105 IMA letter to the CEOs of the member Missions, November 13, 1997.

5

Grouping for Co-operation

5.1 ASSOCIATIONS AND NETWORKS EMERGE

As missions developed they saw a need to strengthen each other by co-operating to meet their common goals and purposes. Associations, National Federations and Networks provided partnership, accountability and exposure to each other. A mission's credibility often depended upon the association or network it belonged to. For the sake of credibility many lone missions joined hands, foregoing minor philosophical or policy differences, bolstering cohesion and growth.

Associations became a necessity to set standards, provide united testimony, leadership development, equal care for the missionaries, standard health care, retirement benefits, development of the missionaries, missionary children's education, recognition of comity arrangements on the mission fields, a voice and a representation of missions to the Government. The networking sets common goals and co-operation until a job is done. It is time and purpose oriented.

The chart below contrasts mission associations and networks.

Associations	Networks
Long-Term Life	Short-Term Life
Multiple Agenda	Single or Limited Agenda
Long-term agenda with long range goals and a long range perspective. The tenure is long.	Short-term agenda with a time limit and specific goals. For example put an evangelist in every pin code area. After the goal is achieved, the network ceases to function.
Structured well with management, membership rules and subscription. It maintains proper accounts, keeps records and minutes.[1]	Less structured or at times not structured at all.[2]

Evangelical Fellowship of India – EFI

EFI was born in 1951 in the same year as the World Evangelical Fellowship.[3] Around 1965 when John Richards was Chairman of the EFI Executive committee, EFI started with a fund of Rs. 720 and grew. It developed IEM as its missionary arm. FMPB and other missions emerged about the same time.[4] Theodore Williams became the first General Secretary of IEM, which was originally known as Indian Evangelical Overseas Mission, begun in 1954.[5]

EFI was an overarching fellowship and a catalyst for many of the evangelical churches, associations and networks assisting evangelicals to achieve their spiritual goals, not another organisation.[6] Its stated purpose was: To provide fellowship among evangelical Christians and be a means of unified action directed towards spiritual renewal in the Church, active evangelism, effective witness to and safeguard of the evangelical faith in the Church.[7]

"The Evangelical Fellowship of India, another co-operative body, gives priority consideration to the recovery of spiritual life in all the churches of India."[8] Rev. Solomon Bodhan, EFI Secretary for Revival and Missions confirmed recently, "During the past year, the EFI continued to Nurture, Outreach and Network with the purpose of building up the body of Christ in our context."[9]

It achieved much by gathering evangelicals in the following congresses: The All India Congress on Mission and Evangelism at Devlali in 1977; the All India Christian Communication Seminar at Nagpur in 1978; the All India Christian Education Seminar and All India Church Growth Seminar both at Hyderabad in 1978; the All India Conference on Evangelical Social Action at Madras in 1979; and the All India Evangelical Women's Conference at Pune in 1979. All of this contributed positively to the growth of evangelical movements in India.[10]

In the first two decades of its existence, the various activities of the EFI served to strengthen the evangelicals. For example, Union Biblical Seminary was established in 1953 for evangelical theological education, All India Christian Book Club in 1953 and the evangelical Radio Fellowship of India in 1957, to name just a few.[11]

EFI, spawned many associations and networks such as IMA, EFICOR, CEFI, EMFI, ENFI and others. As the evangelical counterpart of the NCCI, it sought to counter liberal influences of the ecumenical Church.[12]

However, the EFI identity began to diminish in the eighties as the FECI churches and missions rallied together.[13] Since EFI seemed to lack theological clarity, in 1979 FECI Theological Commission floated an Association for Evangelical Theological Education in India, which, with Asia Theological Association, promoted evangelical separatism, destabilising the Serampore accreditation for theological studies.[14] However, EFI has regained its vision and contributes much to the evangelical churches of India.

Federation of Evangelical Churches of India – FECI.

"In 1974, the position of neutrality towards the ecumenical movement adopted by EFI began to find disfavour with some members of EFI who wished for a more authentic evangelical structure."[15] As a result Federation of Evangelical Churches in India was born at Akola, Maharastra with eight different church denominations joining as members.[16] Daniel Abraham, the President of FECI in his presidential speech during the twentieth anniversary of FECI said that,

> The FECI came as a result of a long felt need in the evangelical churches in India to stand united in upholding the fundamental biblical truths against the attacks of liberalism and other similar destructive forces that are actively at work in the Church today.[17]

While EFI was an overarching body of evangelical missions and churches, the Federation of Evangelical Churches defends the evangelical churches only, and is a Church-oriented Association.[18]

India Missions Association – IMA.

IMA began in March 1977 following a strong call made at the All India Congress on Missions and Evangelism (AICOME) held at Devlali, Maharastra, to bring the emerging indigenous missionary organisations under a national network for mutual help co-operation and corporate expression.[19] For twenty years it has done just that and the missions expect much from IMA.[20] It provides an umbrella as the incorporating body through which the mission agencies associate, lead, influence and benefit from each other.

Becoming a member of the India Missions Association assures credibility, for it requires openness to examination and verification of deed documents and board. IMA grants membership when it is satisfied with the credibility of a mission. Membership of IMA also qualifies a mission for advice to enable it to do its job better—help with leadership development, consultation on management, encouraging missions to become nation-conscious in reaching "all" peoples for Christ, and helping donors to make choices of where they could invest their funds and resources. IMA has a vital role in encouraging mission agencies to develop, help, provide, facilitate, call for consultations and link up with one another.

Dr. Stan Nussabaum, former Training Director, Global Mapping International remarked," It remains clear to us that IMA is the front door to serving a broad cross-section of mission organisations and researchers in India, and we would like to come in the front door."[21] Three workers with the Summer Institute of Linguistics were asked if they would like the Bible translation institute (IICCC) to be independent of IMA now. They said 'No.' They wanted Bible translation to be under IMA to enhance leadership and for IMA missions to take active part in Bible translation.[22] IMA has indeed become the central point of national evangelism and setting general directions for missions.

To help missions, IMA has developed over fifteen departments: Publications (1978), Institute of Cross-Cultural Communications (1980), Missions Leadership Training Institute (1982), Socio-Cultural Study Network (1986), Serve a People (1986), the National Consultancy on Evangelism (1990), the Student Volunteer Programme (1991), Missions Standard Cell (1992), Health Care Network for missionaries (1993), Urban Ministry Consultations (1994), Mission Social Concerns (1994), International Partnerships (1994), Indian Institute of Missiology (1994, now an autonomous body), Tent makers and Overseas Missions (1994), Cell for Assistance and Relief for Evangelists – CARE (1997), Indian Missions Alliance Among Neighbours – IMAAN (1998), and lastly National Institute of Christian Management – NICM (1998). IMA performs many other tasks to assist missions. Most of these departments are led by leaders of various mission agencies under the umbrella of IMA.

Several missions and individuals caution that at times the Association spends more time in survey, research and publication than in interacting with other missions to help them achieve their jobs. They asked IMA staff to make more visits to the missions agencies for fellowship, pastoral counselling related to missions and dealing with the many substantial and immediate issues faced.[23]

Sunder Raj, the GS of IMA, defended his position on the grounds that the research is important and often not available elsewhere. It obtains some research data from the Church Growth Research Centre, but CGRC has moved on from research to training and Church planting. In 1986 the Socio-Cultural Studies Committee, a national research committee, was formed as a loose partnership network, since there are few mission researchers in the country. Although Frontiers Missions Centre (FMC) did some research, more is needed. Other agencies like Discipling A Whole Nation (DAWN) are not ready for the bigger scheme. CONS and Peoples India disseminated Indian census data so that Christians could understand the task of Missions, but did not work on primary research.[24]

Key primary research helps missions decide on their future direction. India is perhaps the first large nation to complete analysis of ethno-linguistic factors and PIN code with a view of reaching people with the Gospel of Christ. Now, all missions have access to the information to make intelligent decisions, to strategise and send their missionaries, and leaders can be specific. IMA continues to update information. As soon as a people group is adopted and workers appointed to reach it, the information automatically changes. IMA offers the updated data on-line. Thus the primary research is essential for reaching the nation; to plan strategy, to measure, evaluate and continuously adapt to the needs of the people of all the ethno-linguistic groups and geographical areas. Each mission according to their convictions can now adopt people groups, language groups and PIN code areas to send their missionaries. Since IMA research and publications are kept up to date, it can effectively aid future strategy for missions in India.[25]

There is also continued secondary research. When a group wanted the profiles of the most unreached peoples of India,[26] a researchers' meeting at Chennai in July 1997 decided that different research agencies would take up different unreached groups for profiling, aiming for completion by December 1997.[27]

IMA felt unable to guide missions when it depended on other agencies for accurate recent research data on the evangelisation of India,[28] so did not regret time on primary research. IMA's effort is appreciated, across the world, as the fruits of this research is made available in books, inter-net, on the web-site and bulletin boards. Every day orders come in from across the world for these research materials.[29]

IMA has lacked an expert communicator and journalists and the right public relations people. Such people are needed if it is to change, for instance, the especially perturbing pattern that the major Muslim population is ignored by most Indian missions. IMA's financial situation also is not yet adequate for the task. In 1985, its annual budget was a meagre sum of Rs. 15,000. Now IMA has mushroomed to twenty full-time workers, and may be the largest Missions Association in the world, upholding at least fifteen thousand missionaries with special concerns like health insurance, school fees for missionaries' children, feasible pension and housing plans.[30] While seeking to provide for the needs of others, Sunder Raj himself does not yet have a pension, or a house to retire to. When questioned about this, he laughed and said that it was not a comfortable position to be in as it affected his family's sense of security. Several Indian veterans, both among the CEOs and in the middle level leadership and those at the grassroots in missions are still in the same situation concerning pension and retirement benefits. This will affect recruiting fresh missionary candidates.

James Kaiser, a former missionary and an Area leader with FMPB for over twenty years, is now the Ministry Co-ordinator with IMA. When he visited two mission stations and their leaders, his visit was heartily appreciated. A mission leader urged him to visit younger missions as they needed much counsel and guidance, and suggested frequent get togethers for mission leaders, so that new CEOs could meet veteran leaders and build relationships and learn from them. This meeting would also help build mutual trust for future partnership, and cross the perceived gap in relationships. Visits from a senior spokesman with IMA helped the missions to unburden and be assured that they were on the right track. These and other initiatives by IMA are appreciated.[31]

Rev. DB Hrudaya, the Director of Orissa Follow-up Ministries, pleaded with IMA to help in finding resources and tools needed for their missionary band of one hundred people. At present Orissa Follow-up Ministry receives a salary subsidy of Rs. 1000 for five missionaries every month from Cell for Assistance and Relief to Evangelists - CARE, a department of IMA. Although this money is not much, it is a relief for many struggling missionaries. Hrudaya was nervous as the subsidy from Gospel for Asia - GFA was being reduced to only fifteen workers out of agreed twenty-five. In this situation CARE has been a help.[32]

Mission leaders appreciate IMA, a neutral body, with whom to unwind and unburden themselves. By listening, praying and helping in times of need, IMA established a credible rapport with the mission leaders of India.[33]

Emmanuel Hospital Association – EHA.

This is an association of Christian hospitals. EHA serves the people through their hospital ministry and also presents the Gospel. Most of these hospitals are in North India, some along the border of India and Nepal.

Evangelical Trust Association of North India [ETANI] and Evangelical Trust Association of South India [ETASI]

These associations help handle matters of property for evangelical churches, including the many properties among the Mennonite, Brethren and other non-ecumenical churches. This trust came under the overarching structure of the Evangelical Fellowship of India.[34] ETASI and ETANI are the evangelical counterparts to Church of South India and Church of North India (CSI / CNI) Trust Association.[35] They are handled by lawyers who help with legal matters of holding and use of properties by the evangelical Trusts and Missions.[36]

ETASI and ETANI have two boards and one executive Secretary who manages both. There has been a suggestion to join them, but consensus had not been reached at the time of writing.[37]

Evangelical Medical Fellowship of India – EMFI

EMFI was organised to encourage Christian medical professionals to be true to their calling as witnesses in the place where they serve.

Other National Associations

Other associations and federations have specific functions: National Council of Churches in India (NCCI); Pentecostal Fellowship of India (PFI); Christian Medical Association of India (CMAI); Indian Christian Media Association (ICMA); National Association for Christian Social Concerns (NACSC); India Association of (Itinerant) Evangelists (IAE); Evangelical Literature Fellowship of India (ELFI); and All India Association for Christian Higher Education (AIACHE). Each has scores (some hundreds) of organisations in its federation representing thousands of staff workers spread all over India.[38]

5.2 Networks

AD 2000 and Beyond Movement.

The AD 2000 and Beyond Movement is a loosely-connected network of agencies and churches focusing on world evangelisation, but with few obligations between the agencies. It did not deeply root in India, as there were already groups at work on similar visions. The Indian representatives of AD 2000 did not register for Foreign Contribution Regulation Act (FCRA) to receive perpetual foreign funds.

North India Harvest Network.

North India Harvest Network (NIHNW) is designed to network state-wise evangelical activities across North India. It encourages evangelism and church-planting in needy places and peoples. "We must move from saturation evangelism to saturation Church-planting as our goal," said Dr. Raju Abraham, one of the initiators of this network. NIHNW is also very keen to establish churches among low-caste Indians especially Chamars in U.P.[39]

Council On National Service – CONS.

CONS, a Southern counterpart of NIHNW, conducts district strategic consultations, saturation Church-planting seminars and training and researchers' training, aiming to increase the effectiveness of grassroots church planters.[40] CONS functions basically in the South with some states in the North such as Gujarat, Rajasthan and Orissa. One mission CEO said that CONS' seminars need more follow up and implementation of its vision which is a church for every village and colony through grass-roots missionaries. CONS reports that CONS related agencies have planted 1000 churches in 1998.

Discipling A Whole Nation – DAWN.

DAWN emphasises evangelism by discipling. The goal is a church for every 500 to 1000 people. DAWN in India, is very small with four personnel trying to pass on this vision. In recent times their emphasis has been on planting house churches.

The FORUM for Evangelism and Missions (NFEM)

NFEM came into being as a result of the National Consultation of Evangelism and Missions held at Hyderabad in September 1996 and organised by the India Missions Association. Mission leaders requested a forum to evaluate missions and evangelism in the country, since much was being accomplished but no one had a comprehensive idea of all that was going on. The network keeps abreast of progress of missions in India. This FORUM represents more missions than the IMA member missions and also large church denominations. It could be the key to understanding the progress and the direction of missionary endeavours in India.

About thirty-five Church Leaders, and mission Leaders gathered in Nagpur in April 1997. They decided to assess results of the following areas: Radio & Television; Literature - Bible, Correspondence Courses & other literature; Christian Films & Audio/ Video Cassettes; Personal and Group Evangelism; Discipleship Groups and Church Planting; Prayer; People Groups; Church Mobilisation; Mercy Ministries; Children Ministries; Harvest Force and Ministry among the College students in different colleges in India.[41] This network is likely to carry on in the next few years. It could have a snowball effect encouraging mission work, and may diffuse tensions in the Church and para-church dichotomy.

Tentmaker Centre, India

The Tentmaker Centre – India, networks with individuals and agencies to mobilise tentmakers in the largely unreached Northern States of India and to nations like the Confederation of Independent States CIS. The Centre publishes *Tentlink*.[42] Higher profile to tentmaking has helped missionaries in secular professions to be encouraged and linked with each other.

Evangelical Literature Fellowship of India – ELFI.

For literature agencies to co-operate, ELFI began through EFI, encouraging professional production and distribution of literature and linking writers, editors, publishers and others interested in Christian literature. ELFI organises conventions for publishers and booksellers to promote co-operation and understanding.

Grass Roots Church Planters Training Network (GRCP)

The GRCP dream is to identify and train at least 50,000 people who will work with their own community and area and plant churches across North India. They will identify and train 2000 GRCP Trainers who in turn will train the 50,000 grass roots church planters. Each GRCP will be encouraged to plant five churches each resulting in 250,000 churches in North India. A special Curriculum has been prepared for training the GRCPs.[43]

5.3 Supporting Agencies

Over the period of the emerging national missions, many groups came into being as support agencies. They are not networks. Cell for Assistance and Relief to evangelists (CARE) – a division of IMA, Christian Aid, Advancing Native Missions (ANM) and Partners International which was known as Christian National Evangelism Commission (CNEC) are some of the supporting agencies. The following are a few others.

Gospel for Asia – GFA.

Gospel for Asia began as a network and subsidised salaries for missionaries by Rs. 800. Eventually, it has become a mission in itself, and the subsidy for non-GFA missionaries dwindled or ceased as it supports its own missionaries.

GFA has multiple approaches to mission and evangelism. Its major emphases are radio programmes, correspondence courses, literature distribution and most of all training programmes of various types with a stress on church planting for graduates. Many training centres have been established across Asian nations.

Its Founder Director[44] KP Yohannan decided deliberately to speed evangelism and church planting and bring the Gospel directly instead of it being entangled with social ministries.

Church Growth Association of India – CGAI, Madras

CGAI provides a research information on the people groups of India and encourages churches and missions to be aware of, and get involved in, people group consciousness. It has advocated Donald McGavran's theory of winning peoples as groups and castes, and then discipling them into a church. The Centre prefers to work with Dalits, poor and the Backward Castes (OBCs).[45]

According to Roger Hedlund, the former Director of the Centre,

> Most religious conversions in India has (sic) been
> through group movements. This is true of Hinduism as
> well as Christianity. The majority of Protestant and
> Roman Catholic Church members in India are descend-
> ants of people-movement converts... Today the issue is
> very much alive. Some 200 million oppressed are

crying out for liberation... This is no time for the
Church (Mission) to draw back but to press forward for
the spiritual and material liberation of oppressed
people. Let the Church become the champion of the
poor and the advocate of justice for all... It is against
this background that the Church Growth Association of
India was constituted by a group of Indian Christians
... for encouraging the movements of Church growth in
India. The CGRC's (older name of CGAI) three functions are research, publication and training.[46]

The CGAI has instilled widely its vision of reaching People
Groups with the Gospel. Their magazine unvaryingly stresses the
ethos of people-group approach in church planting. There is great
mission discussion about whether the Church should be mixed or
monocultural, but CGAI has continued inspiring people to think
one people group at a time. Both arguments have their value.

Vasantharaj Albert, the present Director of Church Growth
Association in India, would like to motivate churches and
missions to win the Other Backward Castes who form a majority of the population in India. He said happily, "I am for encouraging the OBC's to be reached with the Gospel. I am an
OBC man!"[47] Lamentably, he lacks the manpower in CGAI.
The association has however successfully alerted missions to
People Group strategies and kept McGavran's teachings alive
in mission strategy.

Missionary Upholders Family and Missionary Upholders Trust

Sister organisations Missionary Upholders Family (MUF) and
Missionary Upholders Trust (MUT) came in to being in 1984 to
support missionaries. When one family decided to support a
missionary,[48] others caught the vision. At present there are ninety-
five MUF groups functioning all over the country.[49] Each MUF
group raised one thousand Rupees for each missionary as a partial
support. They are raising Rs. 95,000 for ninety-five missionaries in
various organisations. Each MUF group adopts a missionary and
sends their support directly to the mission. They even use the
receipt books of the missions for which they collect funds, so
minimising administration.[50]

MUT, as a registered Trust from 1993, organises MUF groups
which meet some needs of missionaries serving in registered
organisations. These needs include convalescent and rest homes

(1994), medical aid – Medical Endowment fund (1996), setting up a Calamity Relief Fund to assist missionaries' families (IMPACT) in times of the death of a missionary (1997) and providing accommodation for needy missionaries on their retirement.[51]

One rest house was established in 1994 at Vellore for missionaries who came for treatment at the Christian Medical Collage. Maintaining the place was hard, so MUT requested missionaries to be deputed from various missions on two-year rotations to act as the hospitality couple.[52] This is being considered by missions.

MUT's IMPACT programme helps missionary families with Rs. 25,000 from a special fund in the event of the death of a missionary. Later, Rupees five is collected from all the member missionaries across India and the fund is kept ready for emergencies.[53] MUT is joining with IMA to establish medical insurance for missionaries.

This initiative demonstrates how Christians feel burdened to help missionaries in practical ways. If this consciousness is aroused more among Christians, the missionaries on the field will worry less about food and shelter and will be free to concentrate on their missionary tasks.

5.4 Christian Social Action Units

While missions like FMPB, IEM and others were involved in evangelism, there were social needs to meet in the fields. Christian organisations aiming to meet these include EFICOR, World Vision, Inter Mission, Nava Jeevan Seva Mandal (NSM) and others.

EFICOR is an indigenous effort oriented around social concerns. The concern for relief and development led the EFI to set up the EFI Committee on Emergency Relief in 1967. Latter (sic) the Emergency was dropped and the Committee became a Commission in 1970 and the EFICOR was born.[54]

Eventually, the primarily social concerned agencies joined together and formed the National Association for Christian Social Concern (NACSC). They expected to train candidates for social action to help evangelists and the missionaries to serve the people where the missionaries and churches worked. However, this training has not picked up a momentum yet.[55]

Conclusion

Associations, networks, and supporting agencies have added much to the to the credibility and planning of Indian missions.

END NOTES

1 S. Madhav Rao, "Organisational Set Up of Missions—Formation of a Society/Trust—Legal Obligations", Ebenezer Sunder Raj et al (Eds.), *Management of Indian Missions*, (Chennai: IMA, 1992), pp. 3–4.

2 Sunder Raj, IMA, interview, Chennai, 15 July 1997.

3 Siga Arles, "Evangelical Movement in India—An Evaluation" in Arles & Ben Wati (Eds.), *Pilgrimage 2100*, p. 32.

4 Rev. Dr John Richards, the former Chairman of EFI and presently, the Vice Chairman for special projects with AD 2000 and Beyond, personal interview at Nagpur, April 15, 1997.

5 Ben Wati, "Foreword," in Williams, *Sacrifice*, p. 8.

6 Arles, "Evangelical Movement," *Pilgrimage*, p. 34.

7 Ibid, p. 32.

8 Theissen, *A Survey of World Missions*, p. 39.

9 Solomon Bodhan, "A Report of the Ministries of EFI for 1996", presented at the FORUM, Nagpur, 18–20 April 1997.

10 Arles, "Evangelical Movement," *Pilgrimage*, p. 33.

11 Das, "Evangelical Roots: 1793–1966" *Pilgrimage*, p. 34.

12 Sunder Raj, Interview Chennai, 17 July 1997.

13 Arles, "Evangelical Movement," *Pilgrimage*, p. 38.

14 Ibid, p. 39.

15 EFI pamphlet, *To God Be the Glory 1951–1991: 40 years of the EFI*, (1991) 39.

16 Robert J. McMahon, *To God Be the Glory: The EFI of India 1951–1971*, (New Delhi: MSS, 1971), p. 8.

17 Daniel Abraham, "The Historical Development of FECI 1994–1984, *FECI Souvenir 1974–1984*, [n.p.], quoted in J. Jessiah Harris, "The Theological Pilgrimage of the Indian Church: A Study of Contrast–The Futility of Polarisation," SAIACS unpublished D.Miss dissertation, (1997). p. 115.

18 Discussion with Sunder Raj, Chennai, 17 July 1997.

19 India Missions Association Pamphlet.

20 Sunder Raj, lecture to IMA Staff, Chennai, 17 July 1997.

21 E-mail of Stan Nussabaum, Training Director, Global Mapping International to Sunder Raj, IMA. 9 April, 1997.

22 Interview, SIL personnel, Bangalore, July 1997.

23 Bose Meiyappan, the General

Secretary of Church Growth Missionary Movement (CGMM) to James Kaiser, IMA Ministry coordinator on his visit to CGMM at Madurai. 10 July 1997.

24 Primary Research aim to analyse (a) the people groups of India, (b) language groups and (c) the PIN code information. They cover the ethno-linguistic and the geographical areas. IMA finished analysing the unreached people groups list in July 1997. The language analysis was done by 1994 and the Pin Code also finished in by 1997. Refer to the following for further analysis: *Languages of India—Present Status of Christian work in Every Indian Language* and *Peoples of India.* (Chennai: India Missions Association, 1997).

25 Sunder Raj, interview, Chennai, 2 August 1997.

26 It is now known that there are 204 unengaged/unreached people groups in India. Refer to Appendix 4.

27 Researchers' gathering at IMA office at Chennai on July 31, 1997. The task is being carried to 1998 to profile 205 unreached peoples and 300 large cities in India to encourage missions to strategise.

28 Sunder Raj, Chennai, August 2 & September 12, 1997.

29 Raja Kumar, IMA Administrator, Chennai, July 30, 1997.

30 Sunder Raj, IMA Interview, Chennai, 2 August 1997.

31 Report from James Kaiser after his visit to CGMM and ICGM,

Madurai. 10 July 1997.

32 DB Hrudaya, Director, Orissa Follow-up Ministries, Personal Interview while visiting Chennai, July 31, 1997.

33 Derived from correspondence from various mission leaders.

34 [n.a.], Pamphlet on Evangelical Trust Association of North and South India (ETANI-ETASI), Bangalore. [n.d.]

35 Ebenezer Sunder Raj, Interview, Chennai, June 1997.

36 S. Madhav Rao, " Managing of Properties", in IMA *Management of Indian Missions,* pp. 18–25.

37 Daniel Bernard, Executive Secretary ETANI, ETANI. Personal Interview, Bangalore, August 3, 1997.

38 Sunder Raj and Team (Eds.), *Management of Indian Missions* (Chennai: India Missions Association, 1992), p. 136.

39 Raju Abraham, "Networking and Mobilising the Church for North India". Paper at IMA – NCE, Hyderabad, Sept., 1996.

40 Paul Gupta, CONS report for 1996–97.

41 A Report in FORUM at Nagpur from April 16–18th, 1997.

42 Met Castilo, "Here and There— Missions Update," *Missionasia,* Vol. 17, No. 2, Second Quarter (1997) 4.

43 SD Ponraj & Sue Baird (Eds.), *Reach India 2000* (Madhupur, Bihar: Mission Educational Books, 1996), pp. 20–21.

44 Yohannan, *Revolution,* pp. 105–112.

45 Vasantha Raj, Interview, Chennai, December 20, 1996.

46 RE Hedlund, "Church Growth

Ministry in India," S.
Vasantharaj Albert and Roger
Hedlund (Eds.), *India Church
Growth II 1984–1988* (Chennai:
CGRC, 1998), pp. xi–xv.

47 Vasantharaj, CGAI, Interview,
Chennai, 20 December 1996.

48 Nirmala David, "The Birth of a
MUF Group," JJ Ratnakumar
& Krupa Sunder Raj [Eds.],
*Mission and Vision, Who and
What?* (Bangalore: MUT
Publishers, 1996), p. 26.

49 MUT Prayer Focus, Sept.–Nov.
1997.

50 Reported by Shyam Vincent,
August 11, 1997.

51 Ratnakumar & Sunder Raj,
Mission and Vision, pp. 1, 4.

52 MUT Prayer Focus, Sept.–Nov.
1997.

53 JJ Ratnakumar, Secretary MUF,
personal interview at Chennai
IMA Office September 27, 1997.

54 EFI, "To God Be the Glory:
1951–1991, p. 39, quoted in
Harris, "The Theological
Pilgrimage," p. 155.

55 Sunder Raj, interview, Chennai,
August 1997.

6

Stresses and Mission Responses

Financial struggles are not the only difficulties missions and missionaries face. Other stresses fall into three areas – those of the individual missionary, field issues and agency concerns. Often new missions begin enthusiastically without calculating on the many problems they will face.

Issues for individual missionaries include motivation, pastoral care and accountability. Field administrators face difficult decisions on relationship to locals, language learning and enculturation. Missions must be clear about philosophies, ethos and general direction.

Missions made policies as the issues occurred, setting precedents for recurring problems. Many learnt it was better to find solutions before a problem arises. Mission executives need foresight, wisdom and constant interaction about trends on the field, with missionaries and local grassroots workers. Without forethought, small problems snowball and turn into casualties. Some missions have faced major crises and some have collapsed for lack of forward planning.

Dr. Otto Waack, a missionary (1954–1967) with the Breklum Mission, in charge of the Theological Training Centre at Kotpad, Jeypore in Orissa wrote,

> The instructions are divided into three parts: The
> Mission Board, the Mission Society, and the Mission
> Budget.. .... The mission staff knew what was expected
> of them and knew also which direction the work
> should follow. The regulation also had a useful func-
> tion in seeing that the work was done in a unified way
> throughout the area. ...The regular meetings in the
> General Conference made it possible to discuss impor-
> tant subjects arising from the work.[1]

Contrast this with the analysis of Indian Missions by Joshi Jayaprakash.

> The survey shows that most of the agencies do not
> have well-developed structures. Stated policies and
> guidelines are imperative for efficient administration.
> Out of the 82 agencies (surveyed), only 36 said that

they have stated policies. ... Thus the mission agencies can be seen to have a deficiency in their understanding of policy and structure.[2]

Executives are constantly forced to create, recreate and rewrite policies and instructions.

The foundation of Indian mission life lies with the individual missionaries without whom no missionary agency could exist. Therefore the mission will crumble if it does not care for its missionaries. It is one thing to challenge and recruit a fresh missionary candidate and it is another thing to keep him or her going in all the work on the mission field. Holding on to a missionary is more difficult than recruiting. The missionary may simply leave dissatisfied and discouraged – a drop out, often carrying guilt at leaving, even if undeservedly.

6.1 Pressures in Modern Missionary Life

Spiritual Opposition

Many internal and external enemies work against missionaries. Demonic forces are always at work to hinder: Chacko Thomas tells how, whenever he crossed the Barauni bridge on the river Ganges to go to North Bihar, he feared and felt oppressed. He faced much opposition as his mobile team went to preach the Gospel. He had to depend upon God in prayer, to encourage his band of co-workers.[3] Vernon J. Sterk, a missionary to the Mexican Indians wrote, "The major task of preventing God from being glorified is carried out by assignment of specific territorial (evil) spirits for the purpose of halting or disrupting evangelism in their territories."[4] Keith Benn, with SIL wrote the following, showing the work of the devil.

> Since the North East Indian Church leaders and Bible Society representatives gathered at Serampore ... to discuss the initiation of mother tongue translators course. ... Serampore has been under heavy enemy activity. Over the last three months Dr. Daniel has been battered to and fro. His long time friend Dr. Matthew Johns suddenly died. Twice there were political disturbances on the Serampore Campus, which put incredible pressure and troubles within the student body.[5]

Edward C. Pentecost said, "Missionary activity is finally a spiritual warfare. The enemy is not ultimately man, but Satan. The host of anti-God powers works against the missionary, because they are working against God and His purpose."[6]

The next enemy is opposition from those who choose not to believe in Christ. As a result of fallen nature, missions confront people incapable of knowing and doing right. Some cultural practices indicate deformed hearts and minds, turned away from right. Individuals and society suffer. Missionaries love them in spite of their thoughts and actions.[7]

People object when missionaries proclaim Jesus Christ as the only way of salvation. Some fear becoming a Christian means giving up their career, and living as "a holy man", disassociated from the world. Christian teaching of holiness combined with hard work was unacceptable to some.[8] Mary Mead Clark describing the movement of the Nagas in North East India to Christ said the initial period of mission work was hard. When some came to Christ, Satan was not idle. Rumours said the preacher, Mr. Clark, was the disguised agent of the East India Company because he had a white face similar to the people of the Company. Some of the Nagas did not want to leave their cruel customs and old faith. People eyed Christianity with suspicion.[9] Conversions and the revivals increased the evangelistic activities, which in turn stimulated intense persecution and an anti-Christian movement based on the old religion of the Nagas. In fact the anti-Christian movement looked like a Christian ecstatic revival.[10]

Internal Stress

But missionaries at times also caused their own problems. Some entered mission fields carrying inappropriate habits and lifestyles from their past – preconceived ideas, assumptions, ideologies and internal fears. A missionary may struggle with deep insecurity, incompetence, his adverse temperament, the backlash of his family background, pressures both from his immediate family and his parents, peer pressure from non-missionary friends and the temptation to compromise in all issues.

British missionary, Henry Martyn who lived in the early nineteenth century in Rajmahal, Sahibganj, Bihar, serves as an example of discouragement.

Henry Martyn was very much discouraged when he had spoken, scarcely a word had been understood (by the local people). "I was burdened," he writes, "with a consciousness of blood-guiltiness; ... how dreadful the

reflection that any should perish ... how shall I ever
dare to be silent?"[11]

Here are some of the pressures of modern Indian missionaries.
Poulose, a missionary in Bihar, was the only man in his family and
responsible for arranging his two sisters' marriages. Heavy dowry
burdens weighed him down with worries. He found it hard to
concentrate.[12] Another was the first Christian in his family. As he
finished studying weaving technology, his elderly poor parents
had great hopes that he would provide for them. His brother was a
casual labourer. Having chosen to serve as a missionary with a
meagre missionary allowance, he struggled to send even Rs. 300 a
month to help his family, though an Indian is expected to provide
for his parents. Stressed by this worry, he dared not spend on
himself beyond his food expenses.

Missionary Marjorie Collins wrote of self-discipline,

For some, it is not easy to adjust to a new pattern of
living ... . Others feel the whole adjustment is interest-
ing and enjoyable. But one thing that does not radically
change is YOU. And because YOU have to live with
YOU the rest of your life, it is well to consider some of
the little things (and big things, too) in your personal life
which can be or ought to be adapted, adjusted, deleted or
enhanced. And it is never too early to begin![13]

The cost paid is high for the missionary. Recently costs encompass deficient medical care, insufficient salary, inadequate schooling facilities for children, meagre retirement benefits, complete
lack of housing for future and no provision for insurances.

Then there are pressures from their own agencies in the form
of difficult relationships with co-workers, poor leadership, clan
ruled authority structures, disorganisation and inadequate training. Some organisations require too much reporting. Some do not
even make their missionaries accountable.

In the eighteenth century in South India Ziegenbalg boldly and
busily brought people to Christ. Back in Copenhagen his mission
secretary with limited vision could not comprehend Ziegenbalg's
ideas.[14] Such situations continue to occur, and misunderstanding
can kill missionary zeal.

Henry Martyn found no one to whom he could freely unburden himself. Letters from friends in England gave exceeding great
comfort. He was very lonely. His ministry amongst the Europeans
of Dinapore was discouraging.[15] At the end of his life, when he

was only thirty-one years old, he had none with him at Tokat, Armenia as he was travelling towards England.[16] Such loneliness and despair awaited the missionary both then and now. Marjorie Collins writes,

> Loneliness is a fog which arrives out of nowhere to envelope the soul and cause it to feel lost or wayward... If loneliness lasts for a long period of time, it erodes the ability to work well, and produces a number of problems, both in relation to personal matters as well as in the area of ministry. Loneliness often turns to self pity.[17]

Today a missionary carries similar burdens, heartaches and discouragements, though often hidden. Prayer and information letters project Indian missionaries triumphantly winning people to Christ, but often show only the one side of the coin, the flowery side. They encourage Christian partners to be associates, especially in finances, in the work of the Gospel. They are for publicity and, while true, may not show the difficulties of the missionary life. Few missionaries speak honestly of their problems and heartaches. Jayaprakash in his *Evaluation of Indian Missions* warned, "Promotional work should not take the place of working to fulfil the primary objective (the Great Commission.)"[18]

External Stress

Kulothungan, the Director of Maharastra Village Ministries (MVM) said the following were some of his struggles as a missionary and as a mission leader. A balance between ministry and family, between work and health care, between personal relaxation and giving time to others in the mission, between direct soul winning and leading a soul winning agency, between building a person and expecting discipline from him, between choosing priorities and non-priorities, between big heartedness and knowing that he was being taken advantage of, between taking time off to evaluate self and constantly into ministries, between having time with God, study and work and lastly, having home and office together in the same house. Apart from all these he said there were financial struggles especially after marriage and the need for hospitality because of pressure from constant visitors.[19]

One missionary who was "very busy in the Lord's work", was not even aware that his wife had gone astray. He had even challenged others that, as he spent most time for the Lord, the Lord would care for them. He proudly said that, "my wife has not deserted me yet and that could not happen."[20] The truth could be bitter.

> At least three months before your sixty-fifth birthday (or before your retirement), see your nearest Social Security office to sign up for benefits as well as Medicare. Be sure to carry a supplemental medical policy which will provide for the costs which Medicare will not cover. You are very fortunate if your Mission carries the full cost of your medical insurance as part of your retirement benefits. If it does not, carefully consider your need for coverage.[21]

This appears in a missionary manual, but it does not apply to Indian missionaries. When Indian missionaries retire, no Social Security or Medicare facilities are available for them. Anantharaj, an Indian missionary wrote,

> I am a missionary. I do not have access to such facilities (modern equipments (sic)) and programmes (as in the cities), because I am serving God in remote villages where no Christians can be found. I am cut off from friends, relatives and prayer partners and supporters. ... So I can not find believers to have fellowship with me. ... This makes me to feel lonely... I hope you have not forgotten that I am still a human being and not merely a missionary.... . Loneliness, sickness, fruitlessness in the ministry and other such discouraging factors sometimes depress me.[22]

One very prominent well educated, Christian leader in his mid fifties, who would have made it well in the secular world, could not make his ends meet in Christian ministry. His children were very disappointed and felt that their parents were useless as they could not provide many of their basic needs. The missionary parents, though prominent leaders, felt quite heart broken. The whole family asked the same question, "was this the right thing to have done with their lives?"[23]

In another situation, the missionaries' children felt that the parents had no time for them, as they were "too busy in the work of the Lord". The children were bitter about spending time at home in their holidays. The parents were physically present, but actually not available to the children. These children compared other parents with their own quite openly.[24]

Several missionaries interviewed agreed that missionaries and

Christian workers had low or no savings, no health insurance, no retirement benefits and no death relief schemes. They agreed that this resulted from a misplaced overemphasis on "faith", and they were vulnerable to disaster such as a heart attack. One missionary's wife became mad and the finance-strapped mission could not treat her. When the missionary died his wife roamed mad, homeless on the streets.[25]

When some of the workers in a mission wanted to go for studies in the middle of their career, they were given Rs. 2,000 as a yearly grant and study leave. No missionary could survive on this. A study break was unthinkable.[26] FMPB, struggling like other missions, started with no provision for missionaries to take time out for further studies.[27] Now a missionary can apply and receive specified leave time, retaining the normal allowance and as well some study expenses.[28] The UESI allows missionaries to take sabbatical leave for six months with allowance and after that the person has to find the resources for studies, which may last one or two years.[29] The larger missions such as FMPB, IEM and OM have learnt to respond to study needs, recognising this as a valuable investment in lives, enhancing effectiveness and preparing future leaders. Some consciously plan studies at a midpoint of a missionary's career. Smaller missions lacking funds and experience struggle with this. Still most missionaries at times feel inadequately prepared, worn out and in need of refurbishment.

While mission leaders cope with this, making decisions both positive and negative, missionaries caught in the middle may become victims of delayed or wrong decisions and may feel demotivated and inadequate. Two or three years of mid-term training for a missionary may bring a further fifteen or twenty years of service. Study requests will increase. Missions will need to adapt. Without study provision a missionary simply quits and goes to another mission or, with great loss to missions, gives up.

Even workers keen to serve Christ may feel discouraged living in primitive places without modern facilities knowing others operate in the high-speed computer and E-mail age. The pressure to keep pace with new scientific developments and the new communication techniques challenges even a missionary working in cities and towns relating to middle and upper class people.

Coping with the older missionaries can also be a problem for younger missionaries. One forty year old missionary felt frustrated when his senior missionary does not trust him because he was his junior.[30] Another not-so-young-missionary reacted against older missionaries who forced themselves on to committees as "guardians", so the "inexperienced missionaries" would not make wrong decisions. This missionary felt he was not trusted and pleaded for some freedom, space and an opportunity to make mistakes. Missionaries are forced to hear stories of how their elders suffered, inferring the younger missionaries too must suffer. The specious argument says that pioneering older missionaries travelled on cycles, lived in huts, had no tables, no computers, and no office, so neither should the new missionaries, since modern gadgets are not necessary in spiritual work! Such limited vision can cause tension in a modern environment.

On the other hand, some younger missionaries unwarrantedly criticise experienced missionaries causing tension between the two. This is not new. When Henry Martin showed up in Calcutta, the scene of "the Serampore trio" (William Carey, William Ward and Joshua Marshman), there was tension as Martin, though young, displayed better translation skill and a deeper spiritual life than the rest.[31]

When one missionary was married, the mission insisted that his wife stop working, so as to help her husband in the ministry. The wife did not feel that she should give up a profession for which she was trained. She felt that she could serve the Lord by remaining in her profession. Eventually, the mission asked them to resign. Although they were very mission-minded, just because they were married to missionaries, some wives felt that they were deprived of their profession. This tension has been seen in many agencies. OM in the early nineties changed their policy so that wives could work as long as it would not hinder the ministry of the spouse and they were willing to be transferred to other places as their spouse's work required.[32] This will not be a problem when both the husband and wife pledge to serve together in another culture. However some traditional Indian missions are still struggling with such issues.

There are other discouragements in aspects of health and initial adjustment in the field with new food, languages, customs and friends to cultivate. Misunderstandings, shaken ideals, warped unworkable values, non-co-operation from their own families or colleagues, inadequate medical coverage, worries over children's education, future planning and questions over retirement make people insecure. Such stresses cause many to walk away from mission work.

Dr Peter Bierley gives these figures on attrition from mission work in India: 4.1 percent Indian missionaries left the mission field on the health grounds, 5.3 percent on the children's schooling situation, 2.7 percent died in service.[33] The analysis did not show the percentage of people who left missions because of inadequate health care, inadequate retirement benefits, inadequate housing and pension after retirement. Many Indian missionaries will not speak about this for fear of being branded "unspiritual". Instead they quietly suffer insecurities,[34] and presumably a number who join "full time" mission work drop out as they become aware of the dilemmas of their predecessors. This is a cause for concern. A high attrition rate also sends messages to the new generation about mission work.

The emotional burden a missionary carries is high, perhaps very similar to behavioural scientist Warren Benny's description of a company,

One of the obstacles is the emotional and value over-tones which interfere with rational dialogue. More often than not one is plunged into a polarised debate which converts ideas into ideology and inquiry into dogma. So we hear of theory X vs theory Y, personality vs organisation, democratic vs autocratic, task vs maintenance, human relations vs scientific manage-ment and on and on. Surely life is more complicated than these dualities suggest, and surely they must imply a continuum and not simply extremes.[35]

Missionaries' external stresses may come from disunity, poor management, lack of supervision, inadequate non-contextualised training, inadequate or bad leadership, un-healthy competition, unspiritual methods, wrong publicity and wrong statistics. They also may come from non-credible struc-tures such as family run mission or one man organisation or one man control, inability to meet the needs of the parents, family pressures, health care, pressure from the host culture in which he or she ministers, pressure from colleagues for results and more work, judgements, worries about later housing and retirement. With these pressures from within and outside one's personal life, a missionary may become stressed, discouraged and unable to relax with hobbies. This can harm spiritual growth and effectiveness.

Faith and Convictions

Missionaries endure much in the name of "true Spirituality" and "faith". Lawrence O'Richards wrote, "true spirituality is living a human life with God. As we submit ... we will know ... the joys and triumphs of true spirituality."[36] This is a very high aspiration. Gopal Hembrom a missionary at Patna, Bihar said that no one could impose their views on a missionary about whether or not to follow the faith element. The faith element is something that each missionary carried in his convictions.[37] How much a missionary believes God for his needs is his responsibility. On this line of reasoning many have started mission work without adequate physical preparation and some have needlessly suffered. However, on the positive side missionaries have led many non-Christians to faith in Christ. These tensions surface in a crisis, or on retiring with no place to go, or when a missionary dies leaving his family left stranded in the streets with no sustenance.

Warped "faith elements" may be the missionary's personal conviction. Some believe taking insurance means unspiritually depending on men. Some, avoid insurance premiums, take chances mainly because of a lack of funds. Others object to tying money up in insurance premiums when it could be used to support missionaries and buy the tools for evangelism. The slogan is 'Give all to God and He will provide all needs.' Some of these ideas also came from the larger than life stories of famous missionaries such as Carey, or Hudson Taylor who said, "God's work done in God's way will not lack God's supply."[38] Some individuals took such thoughts to extremes.

Some faith elements came from the mission agencies projecting the policies and convictions of leaders. There are strong convictions on appealing for funds. Men like Hudson Taylor did not appeal and seemed to succeed, but others may have taken this to extreme degrees. Some who operated differently were condemned by so called spiritual giants. Operation Mobilisation started this way, but eventually reached a decision to inform well-wishers so they could make intelligent decisions about giving to missionary work. Eventually OM proposed "information without solicitation" with the belief that the validity of some policies could not be determined biblically.

Some agencies embrace obsolete and irrelevant convictions

carried over from the past. Some convictions came from other nations. For instance, till the mid-eighties no one in Operation Mobilisation was allowed to ride or own a moped. It was argued that the accident rates were high. The original policy was designed by the leaders in Europe to counter fast biking and high accident rates. There, they were able to afford a car or public transport was available. In some Asian countries there was less risk because the mopeds were slow, some routes lacked public transport, and most missionaries could not afford a car. The policy had to be changed for this region.[39] Each mission carries its special culture and develops its own convictions and work ethos. Some are biblical and some are cultural and interpretive. But such convictions and faith elements do have a bearing on the life style of a missionary, with the result that often missionaries are deprived of life needs that others would consider normal.

Financial Pressure

Modern Indian indigenous missions do not have sufficient money to do the best for their missionaries.[40] "Pray for financial support and more workers for all the Indian missions," says the Prayer Guide,[41] yet individual missionaries struggle for their survival. Andrew, a missionary to the Muslims in Bengal said that his mission, ten years back, paid him a monthly salary of four hundred rupees. After ten years he received around one thousand rupees a month. His mission insisted both husband and wife must work in the same mission. This meant his wife could not pursue her career. Andrew felt that even if his salary was doubled, he could not survive financially. He left the mission.[42]

"How has it come that we use the name 'evangelist' for the lowest category of church workers – half trained, half paid and half starved? How does it come that respectable Christians feel uncomfortable with the very idea of evangelism?"[43] wrote Lesslie Newbigin. One mission has about eighty-seven workers with no regular pay structure. Each missionary was paid two to three hundred rupees a month. They struggled to survive.[44] One CEO of a mission proudly wrote that his workers probably received the highest salary among all the mission organisations, which was a total of Rs. 2,500.[45] Living in a one bed room house in North India cost a missionary, his wife and two school-going small children Rs. 4000 a month in 1991.[46] Today the minimum cost would be Rs. 4000 to 6000 in a city, and Rs. 6,000 to 10,000 in cosmopolitan cities.[47]

In 1997 some member missions of IMA could not pay their annual membership fee of Rs. 3000.[48] IMA receives only 4.67 percent of its operating expenses from member missions.[49] Some tried hard to fulfil their responsibilities. One mission made the effort of sending Rs. 2000 towards the required Rs. 3000.[50]

Deepu, a missionary with OM, did not remember attending any prayer meeting at which they did not pray for financial needs. OM always seemed short of finance.[51] Within this genuine financial pressure, many took the policy of moving forward in faith anyway. If they wait for all their needs to be met, India and the world would never be reached with the Gospel. However that should not deter Christian supporters from generously meeting the needs of the missionaries who have gone forward in faith.

The missionaries have as many material needs and aspirations as any other person. Just because they have committed themselves to the cause of evangelism, people expect them not to "entangle themselves" in so called, "worldly things". Shyam Winston of IMA who worked to find some solutions for the needs of the missionaries wrote,

> We cannot simply ignore the material and financial
> needs of these missionaries. The missionary is not
> above material needs but has intentionally ceased to
> give priority to his material welfare in presence of call
> to evangelise. His material needs still exist and they
> must be met by those sending him. However, the
> financial resources of most missions are so meagre that
> they can hardly meet the monthly salaries of the
> missionaries.[52]

He rightly identifies five urgent needs apart from monthly allowance for any Indian missionary: a medical scheme, children's education fund, a pension scheme for the retiring missionaries, a housing scheme for the retiring missionaries and death/disablement relief for the missionary family. Even for Western missionaries some of the above were matters of concern. One Western couple in India were in a dilemma as to when they should leave India. The wife felt that it would be better to leave in their early sixties as this might open up doors for them to be in some Christian ministry back home and give time to settle and find a retirement home instead of returning when they would be frail in their seventies not knowing where to go. The pressure then would be far higher than in their sixties. Mission leaders, as part of pastoral care for missionaries, must plan for retirement, rather than fear facing such huge issues. Answers may not be easy, but they must be found.

6.2 Mission Responses

Pastoral Care

Ramesh, a missionary to Bihar from Andhra Pradesh broke down on the field as he felt convicted of his sexual immorality back at home. The mission squad leader found it difficult to handle the situation and needed help from headquarters at Ranchi.[53] In another case one missionary accused another, Stephen, of being possessed by a demon. Stephen's self-image took a plunge, and he needed the rebuilding of much pastoral care and his team needed biblical teaching on demon possession. Eventually, it became clear the root problem was a bad inter-personal relationship.[54] Such a situation can break missionary team spirit and obstruct missionary endeavour. Dr M C Matthew, Chairman of Evangelical Medical Fellowship of India & Health Adviser to India Missions Association, aptly said,"

> Missionaries face emotional, psychological and spir-
> itual stresses which sometimes get conveniently buried
> under the pressure of work that they carry. However,
> they come to surface periodically creating disharmony
> in (family) life.[55]

One of the greatest needs in the mission field is pastoral care. Major missions in India have ten to twenty people who currently need professional psychological care and many more need pastoral care.[56] Rudolfo Giron, the President of COMIBAM ReMap Task Force Coordinator wrote,

> Pastoral care is one thing and supervision is another
> thing... Supervisor is more related to administrative
> and operative matters. ... Very seldom does a supervi-
> sor take time to seek the welfare of the missionary...
> Supervision is necessary, ... to ensure the success of the
> job assigned to a missionary. Nevertheless, pastoral
> (care) work is more important than the former.[57]

Missions in India are becoming more aware they must routinely train people for pastoral care for missionaries. IEM has a training institute catering specifically for the pastoral care of missionaries.[58] GFA sent Jiji Chacko to SAIACS to prepare himself in pastoral care and counselling.[59] OM dedicated several people as "Pastoral Care-net". Marcus Chacko, who wrote a thesis on pastoral care for OM India as part of his studies at UBS, Pune, is now in charge of pastoral care in OM. In that capacity he also trains others to be conscious of pastoral care for the missionaries with OM.[60] IMA is introducing specific training for member missions on pastoral care.[61] IMA and Grace Counselling India (GCI) are exploring partnership to help the missions in caring for their members.[62] "About five hundred plus counsellors across the nation provide professional help at both listening and advisory level."[63]

Health Care and Medical Schemes

Herbert J. Kane, a former missionary to China says, "Health and happiness belong together. According to a study made by the Missionary Research Library in New York, ill health is the greatest single cause of missionary dropouts."[64] "The life and the work of the missionaries was considerably hampered by tropical diseases... It is of no credit to a missionary if he is full of hypochondriac fear, but even less so if he shows a neglectful, brave rashness.[65] Missionaries are not immune to illness. Raja Mohan Das of IEM was affected by tuberculosis and advised to take a year of treatment.[66] Then in November 1997, Das was admitted at Vellore Christian Medical Hospital and diagnosed with lung Cancer.[67] Doctor Matthew wrote,

> From an informal survey done among missionaries of
> two organisations, it was clear that … some of them
> suffer from frequent illness. There are some who
> experience exhaustion because of the nature of work.
> The average age of missionaries (interviewed) may be
> crossing 35 years, with at least 25% of the missionaries
> in their mid-forties. This makes them vulnerable to
> illness of middle age like hypertension, diabetes,
> backaches, arthritis, acid-peptic disease, psycho-
> somatic dysfunction, etc.[68]

So how shall they pay major medical bills? Even minor medical bills can mount up. Missions have different methods. Most struggle. No one system answers. OM pays all the medical bills as they come. Long term workers of OM have medical insurance and the office staff receive a medical subsidy.[69] Christian Life Service (CLS) paid the bills as they came, but recognise if major bills come they will have to devise a more adequate policy.[70] FMPB scrutinises the medical bills and pays legitimate ones, but struggles on large payments. Some missions give no money for medical expenses.

IMA has tried to form a group of doctors in mission hospitals willing to treat missionaries across India.[71] MC Matthew said,

IMA has already outlined some innovative steps to monitor the wellbeing of our missionaries. Many doctors and mission hospitals have been identified to be part of a health care network for the missionaries. The missionaries are being provided with identity cards to enable them to receive health care from these doctors and mission hospitals.[72]

In 1995 IMA issued medical reference cards to over 7000 missionaries of its eighty-five member missions, for missionaries to obtain quality subsidised treatment in the 330 Protestant Christian hospitals in India."[73] But the proposal came to nought because some of the hospital administrators did not understand the payment system, and some missionaries felt some mission hospitals were inadequate or too far away. Some missionaries chose the nearest good hospital. The plan collapsed.

Missionary Upliftment Trust (MUT) gave Rs. 500 for medical expenses of missionaries referred by MUF families, and provided at a nominal charge a house at Vellore to accommodate up to four missionary families for treatment. This system works well for missionaries in the South, but not for North based missionaries due to distance.

Several insurance schemes were worked out and introduced to missions, but none picked up speed. Some felt that the premium money could stay within the mission instead of an insurance agency, letting missions function as the insurance agency. This also did not work because of insufficient manpower and attention to administration. Missions are too busy! Neither the single mission nor a corporate body was willing to take the responsibility of being a para-insurance company. The project died a natural death.

Even if a medical insurance scheme was devised by the insurance agencies, firstly, there was always the question of who would administer the programme. Neither the missions nor IMA was willing to handle medical insurance for all missions. Secondly, the missions were reluctant to take insurance, as the payments did not cover normal medical expenses such as pregnancy and delivery, dental, other common illnesses and the bills of known illnesses at the time of insurance registration.[74] Missions wanted coverage for all medical bills and not just the hospitalisation of certain illnesses. Such schemes were not available. Consequently, while the urgency remained, most missions could not decide which way to go.

One leader of a major mission had critical surgery that cost nearly Rs. 25,00,000. If another missionary in the same mission went through such surgery, it would be difficult to pay the bills.

Winston patiently suggested various schemes during nearly ten years. Missions want IMA to carry the project, but it was restrained by uncertainty whether missions would co-operate. In the meantime the missionaries bore the brunt of the blunders.

Apart from the need for personnel to manage insurance, finance for premiums was critical. Some mission concerned people became frustrated with the delay in meeting the medical needs of the missionaries. MUT tried some schemes which were not feasible. Dr. Raju Abraham in connection with South Asian Concern of UK raised Rs. 2,27,000 for IMA for health care in November 1996, to help in the scheme,[75] but IMA was still bound by uncertainties.

In July 1997 a group medical claim scheme looked good, but the amount, which could be claimed back, would be only eighty percent of the investment. That scheme too fell through. In September 1997 the plan was to encourage all missions to go ahead with individual medi-claim policies for each missionary up to a claim of Rs. 20,000. With a promise of funds from the South Asian Concern (SAC) and Missionary Upliftment Trust (MUT), and part raised by itself, IMA was willing to subsidise about half of the total premium for each missionary who took a policy. The rest of the premium would be shared by either or both the mission and the missionary. This looked like a solution. The IMA pledged premium payment encourages participation and the scheme should cover major hospital bills should the need arise.

However, at the time of writing, December 1997, the scheme was still not launched. IMA Administrative Committee decided as a temporary measure to reimburse up to Rs. 10,000 for major illness for a missionary.[76]

> Though much could have been accomplished in a decade, the progress in real terms has been very little for three reasons: A. The huge finance outlay. B. Bringing together of mission leaders, missionaries, sponsors and donors. C. The low priority accorded to this major need.[77]

However, IMA went ahead and insured their staff as an example for others to follow[78]—which has not happened yet!

Children's Schooling

The Asian Missions Congress II stated, "Each country in Asia must (urgently) develop educational solutions appropriate for their missionaries' children. They should be assisted in this by the resources and expertise of others."[79] Smaller missions in India have made little allowance for the education of the children, and even less for when children enter colleges for higher education as finance is the biggest problem.

OM pays for children's schooling as most children stay with their missionary parents. It also pays for college education. FMPB pays part of the fees for children with their parents. If the children leave parents to attend prescribed schools, FMPB pays the full fees. For higher education, children receive a loan and are expected to pay most of it back when they become employed.[80] FMPB also has the Friends Educational Society (FES) for needs of children of missionaries. It is still in the early stages.

Most larger missions have similar arrangements. Smaller missions among tribals usually encourage parents to send children to prescribed boarding schools, leaving the parents free to concentrate on mission.[81] Some children react to such situations.

> They (the missionaries' children) were born into the
> situation, while their parents were able to decide for
> themselves... This 'sacrifice' was demanded of them.
> Some of them may well just have accepted their child-
> hood as it was. While others felt real bitterness towards
> their parents, even at an advanced age.[82]

Many missionaries in rural areas appreciate the hostels for the children, and feel the children's absence is a sacrifice they make to take the Gospel to the unreached. Some parents see their children only once in a year when they visit parents during summer holidays. "It is never easy for a parent to send a child away for school, whether it is 100 or 10,000 miles away. This is a heartache which must be bravely borne by parents and children alike."[83] Oswald J. Smith in *The Challenge of Missions* summarised,

> Perhaps the greatest hardship of all will be the leaving
> of the children behind, and that cross no one can
> understand except those who have borne it... Heart-
> break of life in a foreign land, with the children at home,

thousands of miles away, is simply indescribable.[84]

Some parents resent sending their children far away to a hostel, but they have no choice. Nearer hostels or schools may cost more. Most parents who live in the city keep their children with them, though they may not get full support from their mission for the city education.

Some missions have no money earmarked for children's education and thus children and parents suffer. One missionary couple pleaded with their mission for a scholarship for their children's schooling and placement in a better hostel. Another couple was full of anxiety over their children's education, as the funds were not available. The struggle has at times made the missionaries leave mission work to seek a ministry close to the cities. Some, who could not afford to send their children to a good school close by because of monetary limitations, suffer agonies. At times both parents and children have difficulties bearing such separations and are affected in their health.

Some missionaries have had their children separated from them on account of better educational opportunities. Others have their children living with them enduring the experience that their parents go through. In both the situations, the impact of the environment and the nature of the work will have their effect on the children, their personality and their future.[85]

IMA, MUT and many individuals carry a burden to help missionaries and their children, but there are no easy answers. Even a nominal amount of Rs. 2000 yearly for each child would require raising twenty million rupees[86] a year for 10,000 children.

Some concerned people run good boarding schools to help Indian missionaries and their children. These are at the campus of Yavatmal College of Leadership Training at Maharastra, Shantosa Vidyalaya at Donavur, Ida Scudder at Vellore and Kotagiri in Tamil Nadu. Based in Delhi and run by Interserve, *Griha Shiksha*[87] is a correspondence school for the children of missionaries studying up to class three. Isaac Israel, the leader of Rural Blessings Mission (RBM) started a hostel for under privileged girls and some missionaries' children at Wardha, Maharastra.[88] Three international schools with a British or American syllabus run at Mussoorie, U.P. and at Ooty and Kodaikanal in Tamil Nadu. Missions and mission supporters could fund schools that cater to missionary kids (MKs) to take in more MKs and also upgrade their standards.

Much social work has been done for many unreached peoples. If the missionary's children are neglected, neither the children of the missionaries nor others who may consider mission work will come into the missions.

> When missionaries do not get sufficient support, ... the parents of Christian children who commit themselves for missionary work hesitate to send their children for missionary work... When there is opposition and resistance from family members and friends, particularly because of inadequate financial support, young people are discouraged from pursuing their missionary calling. If only their basic needs like the children's education, medical care, post-retirement care and calamity relief are given consideration, there will be no dearth of committed and high-calibre people to join the missionary task force.[89]

On a positive note, Herbert Kane observed that separation from children was a part of missionary life. Sending children away to school was not as difficult as some people imagine. Missionaries were not the only ones with this problem. Life in the mission school was usually happy and wholesome. The vast majority of MK's[90] turn out well although there were some casualties.[91] This is only one of the opinions.

To meet the needs of college going missionary children the suggestion was to set up "A self financed multi disciplined college with 50% reservation to MKs at a highly subsidised fees and/or with sponsorship."[92]

Pension and Retirement Benefits

As missionaries retire, missions slowly become aware of their needs. They need some security to live. Most missionaries did not feel comfortable to live in the shadows of their children, as is the case for many Indians in the country. Very few of the present missionaries have any income from ancestral properties. Thus, there have been anxieties on both their part and the mission. Pensions would assure a regular income, but preparations are lacking.

MUT was grappling with the following needs of post retirement: 1) Pension scheme to ensure regular monthly income; 2) A scheme to facilitate those who still wish to serve the Lord in outreach work nearby; and 3) Accommodation for those who do not have children/house on their own.[93] Younger missionaries are encouraged to pay in money for a pension.[94] The Executive Committee of IMA requested that all the IMA staff be put under a pension scheme as soon as possible for a regular income in the future.[95] In the same way some missions are planning to start pension schemes.

Most missions have been following a Provident Fund (PF) policy, deducting a sum from the missionary's salary to invest for the missionary's future needs, usually in recurring fixed deposits.[96] Thus when the missionary retires, there will be some money available. Even before retirement, he may take loans for special needs of his family such as marriage for his sons or daughters. Also, there are gratuity schemes. Depending upon the years missionaries invest in an agency, they will be paid a certain amount when they retire or leave the mission.

Perhaps different Indian companies should be contacted to arrange the best pension schemes for missionaries. As done by the European Missions Association (EMA), IMA could help the mission agencies to get the best pension scheme.[97] IMA could do this through its National Institute of Christian Management (NICM). Or this could be carried out by an independent agency such as a Missions Standards Association (MSA), if and when it is formed. MSA, if it becomes a reality, also could help the missions to set standards as compatible as possible.

Personal Housing

A missionary working for many years in West Bengal establishing churches reached fifty-five and had nowhere to go. He asked another missionary, his distant relative, if he could live with him as he was a refugee to the country and had no parents or property. The best years of his life were spent in winning people to Christ. He had two grown up daughters to be married. He worried about the dowry that he might have to pay for his daughters' marriage. He was strong in the Lord, but worried since he had no answers for his wife and children.

A CEO who served in cross-cultural mission was left stranded as he was approaching his sixties with retirement around the corner. He was confused about housing and wished that he had a small plot with a house to retire.

In the Western situation Marjorie Collins notes,

In many areas it is possible to find adequate, yet

inexpensive housing near a mission oriented church, or in a community where Christian workers are well accepted and also utilised in ministries... Single retirees are sometimes invited to share a home with a friend. Couples are sometimes provided for by their children. Mission minded churches have occasionally provided retirement facilities for those whom they have supported on the field for many years.[98]

Her suggestions are excellent, but still there is a basic insecurity. What if they have no friends, nor mission minded church to provide housing, nor children of their own. Some retirees have all of the above. Some do not. Solutions are needed. Mission leaders as a pastoral responsibility should discuss this with their missionaries. They may even negotiate with sending churches, and not at the last minute before retirement, but as a process early enough in the life of a missionary.

Some thought has been given to housing for retired Indian missionaries. Patrick Joshua of FMPB felt there should be homes/flats where retired missionaries could live the rest of their life with dignity.[99] Winston said that a few years ago he designed houses for missionaries in Danishpet, Salem, but no one took it up. It is a big project. The way forward is to call for interested partners like the Esther Enterprises of Bangalore and work through them. Let such Christian companies carry on the job and slowly provide housing. Such ventures could be undertaken across India.[100] Recently Esther Enterprises announced the availability of plots for missionaries near Virudunagar and Thirunelveli at low cost, and were even willing to give them on instalment payment basis.[101]

If when a missionary joined, a mission bought a house with a housing loan and rented it to pay the mortgage, by the time the missionary finished his service the house could belong to him. If the missionary did not want the house in that location, he could sell it and buy at another location. Winston disagreed with the reasoning that a missionary does not need to have a house because he is a servant of God. The legal implications could be easily worked out.[102]

Providing a house for retiring missionaries would help them not to move from one mission to another also, and would give a deep sense of being cared for, a feeling of self-worth and belonging. Jesus said, "In my Father's house are many mansions; ...I go to prepare a place for you."[103] Home is a place of rest and care, of belonging and security.[104] A home for the missionary is a blessing and it is not unspiritual to have a house to rest in and be encouraged.

Death Relief

Sunder Raj wrote the following to MM Maxton, the Director of India Every Home Crusade, "We are saddened to learn of the untimely death of a young IEHC evangelist in lightning in Bihar. Please convey our condolences to the bereaved family. We are trying to send some small contribution towards that family."[105]

In another story Bose Meiyappan, the General Secretary of Church Growth Missionary Movement (CGMM) wrote to well wishers,

P. Jacob working in CGMM for nearly ten years needs open heart surgery on twenty-third of September 1996 at Christian Mission Hospital, Madurai. This operation and follow-up treatment cost above Rs. 1,20,000. He comes from a poor family. We covet your earnest prayer and also your financial support for this cause. Whatever the Spirit of God induces you to give, please give.[106]

However, Brother P. Jacob in his thirty-sixth year died.

"Sister Mary, wife of Brother Immanuel Paul suffered from cancer for more than one month before she died, leaving behind her husband and five children."[107] Brother Mangal Panna, in a riot instigated by anti-Christians, was pelted with stones and bricks and was killed by an injury from an axe. This happened after a mini Crusade. His brother was also left in a critical state. Mangal Panna left behind his wife and four children. He was strong in the Lord.[108] David Johnson's wife was critically ill and died during her delivery at Bhagvanpur village. The village had no medical facilities.[109] The above "three families of the deceased evangelists and missionaries have received a death relief fund of Rs. 10,000 each and one family Rs. 5000."[110] The families of Stephen Ekka of IEHC and Amalraj Peter of BYM who died recently were also given Rs. 10,000 each.[111] Chellappa of FMPB went to be with the Lord following a heart attack. On fourth July 1997, Matthew Philip from Nilambur, Kerala, working in Maharastra as a missionary with OM, was killed in an OM vehicle accident near Nasik. Their truck skidded and turned upside down when he and the team were returning from a prayer meeting. Matthew was caught under the truck and died in the hospital.[112] "On average about twenty missionaries die every year."[113]

As early as 1989 Jeyasingh, the administrative Assistant of GEMS wrote,

> Since a few months, I have been thinking of the fami-
> lies of missionaries who die suddenly or go under
> major treatment. To add to my burdens recently I heard
> about the death of a young missionary of IEM and also
> of a FMPB sister suffering from blood cancer .... After a
> long prayer I am inspired to write to you the following
> suggestion. As Government establishments, we can
> have a simple group financial assistance scheme like
> group insurance. If every missionary can contribute Rs.
> 20 per month, the collection from a thousand mission-
> aries will annually yield Rs. 2,40,000. By this money we
> can pay Rs. 50,000 immediately to the next of kin of the
> missionary who dies in action and also finance the
> missionaries who need major medical treatment.[114]

"Either a sum of Rs. 1,00,000 or Rs. 1000 per month as relief to the bereaved family would be very beneficial."[115]

From 1977, MUT has had a plan of providing Rs. 25,000 to the deceased missionary's family. This Calamity Relief Fund was called IMPACT. The Rs. 25,000 was sent to the family of the deceased missionary through the mission in which the missionary worked. MUT collected this fund from all the missionaries who became members of this project. Each missionary was encouraged to contribute five rupees each and then the amount was re-depos-ited in the fund. Thus a rotation of endowment fund was made available.[116]

There is a dawning awareness of responsibility on the part of the Indian Church and mission bodies to help families of mission-aries who die in action. IMA prescribed the following conditions for the families of the deceased missionaries: that the missionary should be under sixty years old when he died irrespective of the retirement age in his mission, full-time paid staff with a minimum service of two years with a member mission of IMA in good standing. His gross monthly family income must not exceed Rs. 6000 per month including all allowances and perks.[117] The gross wealth and savings of the family apart from one house must not exceed Rs. 50,000.[118] Missionaries working in organisations with no field staff engaged in evangelism, church planting, or Bible translation are not eligible. Those who are working in organisa-tions which already have a similar scheme will not be eligible, but the shortfall will be met if the amount is less than the prescribed IMA scheme. Lastly, the scheme is not available to those who are employed after their retirement or voluntary retirement.[119]

In response to these conditions for death relief for families of a deceased missionary, Shunmugam said that all missionaries should be treated equally and honoured for their service irrespective of their salaries. He compared it to a medal for a soldier who falls in battle. Right now, most missionaries receive a gross income greater than Rs. 6000 per month if house rent and children's education expenses are counted. The limit of Rs. 6000 would mean for most part that only families of missionaries to tribals would qualify for the death relief. For how many years will this Rs. 6000 figure stand? Who will revise the amount? If a particular missionary's family is well off, they could always return the amount as a gift to the same fund in order to benefit needier missionaries.[120] Winston defended the policy as safeguarding the sacrificial giving of Christians in order to make sure the most deserving families benefit.[121] Discerning just who is 'deserving' is no easy task. On the other hand an honour is an honour. There needs to be flexibility so that each missionary can be honoured.

Conclusion

Missions must look after missionaries. They are the backbone of the agency. If the backbone is weak the agency will not last and the agency and also evangelisation of India will fail. We must strengthen the missionary to better evangelise this nation.

For comparison, we may look at The *Waqfh* Board[122] of the Muslims and the Hindu Temple trusts. They do their homework in caring for their priests. Each State in India has schemes to care for them. The following is the scheme for the Hindu priests from the Tamil Nadu Hindu Religious Charitable Endowments.

Archaha's[123] Schemes: Death Benefit Rs. 25,000; Medical benefit Rs. 15,000; for marriage of each child Rs. 15,000 and pension Rs. 500. In addition there are scholarships for the education of their children.[124]

Much more so, Christians need to systematically care for their missionaries who carry the good news of Christ. They need care in order to do their work, which means training them and giving them the best tools. They need care to relate to their own co-workers. They need assistance in relationship to the non-Christians to whom they are witnesses. Merely recruiting missionaries and leaving them alone will not achieve the Great Commission of Christ in India.

We need to respond to their anxieties by providing for their needs for the family, starting with a salary compatible with that of a normal secular task. We need to take care of children's education. Some can cope with sending their children to hostels, at times, a thousand kilometres away. Others need the funds to keep their children nearer, where they can see them more often and where they feel comfortable with their children's education.

Most missionaries have no medical insurance and when they fall ill, struggle to pay the bills. The missions perhaps are willing to pay the big bills, but have no money to do so. When missionaries fall ill, they may feel a burden. Their self-worth and security deteriorate. This must change so that missionary children and others who consider mission will not hesitate thinking a missionary is not taken care of.

Missions can recognise the worth of missionaries by planning for their housing and pension after their retirement. A missionary who has given a life of service to the Lord Jesus Christ, in the front-line, is worthy of a house and a respectable retired life. Even godless secular companies recognise this. Mission leaders must be wary of the false teaching that the things of this world will not last and so missionaries do not need a house when they retire. Some mission leaders make the missionaries feel guilty by messages of a lost world, and Jesus' quick return. This automatically makes a missionary feel that even thinking of a house and pension after retirement is sinful. This attitude perpetuates insecurity both in the person and in family members.

Our ability to recruit missionaries and reduce attrition hinges on the way present Indian missionaries are looked after by their agencies and sending churches. We must not accept a double standard – a lower one for the missionaries and a higher standard for the rest of the Christians. Both missionaries and other Christian believers are called to be disciples and bearers of the message of Christ.

Missions must care for missionaries or mission work will decline. On this depends a large portion of the success of the missions. Good mission strategy is only a second reason for the mission's success. Care of the missionary and strategy must go hand in hand. Strategy without care for missionary personnel will achieve little and will collapse in the long run.

END NOTES

1 Waack, *Church and Mission*, pp. 303, 316.

2 Jayaprakash, *Indigenous Missions*, pp.17–18.

3 Chacko Thomas, interviews while working at the state of Bihar.

4 Vernon J. Sterk, "Territorial Spirits and Evangelisation in Hostile Environments," C. Peter Wagner [Ed.], *Territorial Spirits*, (Chichester, England: Sovereign World Limited, 1991), p. 154.

5 Dr Keith Benn, Bible Translation Consultant, SIL, Letter to IMA. November 16, 1996.

6 Edward C. Pentecost, *Issues in Missiology* (Michigan: Baker Book House, 1982), p. 199.

7 Ibid, pp. 195–196.

8 Waack, *Church and Mission*, pp. 348–349.

9 MM Clark, *A Corner in India*, (Gauhati: Christian Literature Centre, 1978), p. 17.

10 Frederick S. Downs, *Christianity in North East India*, (Delhi: ISPCK, 1983), p. 123.

11 Jesse Page, *Henry Martyn of India and Persia*, (London: Pickering & Inglis, [n.d.], pp. 78–79.

12 Poulose, missionary to North in 70's, interview, Bihar, 1975.

13 Marjorie A. Collins, *Manual for Today's Missionary*, (Pasadena: William Carey Library, 1986), p. 25.

14 Lehmann, *It Began at Tranquebar*, pp. 33–34.

15 Sargent, *Letters of Henry Martyn*, pp. 183–185.

16 C.E. Padwick, "Henry Martyn," JD Douglas [Ed.], *The New International Dictionary of the Christian Church*, (Michigan: Regency Reference Library, 1994), p. 638.

17 Collins, *Manual for Today's Missionary*, p. 216.

18 Jayaprakash, *Indigenous Missions*, p. 3.

19 Rev. Kulothungan, Director, Maharastra Village Ministries, personal interview, Nagpur, April 17, 1997.

20 Personal interview, name withheld, July 1997.

21 Collins, *Manual for Today's Missionary*, p. 360.

22 E. Anantharaj, Neemkathana, "Longings of a Missionary", *Mission and Vision—Who and What?* (Bangalore: MUT, 1996), p. 15.

23 Personal interview, name withheld, July 1997.

24 Personal interview, name withheld, May 1997.

25 Shyam Winston, IMA Management Consultant, personal interview, Chennai, September

1997.

26 James Kaiser, IMA Ministry Coordinator's report of his visit to a mission, (name withheld), September 10, 1997.

27 Abubakker, an ex-FMPB missionary, Vellore, July 1997.

28 George Edward, FMPB, interview, at SAIACS, Bangalore, 1997.

29 Sunil and Suma, interview, SAIACS, Bangalore, February 14, 1988.

30 Kingsly (real name withheld), personal interview, Bangalore, October, 1997.

31 Page, *Henry Martyn*, pp. 64–65.

32 OM India policy.

33 Jonathan Lewis, "Investigating the Causes and Cures of Attrition" [n.p], [n.d.] p. 5.

34 David and Grace Shunmugam, ex-missionaries to North India, personal interview, Chennai, July 1997.

35 Warren G. Bennis. "Theory and Method in Applying Behavioral Science to Planned Organisational Change," Alton C. Bartlett and Thomas A. Kayser (Eds.), *Changing Organisational Behaviour*, (New Jersey: Prentise-Hall, Inc, 1973), p. 80.

36 Lawrence O'Richards, *A Practical Theology of Spirituality*, (Michigan: Academie Books, 1987), p. 246–247.

37 Gopal Hembrom, personal interview when he visited Bangalore on September 14, 1997.

38 Hudson Taylor's quote— inscribed on the stone at the entrance of SAIACS, Bangalore.

39 David Shunmugam, a former OM Leader and at present a pastor with the Free Evangelical Church at Madras, personal interview, July 1996.

40 Winston, Consultant, interview, Chennai, August 1997.

41 IMA, *My Prayer Guide*, (Madras: IMA, 1996), p. 3.

42 Andrew, an ex-missionary to Assam, personal interview, Vellore, September 1997.

43 Newbigin, *The Good Shepherd*, p. 54.

44 Reported by James Kaiser as he visited *Samrajya* Ministries, September 1997, (Real name has been withheld).

45 Correspondence, the name of the CEO is withheld.

46 Roy. T. Daniel, "Evangelists Need More," *Insight India— Assembly Testimony Journal*, April–June (1997) 6.

47 Roy. T. Daniel, "Missionary's Cost Index," *Insight India— Assembly Testimony Journal*, April–June (1997) 8.

48 IMA Annual General Body Meeting, discussion held at Chennai on October 17, 1997.

49 IMA 1996–97 audit report, for AGM, Chennai on October 17, 1997.

50 Letter received from an IMA member mission (identity was with held) on October 17, 1997.

51 M. Deepu, OM, personal interview, Hyderabad, 1994.

52 Winston, "Life Savers," Rathnakumar and Krupa, (Eds.), *Mission and Vision*, p. 21.

53 The writers experience, Hazaribagh, 1973.

54 The writer's experience, Banmanki, N. Bihar, 1973.

55 MC Matthew, IMA Health Care Support for Missionaries, a proposal, September 1995.

56 Winston, personal interview, Chennai, November 26, 1997.

57 Rudolfo "Rudy" Giron, "An Integrated Model of Missions," A paper presented at Mission Commission Workshop, World Evangelical Fellowship, U.K., April 9–13, 1996. p. 1.

58 Johnny Desai, personal interview, SAIACS, Bangalore, February 1997.

59 Jiji Chacko, personal interview, SAIACS, Bangalore, September, 1996.

60 M. Deepu, OM, interview at Calicut, November 16, 1997.

61 Winston, Sunder Raj and Rajendran's discussion on involving Grace Counselling India, November 25, 1997.

62 John Zachariah's letter to IMA, November 11, 1997.

63 [n.a.] *National Consultation on Evangelism*, Hyderabad, September, 1996.

64 J. Herbert Kane, *Life and Work on the Mission Field*, (Michigan: Baker Book House, 1980), pp. 189–191.

65 Waack, *Church and Mission*, p. 381.

66 Raja Mohan Das, late IEM Associate General Secretary, personal interview, ICSA, Chennai, October 17, 1997.

67 David Shunmugam, after visiting him at the Vellore CMC, November, 1997.

68 MC Matthew, IMA Health Care Support Proposal.

69 OM India policy on Medical needs.

70 P. Gnanaraj, CEO, Christian Life Service, person interview, Bangalore, October 14, 1997.

71 IMA Health Care Network, planning meeting, held at Madras on October 12, 1995.

72 Dr MC Matthew, Chairman, Evangelical Medical Fellowship of India & Health Adviser to India Missions Association, "Forward", Dr Kuruvilla George, *A Health Manual for Indian Missionaries*, IMA Publication.

73 Ebenezer Sunder Raj's letter addressed to all the mission hospital doctors and copies to mission leaders, September 28, 1995.

74 **Health Insurance – Exclusions**
   1. Diseases in existence at the time of taking this insurance.
   2. Expenses incurred in the first 30 days from the date of Insurance except in the case of renewal or injury arising out of accident.
   3. During the first year of the operation of insurance, the expenses on treatment of diseases such as Cataract, Benign Prostatic Hypertrophy, Hysterectomy for Menorrhagia or Fibro myoma, Hernia, Hydrocele, Congenital Internal diseases, Fistula in Anus, Piles, Sinusitis and related disorders.
   4. Circumcision, change of life, cosmetic or aesthetic treatment of any description, plastic surgery other than as may be necessitated due to an accident or as a part of any illness.

5. Cost of spectacles and contact lenses, hearing aids.

6. Dental treatment or surgery of any kind unless requiring hospitalisation.

7. Convalescence, general debility, "Run-down" condition or rest cure, congenital external disease or defects or anomalies, sterility, venereal disease, intentional self-injury and use of intoxicating drugs/alcohol.

8. Treatment of AIDS.

9. Charges not consistent with or incidental to the diagnosis and treatment.

10. Expenses on vitamins and tonics unless forming part of treatment.

11. Treatment of pregnancy, childbirth including Caesarean section.

12. Voluntary medical termination of pregnancy during the first 12 weeks.

13. Naturopathy treatment.

Domiciliary hospitalisation:
Claims for treatment taken at home will be paid only up to 20% of the Insured amount. However many diseases are excluded for this purpose. Further it has to be proved that treatment was taken at home as there was no room in the hospital or that the patient could not be removed to the hospital.

Source:

Shalom Advisory on Finance for Evangelists, *SAFE*, 47, Srinivasa Nagar, Koyembedu, Chennai 600 107. Phone: 487 1009.

75 IMA Staff Meeting minutes, Chennai, November 11, 1997.

76 Ibid.

77 [n.a.] National Consultation on Evangelism, Hyderabad, September 1996.

78 Raja Kumar, IMA Office Administrator, personal interview, Chennai, November 30, 1997.

79 Asian Missions Congress II – "In to the 21st Century," Pattaya, Thailand, September 29–October 3, 1997.

80 James Kaiser, Former FMPB missionary, Chennai, July 1997.

81 John and Mercy Matthew, IEM missionaries, personal interview at SAIACS, Bangalore in October 1996.

82 Waack, *Church and Mission*, p. 387.

83 Collins, *Manual for Today's Missionary*, p. 194.

84 Oswald J. Smith, *The Challenge of Missions*, (Bromley: STL Books, 1983), p. 103.

85 MC Matthew, IMA Health Care Support Proposal.

86 Approximately US $ 686,400. Presently US $ 1 = Rs. 42

87 Premi Koshy and Tracy West, "Griha Shiksha; Home Schooling in India. Development Plan Proposal 1997–2000", March 1997. C/O Interserve, C–20 Community Centre (First Floor) Janakpuri, New Delhi 110 058

88 Isaac Israel, CEO Rural Blessing Mission, personal interview at Wardha, Maharastra on October 31, 1997.

89 [n.a], "Longings of a Supporter", *Mission and Vision—*

Who and What? (Bangalore: MUT, 1996) p. 34.

90 MK's—Missionary Kids.

91 Kane, *Life and work on the Mission Field*, pp. 189–191.

92 [n.a.] *Consultation on Evangelism*, Hyderabad, September 1996.

93 MUT working paper of polices for a consultation on Missionary Welfare sent to IMA for feedback, [n.d.]

94 Raja Kumar, IMA Office Manager, Chennai, Sept. 1997.

95 IMA Executive Committee, Chennai on October 16, 1997.

96 OM cuts 12 percent of the salaries of their missionaries and adds 12 percent and invests it as Provident Fund.

97 Winston, IMA, personal interview, Chennai, August 1997.

98 Collins, *Manual for Today's Missionary*, p. 362.

99 Patrick Joshua, General Secretary, FMPB, personal interview at SAIACS, Bangalore, October 15, 1996.

100 Winston, personal interview, Chennai, August 1997.

101 Letter from the Esther Enterprises, December 1997.

102 Winston, personal interview, Chennai, August 1997.

103 John 14:1.

104 Carol Houghton, Lecture on Christian Family, at SAIACS, Bangalore, November 1996.

105 Sunder Raj's letter to MM Maxton July 24, 1996.

106 Bose Meiyappan, GS of CGMM, an open letter September 18, 1997.

107 News, GEMS Flashes for Praise and Prayer, July 1997.

108 Ibid, July 1997.

109 Letter, GEMS Flashes for Praise, July 1997.

110 IMA GS' Report for the Year 1996–97.

111 IMA Staff Meeting, Chennai, November 11, 1997.

112 OM *'India Area Communique,'* July 1997.

113 [n.a.] *Consultation on Evangelism*, Hyderabad, September 1996.

114 Jeyasingh, GEMS Administrative Assistant's letter to IMA General Secretary, July 13, 1989.

115 [n.a.] Consultation, Hyderabad, September 1996.

116 Rathnakumar, Secretary MUT, interview, Chennai IMA Office September 27, 1997.

117 Family, here, means self, spouse and unmarried children in case the missionary was married; self and parents if the missionary was unmarried. Even this is a low amount for a missionary in the city. This basically means only the missionaries who worked among the tribals will get this benefit. The author suggests a gross income of 12,000 including all the perks, especially if this includes all the allowance of children's education etc. This needs more thought.

118 Sunder Raj's letter to all member missions on "Missionaries Death Relief Scheme," Ref. No. M/Relief/71, March 18, 1996.

119 IMA–"Missionaries Death Relief Scheme Launched." Draft Proposal, [n.d.]

120 Shunmugum, former mission-

ary to Bihar, personal communication, Chennai/Bangalore, November 1997.

121 Winston, Interview, Chennai, December 2, 1997.

122 *Waqfh* Board—Islamic mosque management board.

123 *Archaha*—a Hindu priest.

124 Winston, IMA, Interview, Chennai, September 22, 1997.

7

Mission and Strategy

After all the challenging stages of recruitment and orientation missionaries arrive on the mission field, shocked, confronted by issues previously only theoretical. They must find solutions. Some problems have no solutions, and solutions that work in Tamil Nadu or in Kerala may or may not work in Haryana or in Bengal and vice-versa. Fields differ in languages, cultures, ethos, worldviews and even geographical context.

"You cannot have water from my tap," said Arun's neighbour. Arun and his co-workers were surprised that all of a sudden his neighbour whom he had known several months refused drinking water. This was because the team was associating with lower caste people in the town. This neighbour who is of a higher caste did not like that. How sad![1]

Arun and his mission team in Gujarat had to make decisions about whom they should associate with.

Mass Movement versus Individual Conversion

December eighth of the year 1977 is a red-letter day in the history of the FMPB's mission among the Kuknas.[2] On this day in the village of Halmoody forty-two tribals have accepted Jesus as their Saviour and pro-claimed it openly by entering the water baptism. These believers were from nine different villages ... . According to the statistics gathered in January 1997, not less than 22,605 Kukna tribals have joined the local churches. Their 296 prayer groups and churches have been built in 121 places. Fifty-two local evangelists ... and eighty catechists.[3]

Much argument goes on among the mission agencies about mass movements as opposed to individual conversions and numerical growth as against qualitative growth. Mission views are coloured by the theological tint of individuals. This seems more a problem in the newer evangelical churches than in the mainline churches, since personal conversion and piety are emphasised more in the evangelical churches.

Roberta Winter, looking at the history of the Celts and the Goths AD. 400 to 800, commented, "The Barbarians had been 'Christianised', somewhat, but their understanding of the nature of Christ was imperfect. They were eventually won over to the theology of those they invaded."[4] In other words, they were eventually discipled. Graham Houghton, Principal of SAIACS, believes that in the process of conversion more is changed than is usually implied by the word "conversion".[5] Conversion is a process, not just an event although it may start with an event.

The question of mass movement or individual conversion resurfaced with the Homogenous Unit Principle (HUP) of Dr. Donald McGavran. It was not that McGavran was against individual conversion, but he wanted a whole group brought to Christ first and then discipled one by one, as part of the group.[6]

Peoples become Christians as a wave of decision for Christ sweeps through the group mind, involving many individual decisions... This may be called a chain reaction. Each decision sets off others and the sum total powerfully effects every individual. When conditions are right, not merely each sub-group concerned decides together.[7]

McGavran called this a people movement, and saw its strength in people acting together. Without it they may be unstable in their faith. This theme is close to the ethos of movements like DAWN, CGAI, Evangelical Church in India and Brethren in Christ in Bihar. Francis Xavier employed mass conversion methods to Christianise people.[8]

Evangelicals and evangelical missions are afraid that mass movement will result in syncretism and compromising of Christian faith. This makes it sound as if there are no problems with individual conversions. Many quote circumstances like the mass conversions and baptisms years ago in parts of North West India and note that today few Christians remain in those places.[9] Ironically however, this fear is often voiced by people whose great-grand parents themselves were the fruits of mass conversion in places like Tirunelveli and Tuticorin.

From 1810 members of the caste now called the Nadars began to ask for baptism. Though he (Ringeltaube) refused them at first, not being satisfied with their motives, he baptised four hundred of them during the following year. ... After the arrival of his successor,

Charles Mead, in 1817 a great mass movement of Nadars into Christianity began, which continued throughout the nineteenth century.[10]

Several other mass movements took place in the North Eastern States of India, Bihar, UP, Gujarat, Maharastra, Punjab and AP.[11] Of the Punjab mass conversion Frederick and Margaret Stock wrote, "In the first twenty years of mission work in Punjab, the problem of caring for converts became increasingly acute. In this way the mission station became the centre for the new band of believers."[12] The presence of Christians in Pakistan was attributed to the mass movements of people to Christ in the mid-1800's to early 1900's.[13]

They[14] had found that to convert a family rather than an individual could readily start a chain reaction of conversions... Since there were no artificial barriers within the caste group, sometimes the entire caste group would enter the Christian community by virtue of a group decision. This pattern conserved the immediate social relationships of the individual convert and by utilising them as lines of infiltration within the caste walls, the missionaries often immensely speeded up the evangelising process.[15]

The study showed that most Christians in India and Pakistan were the result of mass movements in early missionary endeavours, so most certainly we cannot discount the value of mass conversion to favour exclusively individual conversion. When the mass were given attention and follow-up with biblical teachings and examples, they could be as spiritual as an individual convert. Bishop Neill summarised,

Bishop Pickett of the Methodist Church showed,[16] first that an overwhelming percentage of India's Christians owe their origins to group movements, ... secondly, that for India, ... group movements are to be expected, and to be accepted as the natural way of movement of the Spirit of God. Of course individual conversion must remain the aim, but this is much more likely to occur and to bear permanent fruit within the frame work of the family and a community which has already been in part Christianised.[17]

The key was follow-up. The missionaries who baptised many at Tirunelveli struggled to provide follow-up due to a lack of workers. "Hough (1816–1821) did what he could, supplying Bibles and prayer books, teaching catechists and teachers and superintending."[18] In Tirunelveli the number of the baptised in the SPG area alone increased by 12,000 in the six years following 1877.[19]

Although mission compounds are heavily criticised by some today, there was often no choice in those days. However, in recent times, as a reaction against mission compound cultures, attempts have been made to place new believers in the mainstream society, but it does not work in all cases. Some new believers from difficult backgrounds have to be rescued and rehabilitated, or else they will backslide. The Church in general is not willing to accept new people, especially new Hindu and Muslim converts, to be discipled.[20] Follow-up must strengthen believers. "The late Samuel Shoemaker rightly said, 'The test of a man's conversion is whether he has enough Christianity to get it over to other people. If he hasn't something is wrong in it.'"[21]

The way forward on individual or mass conversion lies with balance and good follow-up. In missions today in the midst of the vehement debates, many individuals and large groups become Christian believers.

Many people who moved with mass movements were eventually discipled and led into deep-rooted faith in Christ. In the beginning many turned to Christ for reasons other than spiritual. The Kukna people are one example of what God did in a community.[22] Society can be built with a mass turning to Christ. In one sense it is easier to disciple the mass rather than one individual, and the subsequent discipling of individuals could be significant in bringing the nation to Christ. This does not rule out the need for personal faith in Christ, for each person to be accepted by God through Christ and through His sacrifice for each individual. A balance is needed to include both mass and individual conversions.

Integration of Converts vis-à-vis the Christian Mindset

When Gandhi was in South Africa, one of his close friends tried to persuade him to confess Christ. As he considered this, Gandhi went to a famous church and was evicted. After that for years he never went inside any church. In later years he occasionally went into churches. Worship in public was not common in Hinduism, but he conducted services in the open-air with strong similarities to Christian worship.[23] It is food for thought that since then any number of Gandhis may have been thrown out of churches due to colour, caste and other prejudices. The famous Tamil cinema music composer, Illaya Raja, was one who left the church in his early years as he was considered "odd" by church traditions and did not exactly fit in.[24]

John Vandayar said that he was welcomed into each church, because his presence added to the number in the church, but he never felt accepted by the people and eventually left one church after other. He felt that not many missed him.[25] Abubakker, Shunmugam and Karpagam – all from other faiths testified to similar experiences.[26] Suresh became a Christian and a member of a Pentecostal Church and studied at SABC at Bangalore. One pastor insisted on the importance of changing his "Hindu" name to a Christian one! Suresh tried to explain that his relationship to Christ was more important than his name and it was a help to witness to his friends that being a Christian was actually not about changing names. There was also the hassle of legal complications in changing one's name. Eventually Suresh gave up explaining anything to this Pastor.[27] Many converts still find it difficult to enter and adapt to the traditional Christian cultures. The brave survive. Some others return to their comfortable communities. Those who survived with the traditional Christians said it took a long time to establish their credibility, unlike second and third generation Christians who had families to vouch for them. Ravi Kumar, a headmaster in a school, felt this even though he attended a Brethren Church. He felt they lacked concern. His marriage was delayed, due to the difficulty of finding a bride who would be able to adjust to his family members. There was pressure from his family to marry a Hindu if he did not find a Christian bride.[28] Girls converted from other faiths find life even more difficult. Unless the Church is willing to receive and train the new converts with sensitivity, it will be hard to establish them in the existing churches. Converts tend to wander from their present churches, slowing the number who could turn to Christ. With the current mind-set of Christians, there is much less hope for a mass movement to Christ by middle class and upper middle classes. We need a shift in the mindset to receive and nurture converts. Missionaries may like to be innovative here.

Ashok Kumar, a former State cycle champion of Kerala and a winner of awards, started a fellowship called *Kristanugami Sangh*.[29] They gathered contacts from the majority community and followed up in discipling them for Christ.[30] In the same manner Abubakker named his centre the Fellowship for Neighbours. He gathered interested Ishmaelites and taught them before they returned to their communities as witnesses for Christ.[31]

We need to teach, demonstrate and train church people on this issue. Caste churches or homogeneous groups or missions are in a disadvantaged position if they are not open to receive any other "people" in their midst and disciple them. However, if they are trained, according to Bishop Waskom Pickett, "Every convert is a potential evangelist and the potentialities of many converts are enormous."[32]

Christianity and Contextualisation

The returning crusaders, ... in Constantinople saw the enormous, shining St. Sophia mosque, built by a Christian emperor as a cathedral but later taken over by Muslims. This led to the desire of cathedrals, some- what as a fad. All of the major cathedrals in Europe were begun within a fifty year period. This thrust, while not inherently evil, became the focus of the Church while evangelisation was neglected to the side-lines.[33]

For some, the cathedral is synonymous with Christianity. "There is sometimes a tendency to forget the wide difference between the two and to think that to introduce Christianity means also introducing Western ways of life."[34] When Christians are diverted from the finality of Christ, they get side-tracked from their goals and neglect evangelism.

The famous Jesuit, Francis Xavier, who worked in India 1506– 52, followed the thinking of the medieval missionary church that everything in non-Christian life should be abolished before Chris- tianity could be introduced. Of course he changed his mind when he reached Japan, where he saw a culture superior to that of the West.[35] Frederick W. Norris called this "Radical Displacement", where Christianity with its entire Western (or whatever the na- tional culture of the missionaries) cultural baggage was trans- planted whole and ethnic religion was brushed aside as value- less.[36] This mindset worked against contextualising Christ's teachings to the cultures in India.

Asking why Christianity did not take root in India, Khushwant Singh observed,

That Christianity was never able to erase the taint of

being alien to the soil of India ... . India did not produce a Christian saint of its own ... . Sadhu Sunder Singh came close to it. ... Indian Christianity needed a *Mahatma*; all it produced were men and women, good scouts, girl guides, directors, YMCA and YWCA.[37]

Khushwant Singh's desire for a saint seems to have been fulfilled in Mother Theresa of Calcutta. Her funeral was glorious with full military honours, second only to the funeral given Gandhi. She was called the "Saint of the Gutters". Prime Minister Gujral said, "A beacon of light and hope for millions of poor has gone out of our lives."[38] She became a saint to millions of Indians and others even during her lifetime. She was up front with her faith in Christ and as an expression of it, loved by all people. Neither the BJP, the Hindu communal tinted party or Arun Shourie could point their fingers unfavourably at Mother Theresa. A saint was established and now it is time for Christians unashamedly to work, demonstrating the love of Christ.

Given the varied and changing cultures of India, one must contextualise the teachings of Christ in multiple ways of service, worship and proclamation. Neill Anderson, the President of Freedom in Christ Ministries says, "The world is changing at an alarming rate. ... The ecclesiastical challenge is to give anxious people the timeless message of Christ and present it in contemporary way that relates to a changing culture."[39]

Mangalwadi and Richard want an inward change in Christians rather than outward. Then there is less risk of losing the timeless message when contextualising to Indian culture.[40]

In both churches and missions the debate is not over. Many see a need for a change, but what and how to go about it is the question. Acharya Daya Prakash Titus through his ministry of Indian Evangelical Fellowship (IEF) reported a seven-hour seminar at Kottayam on August 2, 1997, for eighty clergy and churchmen. Towards the end of the seminar forty people stayed behind and concluded that the time was ripe to reach the educated classes.[41] Except for such minor efforts to contextualise, little has been done to swim against the current of Christian Traditionalism with a Western link. Most people are traditional and it is hard to change them.[42] The lesson for the church is not to change too much of a local culture unless it is harmful or a sin against God.

According to Bruce Nicholls, indigenisation is relating the

Gospel to the traditional cultures of the people. Contextualisation includes all that is right in indigenisation but in a wider context including contemporary and changing cultural patterns of life. Increasingly Christians world-wide are recognising that the Gospel must be contextualised from one culture to another if God's kingdom is to be established on earth.[43] Ponraj explained that contextualisation means to interpret the Gospel and its implications in terms of the needs of the whole man and society. Contextualisation is not another word for indigenisation, but includes the concept. Both words have important meanings in the context of planting churches in India.[44] In a cross-cultural church-planting situation Doug Priest Jr. suggested that the Church should retain as many of the indigenous forms as possible, and explore the need for functional substitutes, but remain alert to safe-guard the faith against the incorporation of pagan beliefs.[45] This is where the tension exists. Rao reflects the same and adds that it involves risk. No interpretation is valid if the core of the Christian faith is sacrificed on the altar of adaptation to the Indian situation.[46] Norris proffers six ways to contextualise.

* the *radical displacement* of the culture, where the old host culture is completely shelved.
* the *discontinuity theory*, where the Christian superiority feels no comparison with the local culture, while it seeks to adapt itself to the cultural forms of the people.
* the *uniqueness theory* which recognises both religions unique but assumes Christianity is superior.
* the *legitimate borrowing theory*, where the commonality from both religions is accepted and borrowed to be truly indigenous.
* the *fulfilment theory*, where the Gospel of Christ is accepted as the fulfilment for people's quest in that culture.
* *relativistic syncretism*, which accepts that all religion contains different truths to lead to the ultimate Truth.[47]

Indigenisation, contextualisation and 'de-Westernisation' are interrelated themes. Rajaiah D. Paul way back in 1952 furiously proclaimed a need for de-westernisation.[48] Ralph Winter at GECOWE conference in South Africa in August 1997, challenged people to de-westernise Christianity to accommodate mass move-ments to Christ without a hangover of Western imperialism attached to the message. Sunder Raj said de-westernisation is no longer an issue for the Church in India which is a hangover from the colonial days. Now all that the missions and the churches need to do is to think and act responsibly to accommodate mass movements to Christ.[49] In this view we need not de-westernise, but develop strategies to present Christ without compromising the message. For this, the Church and missions must present the Gospel with flexibility as to the forms so that it will be palatable to the majority of the people in the country.

However, all the above men agree we need to change our approach to the evangelisation of India. Stanley Soltau, a missionary to Japan, emphasised that the introduction of Christ will inevitably bring changes even in their customs. But the changes are not introduced by the missionaries themselves but by God.[50] As Rao said, missionaries do not need to inject other cultures into the community to "make" them Christians. "The present task of indigenisation is to apply some surgery, separating the Christian message from Western Culture, then translate that same message into the context of Eastern Culture."[51]

SD Ponraj suggested three broad areas to consider: contextualising the theology of Gospel interpretation, contextualising the forms of Gospel expression, and contextualising the Church – its leadership, finance and witness.[52] There should be more detailed focus on witness, evangelistic methods, leadership and church government, finance, worship which includes seating, reading, posture, church buildings and life styles.[53]

However, Rao gave five cautions against extremes in contextualisation and indigenisation. Indigenisation is not being more Indian than Western. There is a great temptation for the *Ashramites* to try so hard to identify with things Indian that they compromise with Hindu thinking. Christians must work on separating Western culture and the message of Christ. They must identify the essential and non-essential elements in Christianity in order to keep the essential.[54] Christians must overcome the fear that ordinary people will equate the indigenised forms to Hindu forms and avoid indigenisation.[55]

According to Soltau, the results of the indigenised churches or missions are their strength, rapid growth, more wholesome relationship between the missionaries and the locals, more effective presentation of the Gospel and a wider outreach.[56]

S Pillai, a first generation follower of Christ asked, "Why can't churches be kept open for all people to visit at any time of the day and night?"[57] Pillai was asking culturally relevant questions.

Evangelism and/or Social Work.

Some missions are reluctant to start any community project as they do not have the funds. Others are afraid a community project would siphon funds away from evangelism, church planting and training.[58] Some even believe that both evangelism and social work would repel each other. Some are aware of the danger of community projects yet feel that there has to be a presence for evangelism.[59] Some believe only in community work and do not feel it is essential to proclaim the Gospel.[60] Some see community development and social work as on a par with leading people to Christ and discipling, making community development synonymous with evangelism. These are different perspectives.

Jayaprakash Joshi wrote, "The City of Calcutta has thousands of rickshaw pullers. Did any one think of reaching them? So far as it is known there is no effort to rehabilitate or to evangelise them."[61] It seems as though he was equating rehabilitation of the rickshaw pullers to making them disciples of Christ. Or perhaps a holistic theology places rehabilitation and evangelism on a par!

A priority shift in the churches of America has affected the Church world-wide so that they are now more socially and culturally conscious. The priority shift, based on a theological shift known as New Mission,[62] had the determined effort of the WCC to replace the Great Commission by a programme of humanisation and social liberation.[63] "New Mission" used the same key words such as mission, evangelism, conversion, salvation, liberation and Church, yet all these words meant something quite different from classical mission concepts.[64] Words like sin, salvation, sanctification and justification are regarded as outgrown and irrelevant.[65] Peter Wagner pleaded for balance. "The evangelistic mandate should have the top priority in carrying out God's work in the world. The great priority shift would lesson the effects of both the evangelistic and cultural mandates in the main line churches. This, in fact, has happened."[66] "Cultural mandate should not eclipse the evangelistic mandate."[67]

Wagner reasoned that if the church used its money for anything other than bringing people to Christ, and instead politically changed society, what would happen? Could the church replace local politics and take things into its own hands?[68] He insists that only the Gospel will change peoples' lives. People like Peter Wagner have been considered lone voices and fanatics. They have been accused as followers of the "Imperial Mission Model" from European and North American Missionaries, opposed to serving the total man.[69] This idea has been firmly implanted in the minds of some mission leaders even in India, especially the ones in leadership who feel strongly about the rise and the thrust of the third World leadership. They subtly dominate the guilty European and American Christian leaders, almost as a reaction to what white missionaries have done. One prominent Indian leader blatantly accused Americans of being "preaching" minded rather than meeting the physical and spiritual needs of the people.[70]

Ironically, most of the funding for these social projects comes from some of the same European and American Christians who were accused of being "preaching" minded. Every organisation which worked socially among the people, received most or a large amount of its income from overseas especially from Europe and America. Even Indian-funded missions divided their work in two. The missionary wing, funded from within India and the social wing funded from overseas. So arose a dichotomy among mission agencies across the nation. Some explained this by saying that if ever the social projects closed for some reason, the missions would carry on proclaiming the Gospel with Indian funds which supported the missionaries who were directly involved in evangelism. However, the groups that did social work had good resources. John Austin did say that in the West very few now give money for the preaching of the Gospel, but they give much for the social needs of the people. Therefore, designated money should be used for specified social purposes. Many of his long-term missionaries are now challenged to move into this aspect of work even if they are not fully convinced about its priority, or else they faced the sack.[71]

On this issue KP Yohannan rightly said,
Mission monies, once used to proclaim the Gospel, were more and more side tracked in to the social programmes towards which the new governments of the former colonies were more sympathetic. A convenient "theology of mission" developed that today equates social and political action with evangelism.[72] ... Social Concern is a natural fruit of the Gospel. But to put it first is to put the cart before the horse; and ... we have seen it fail in India for over 200 years.[73]
However, Ponraj, who mostly worked among the tribals in

Gujarat and Bihar, feels that social uplift of the tribals and Church growth are interrelated. He advises that any community development should be planned and set up with research and wisdom in a place where there already is some Christian presence to support it.[74] Social work should complement the growing Church.[75]

All do not subscribe to this view. Some feel that, in certain geographic areas or among some peoples, whether there is a church or not, the church has to make an entry point to find a beachhead. These agencies relentlessly work to establish a rapport with the people whether they are responsive or not. They feel that the proclamation of Christ necessitates compassion for all peoples and community development projects do motivate people to follow Christ. One Christian leader believes people have to be served whether they are Christians or not. He believes he must provide social benefit for all, so he does not want to link evangelism with it. Much money of this evangelistic agency goes into social work, with social ministries the focal point for raising funds.[76]

However, Ponraj was clear that development should not take priority over evangelism.[77] "Only changed men can change the society."[78] There has to be a perfect balance or else the mission will be sidetracked, as has been the case of some well-meaning missions in India.

Joseph D'Souza, the Director of OM India, asked why millions of Indians, although attracted to Christ, held back from following Christ. He answered his question thus,

The Church has been a bystander, seen as on the periphery of Indian society rather than an integral part … There has not been a sustained Indian expression of the reality of Jesus at the practical level during the last fifty years.[79]

Although D'Souza felt that the Church has been a bystander, it is necessary for the Church and missions to retain an unbiased view and a healthy image. In a previous chapter, the writer pointed out that most of the renaissance in India came about because of Christian input into society by the churches and missions. The Church has not been a bystander. Churches and missions have contributed much to alleviate the pain of the common people of India. In fact, the foundation for modern India is what the missionaries sacrificially have done for her.[80] It is inappropriate to thrust guilt and pressure about social work upon the Church and missions where people are in some cases breaking their backs to build India. Instead Christians must plan to maintain their social contribution as an expression of the compassion of Christ to our people in India. Thus people will be helped to admire and follow Christ.

As a policy, OM stayed away from becoming too involved in social work full-time except in cases of calamities when emergency relief work became necessary. This policy helped them to concentrate fully on training people for the mission field. If the focus shifted from training, they could have long ago side-tracked into other issues. OM always believed in social work as a complement to proclamation of the Gospel, but it empowered other missions to do the job while it concentrated on training people to communicate the Gospel effectively in different situations.[81] Now, as a new policy, OM is also directly involved in continuous social projects and development. According to D'Souza, less than ten percent of OM India's work is to help people in need.[82] However, in OM newsletter, nearly twenty-five to fifty percent of the news highlighted the aspect of the "Good Shepherd" social work. The explanation is that the reader likes to be made aware of such work and participates more in prayer and in resource sharing.[83] It is a challenge to all mission work to keep a correct focus and not drift into a totally humanitarian work for which there are other organisations.

The one hundred IMA Missions with fifteen thousand missionaries are now equally involved in Church planting and social work. Interestingly a survey of missions in 1987 found 57.17 percent of the missionaries were involved in church planting and only 7.17 per cent were doing development work. 20.99 per cent were not clear what they were doing.[84] Social work by the missions has increased and may grow more. We should keep a balance.

Church/Missions Relationships

The place of the Church in Indian missions is crucial, yet the debate on the role of the Church and Mission is on-going and never ending. Para-church missions have grieved the Church by imprudence. Some injudicious behaviour came from over-zealous, grassroots workers who insensitively annoyed each other. It was like what happened between the servants of Lot and Abraham. The problem was not with Lot and Abraham but between the workers.[85]

GW Peter regards mission structures as an "unfortunate and

abnormal historic development, which produced autonomous mission-less churches and churchless missionary societies."[86] Orlando Costas argued that the "existence of the missionary societies apart from the church bodies, in reality represented God's judgement upon the Church."[87] Ron Penny, working with the Brethren Assemblies, said that the Church must provide the base for mission as in Acts Thirteen, where Paul and Barnabas were set apart for missionary work. The Church had to take the initiative, as the sending headquarters for missions.[88] However, Ralph Winter insists that both structures were in God's plan and always existed simultaneously both in the Old and in New Testament periods. He called the Church structure the "modality" and the mission the "sodality". Both modality and sodality have uniquely contributed to Church growth and strengthened each other in the past.[89]

Both churches and para-church agencies struggle with biblical concepts, missiological concepts and the funding constituency – the church members and others. Rev. Jeevan Babu, the mission Secretary of NCCI identified second baptism, sheep stealing, pluralism, partnership, comity, and understanding the concept of mission as some of the tense issues that need to be addressed.[90] Instead of sorting out these issues, the chasm has become wider. We need to build bridges for the two to meet to carry on the task.

The churches in North East India have done well on this.[91] They sent nearly four hundred cross-cultural missionaries to other parts of India, Bhutan, Nepal, Melanesia, Africa and very soon to Thailand. This could be multiplied three to four times judging from the amount of giving and number of Christians in this area.[92]

Some constantly try to bridge the gap. IMA organised a National Consultation for Evangelism at Hyderabad in September 1996. The National Forum for Evangelism and Missions was convened by some concerned people in April 1997 in Nagpur. These resulted in a joint mission consultation by the national, mainline, evangelical churches and mission leaders, perhaps for the first time, in Bangalore on 20–22 January, 1998. Perhaps this can begin to iron out the differences between Church and Mission so they can move together taking the Gospel to the whole nation.

Many churches are increasingly aware of the needs of Missions and have started to support them. Rev. Vijaya Kumar of the Richmond Methodist Church, Bangalore, says forty to fifty percent of that church's budget goes to missions in India.[93] One-third of the budget of the Lalbagh English Methodist Church at Lucknow

UP, went to the support of missionaries who work with various agencies. This has developed only over the last twenty years under the pastorship of Rev. Kuruvilla Chandy, whose messages and commitment to missions inspired the people of the Lalbagh congregation.[94] The inspiration of churches and Missions depends on the pastors and the leaders, their own exposure, understanding of missions and their ability to move their congregation to realise the need to contribute to mission. Rev. James Nathen of Lucknow in the Methodist Church, the Executive Secretary for Council of Evangelism for Methodist churches in India, called all the pastors to create an awareness for cross-cultural missions and evangelism. He felt this would also help them avoid church politics.[95] The Great Commission of Christ is too big for petty competition between churches and missions.

Prayer, Truth and Action

There is a dichotomy between spiritual life and work. Often work is considered secondary to spirituality. Many Christians dichotomise spirituality and missions so much they appear to have no connection. Many feel Christians can be totally spiritual without the necessity to witness to Christ to their neighbours. Theologian John MacQuarrie wrote,

A theology without spirituality would be sterile academic exercise. A spirituality without theology can become superstition or fanaticism or the quest for excitement. Theology and spirituality need one another within the unity of Christian life.[96]

Placing spirituality, theology, and implementation in opposition disregards the Great Commission. We need a balance of all three. We have not obeyed till we give weight to them all. Rao, concerned about a church, pastor and congregation not engaged in evangelism said,

A minister who concentrates on his congregation of a few hundred will finally find himself often ineffective in his service. The congregation too become "sermon proof" and their lives become hardened ... because no new vigour comes to the church without outside experiences.[97]

Spiritual life is expressed in sharing Christian faith, and, as Rev. James Nathen points out, the missionary has an influence on the Church.[98]

During a mission leaders' get-together at Nagpur to evaluate evangelistic and mission progress in the country, some leaders felt that the meeting could have had a day of prayer. Others felt there was insufficient time and wanted the business to be over so as to head to their next activity.[99] This tension between prayer and activity exists at many levels, both within the same organisation and inter-mission gatherings. This requires a fine balance, as most executives are really busy.

Many prayer walks have been arranged in different states and many full-day prayers. To encourage such prayer ventures, books and other study materials are being planned. To move women in mission there is an effort to identify two women in every State who will encourage prayer in their respective states.[100] There are at least two such networks to mobilise women in prayer for evangelism and in spiritual life. One is under the leadership of EFI women's ministry coordinator, Leela Mannasseh. The other, led by Juliet Thomas, is called *Arpana Ministries*, a ministry of OM. These efforts are helping women to pray and become involved in mission activities in their own areas and also help their husbands and churches in their ministries. However, there were difficulties, frustrations and tensions at times as some of the ladies who were part of one network were abducted by the others with similar ministries in the area.[101] Tensions are apparent between leaders with similar ministries under different organisations. When this was recognised by some of the followers in prayer networks, they tended to get discouraged by the rivalries. One woman felt these groups try to "own them" for "their" organisational cause. Although there is a spirit of prayer, tensions occur between activities and prayer. Women have done well in mobilising the women of India to prayer, but need more partnership.

Differences on How to do the Task

There is much confusion about the means to use to reach India with the Gospel of Christ. Many missions feel their methods are right and, in some cases, better than the others. Yet each mission reaches a different segment of the Indian population. They complement each other. Until this is understood, there will be incidents of misunderstanding and friction between missions.

Operation Mobilisation was strongly criticised for distributing tracts when members went to the extent of tossing some tracts into each village as the team passed by to the next major town. Chacko

Thomas, a leader of the organisation, said that it might provide the only opportunity for some of the villagers to hear the Gospel. He also hoped that someone from that village would be stimulated into writing to the Bible Correspondence school mentioned in the tract. Even if only one or a few of them responded, then the effort would have been worth it.[102] The past had shown that, even without a witness, villagers have written in for correspondence courses and come to Christ through tracts and literature.

> Ramesh found a tract on the roadside and came to know Christ through reading it. He asked for more information, by filling in the response coupon ... . His is one of the dozens of response cards the team is getting back.[103]

A policeman on a tollgate in Bengal came to Christ through reading a tract given by an evangelist.

Similar stories are told by CCC, IEHC, SGM and many other literature bodies.

Pamela Ninan strongly believes that to influence the educated, Christians must offer the right kind of literature.[104] Literature is a good tool for cross-cultural missionaries and also for others to start a conversation with people. When missionaries initially do not speak the language of the area, it is still a good way to communicate Christ.[105]

Transworld Radio claimed that they were broadcasting the Gospel in forty different languages, from four stations, thirteen hours a day. They received letters from 60,000 listeners, had eighteen follow-up centres, 178 bases and 235 worship centres with 174 workers.[106] Similar stories were heard from the other broadcasting ministries. Emil Jebasingh, the Director of Transworld Radio said, "It is now possible to reach heterogeneous people groups ... . Today one radio evangelist can reach in one hour more people than St Paul in his whole life time could."[107] PA Sundara Rajan, the Director of World Cassette Outreach of India emphasised that audiocassette is a powerful form of media to reach the people.[108] Ron Beard believes that pictorial flipcharts are a tool of communication.[109] Kathleen Nicholls says that art and drama are the best traditional media to effectively reach people.[110] Missions may emphasise varied means to reach a certain segment of people. The variety of ministries and evangelistic efforts with different methods reach different sections of people.

Integrating within Missions

The Indian Government tries to get Indians of all states and castes to unite and feel Indian, rather than regionalists, but people still tend to be regionalist. On the other hand, perhaps Christians lead the amalgamation, identifying as the recreated children of God, one body in the Lord Jesus Christ. However, this is not the case in the missions. Confusion continues about the ministries and leadership centred around regional and caste divisions.

Christian leaders group by languages, castes and regions. Many leaders of Indian missions have been or are connected as relatives in one way or another. Some say the baton will pass only to relatives and people of the same caste, language and region. This unfortunate trend was echoed by PC Muathunga from the North East of India.

> Our weakness as Christians in India is we are so vocal in condemning racism in the West, but our own house here in India suffers from a virus worse than racism ... [The] jet-set Christian leaders from mainland India do not really understand the Church in this region... Of course missionaries should be sent out [from the North East], but ... how many churches or Christian groups are prepared to really work with us on equal partnership?[111]

Another North Easterner in his mid-forties commented that his own mission would not select him or any from his region as General Secretary, but only persons from the region from which most missionaries originated. Another pointed out that missions from mainland India came to the North-East to promote their missions and collect money from churches. They made no joint-efforts to reach his own North-East people. One leader from a mission complained and abruptly resigned, feeling only people from one state and language were chosen or developed as leaders. Others, neglected, missed the opportunity to grow.[112] This person might have been too sensitive but there is an element of truth, which must be dealt with. Jacob King, who watched a meeting launching a new mission, said, "The saddest part in this is, that I very clearly sense the North-South regional spirit. Using this North-South divide as a trump card the organisers of the new Mission led the reporting and the discussion time to achieve their agenda."[113]

Partly Paid and Fully Paid Missionaries.

Many missionaries are partly paid and raise their rest of the finances by themselves "by faith". These usually reside near a city and receive supplementary income from the Christian community. Such "faith missionaries" often struggle to survive, and many are accountable to no one as they are only partly paid.

> It is relatively much easier to "live by faith" in
> Kottayam or Madras ... "Faith missionaries" who go to
> the North, an overwhelming majority of them are stuck
> in the major towns (where there are) ... some sizable
> Christian communities – with a good number of South
> Indians, among whom they can exercise their "faith
> living."[114]

That is one of the reasons why two-thirds of the PIN Code[115] areas have no Christian worker. Many comity problems occur with these "faith missionaries".[116]

Full-time Missionaries, Tentmakers and Lay Evangelists

In a UESI mission convention for their students and graduates at Kerala in October 1997, the calibre of the people who attended the meeting was high. Nearly one hundred professionals indicated a desire to become missionaries in the future as tentmakers. Some mission leaders were there to encourage, direct and recruit prospective missionaries.[117]

This is a growing trend. In the midst of a great emphasis on full-time evangelists and missionaries, the conviction grows that the ethos of tent-making missionaries may suit well in India and South Asia. The method is promoted by Tentmakers.[118]

During the National Consultation on Evangelism (NCE) at Hyderabad in September 1996, sixteen mission executives discussed and willingly considered sending tent-making missionaries, though they needed advice. They decided to profile jobs available to tentmakers, and to call a two-day consultation to deliberate further on this issue. OM India was keen on sending tentmakers to Islamic countries.[119]

Although Patrick Johnstone encouraged tentmakers to go to countries where a traditional missionary could not go, as in the case of the Maldive Islands, he cautioned that some tentmaking missionaries at times merely survive in a new culture. Much is required from them, and some dry out from the pressure of coping with a secular job, earning as well witnessing. Each case must be individually decided. If tentmaking helps a person to enter a country legitimately, then his or her presence and outreach as a witness could be positive. However, missions should not expect too much through one missionary, but support their efforts.[120]

Some feel that lay people offer a key to evangelism. While most pastors train their lay people to be faithful church members, others see the potential of the laity in E1 and in E2 evangelism and in some cases E3 evangelism also.

Raja Bahadur and Beulah Herbert wrote, "The lay people are trained (to) establish contact, gather their neighbours, conduct the house church meeting, follow through and give reports ... The house church provides the training ground for the laity."[121] Rev. Imotemjen Aier, the General Secretary of the Council of Baptist Churches of North East India (CBCNEI), wrote,

The task of evangelisation rests both on the people of the pew and the people of the pulpit ... . Lay men and women are the spearhead of the church's mission to the world. The lay people have an advantage ... (to) witness in families, shops, labour unions, political centres, social clubs, etc.[122]

The Church Growth Association of India plans to mobilise 10,000 lay leaders for evangelism and missions, by the year 2000. CGAI will train 250 lay leaders through the Harvest Training School. Then each graduate in turn will train 40 others in a proposed five-year plan. Lay leaders will be trained in their local setting through the Portable School method. CGAI have already linked with twenty-five churches, missions and networks.[123] CONS,[124] Orissa Follow-up[125] and OM Bihar[126] have started setting up Portable Schools and schools of evangelism to train lay women and men and grassroots workers for planting of churches across India.

FMPB has been a strong force in mobilising lay people to spread the vision and raise funds. Care, time and training groom these lay leaders for the task.[127] According to Dr C Barnabas, the Director of IIM, over twenty FMPB lay leaders registered for a correspondence course on mission and leadership.[128] Several South Indian missions and networks like BYM, CGMM, FFNI, CLS, MUF and others mobilise laity for mission. North East missions similarly use their Laity Church Associations.[129] Lay people are now active in education, fund raising and in E1, E2 and E3 evangelism.

Short-term and Long-term Missionaries

Most Indian missions concentrate on recruiting and training long-term missionaries, allocating long-term tasks to reach specific peoples. Although this is good, very little has been done to harness others through short-term exposure to missions. Short-termers could become witnesses in their own geographical areas and also become missionary up-lifters. Glandion Carney, the Director of Inter-Varsity Missions Fellowship said, "Deepening values lie behind a call to short-term mission. It's part of a process—of knowing God and drawing closer to Him."[130] Analyzing "Mission - Motivating Factors" in USA, Elouise Corwin wrote, "Students of the 60's and 70's who had short-term opportunities were motivated by such exposure. It was a single most outstanding factor for those of the 70s."[131] Tim Gibson, the Director of World Servants said, "There's a wave of enthusiastic Christians embarking on short-term mission with the help of a dedicated short-term agency."[132]

Project Light is OM's multi-pronged short-term evangelistic venture. The introductory pamphlet announced that, one hundred million people in ten states will be reached with literature in four years. OM called for 3000 short-termers to join hands with the 600 long-term OMers. "One of the objectives of this programme is to train and mobilise Indian Christians for mission."[133] One such short-term worker testified that he came for six months but continued on in mission for over twenty-five years as a result of his short exposure.[134]

IMA has initiated programmes for university students, Student Volunteer Programme, SVP. Organised by UESI, SVP encourages students to catch a vision for mission. In 1996–97 nineteen students joined this programme.[135] IMA wants to increase this to 1000 students annually, including other student bodies.[136]

YWAM and OM actively train young people, including many Bible college students on summer internship in evangelism. YWAM and OM have a policy to train any person to witness for Christ, even if they do not have a theological degree, by training team leaders and using study programmes specifically for short-term ventures. Steve Hoke, Vice President of Training at Church Resource Management affirms, "Training by apprenticeship is the most natural preparation for ministry. (Find a mentor and) learn to receive instruction from a person who is further along in the spiritual walk."[137] Working in a small team also enhances the skills of each person in the team, strengthens spiritual gifts and confirms their calling for a full-time missionary task in cross-cultural situations.[138] Robert McQuilkin, the Chancellor of Colombia Bible College and Seminary said, "The short-term experience can infect you with the excitement of God's plan for the ages. It can transform your life and bubble over to others."[139] George Verwer challenged Keith Danby, the Chief Executive of OM Books UK to go to India and be exposed to mission. Danby acknowledged his life has never been the same.[140] Obviously short-term programmes achieve more than one objective.

A survey by Interserve showed approximately ten percent of those who come for short-term programmes become full-time missionaries.[141] This is true in the missions in India. It could be true of the 10,000 who were trained by OM India who serve with several missions in India and abroad.[142] Some of the supporters of OM India's work are men and women who graduated from OM who now serve in several professions across the country. Although OM started as a short-term venture for young people, it expanded into many long-term projects. Today OM has nearly 3000 full-time missionaries across the world, plus thousands of short-termers.[143]

Missions like FMPB and IEM attempt to give short-term exposure tours for their prayer partners and donors, but they cannot handle many short-termers in their programmes. Exposure tours and training short-termers demand specific goals, effort and specially trained leaders, with skills other than those of regular field missionaries. The latter may feel short-termers are more hindrance than help, with all their enthusiastic questions, reasoning, suggestions and judgements, as they often do not understand the struggles of the long-termers. However, once the short-termers make contact with long-termers, their commitment to missions increases. Training short-termers needs patience and planning.

At times, training short-termers has suffered because of the lack of trained leaders, proper mission entry orientations,[144] re-entry or exit orientations,[145] proper study programmes for them while they are on the field and especially a lack of funding for such programmes.[146] Yet, the more people exposed to missions, the greater will be the education, participation, prayer, empathy and finance for missions and workers. YWAM and OM, with their graduates permeating society and missions, have already brought vision and vigour to churches and missions. If mission education is to come to the Church as a whole in India, short-term training is a must.

Missionaries and Local Workers

On the issue of Westerners or Indians, KP Yohannan, the founder of Gospel for Asia said some years back that foreign missionaries from Europe and America were ineffective in reaching the "hidden People" and Asians.[147] He later modified this opinion. Rao writes,

> The presence of the (foreign) missionaries is considered in many ways a hindrance to the growth of the Indian Church particularly in the context of indigenous leadership, self-support, dealings with the non-Christians and the Indian Government. ... There should be healthy understanding and real transfer of leadership by the missionaries who should work along with Indians as true partners. ... The Indian Christians on the other hand, should not resent the overseas missionaries from any petty nationalism or perverted patriotism.[148]

Yohannan asserted that spending high levels of money on American missionaries to Asia was not good stewarding of God-given money resources. He implied it is better to send Asians to reach Asians because they will relate better to their own cultures.

Then the suggestion is made that money given to Western missionaries could be better used to employ more Asian missionaries.[149] Yohannan originally asked support of US$30 per missionary in Asia,[150] but a dollar a day was unrealistic and far too little for the Indian missionary to live on.[151] Eventually, at the request of many Asian Christian leaders, he changed the figure to a minimum of US$50 per missionary.[152] Yohannan's blunt statements caused sharp dispute, confusion and dissension. However, with the funds from donors, GFA subsidised many thousands of national missionary salaries.[153] More recently GFA supports its own missionaries.

Sunder Raj observes that the apostle Paul's colleagues were people of other nations and cultures. Paul welcomed Jewish Christians to work in Gentile cultures as long as they were not spreading Judaism instead of the Gospel.[154] Yohannan is right about Asians sharing the Gospel effectively in Asia, but it is unbiblical to stop others who want to carry the Gospel to other nations. The Great Commission is for all, even though there is a high cost. If one group of missionaries is restricted into India, then equally Indians should not aspire to work cross-culturally elsewhere.

Besides this, although Indians may look somewhat alike, the cultural diversity is enormous, especially between South Indians, North Indians, and North East Indians. Culturally, a person going from Kerala to Haryana will find it as different as going to Saudi Arabia in culture, customs, language, geography, politics, economics and agriculture. It may not be as difficult as an American going to Haryana but it is still a challenge for a Keralite to go to Haryana.[155]

Another aspect is Christianised locals reaching out to their own people. In recent years Indian cross-cultural workers have tried hard to raise leadership and missionaries from among the local people who would be able to reach either their own people or their neighbours with different cultures. They called these local workers the *swarthics*.[156]

God uses all groups of missionaries in evangelism and Church planting. With no European and American missionaries in the eighteenth to twentieth centuries the Gospel would not have reached some of the peoples of India. Although South Indians received the Gospel before the Europeans, they were not proactive nor able to reach India by themselves until the European and American missionaries came to India. Cross-cultural or E3 evangelism was necessary before local workers could get involved in the E1 and E2 evangelism.[157] Once Indians came to Christ, foreign missionaries could get them evangelising their own people and their neighbours. However, the terms of partnership must be spelled out carefully. Missionaries who are partners with the local Indian Christians are called "Regular missionaries."[158]

There need not be a question of who should fulfil the great commission as long as there is a clear demarcation of responsibilities and learning together as they reach the peoples of India. This applies also to Indian missionaries to North India.

Cross-Cultural Evangelists and Local Evangelists

Most missions working cross-culturally to other states have done well with cross-cultural adjustments. Some missions arriving in other states of India have recruited local workers and integrated well. Maharastra Village Ministries (MVM) has been working for sixteen years in Maharastra.[159] Although Kulothungan, the General Secretary of MVM, is from Tamil Nadu, most of his workers are from Maharastra.[160] Most major indigenous missions have recruited the majority of their workforce from the states in which the mission originated. The *swarthics* or local workers are mostly in the second level of leadership. Sometimes because the majority of these missions are from the South, they are called the *Madrasi* missions.[161] Both these and the North-Eastern missionaries have had some difficulties mixing with workers from the North and training the locals. They risk repeating the mistakes of the foreign missionaries in not giving the work over to locals, looking down on then with an excuse that they are not yet ready for leadership.[162] Hedlund observed that, "South Indian Christian workers in the North lack cultural sensitivity and create difficult personal relationships ... (and) impose their alien social patterns and violate local norms and feelings."[163] Similar cases have been found among the North East workers to other parts of India.

There are some independent South Indian missionaries who, when called to the North, established churches among their own people in diaspora. This produced Malayalam and Tamil churches in cross-cultural regions of India, especially with missionaries sent out by both the many Pentecostal and Brethren missions. Some have bilingual churches, but the majority plant churches among their own people even though they physically crossed cultures.[164]

Bruce Graham, the former principal of Bethel Bible Institute noticed that there was very little cross-cultural training for prospective missionaries. Most missionaries get trained in their own culture even though they go to other States for their work. Graham wanted to expose his students at least for a month or two in cross-cultural circumstances with OM or YWAM or any other groups which gave positive education and experience to cross-cultural evangelism.[165] Hedlund expressed similarly, "The 4,000 or so Indian missionaries serving under more than 100 Indian missionary societies do not receive cross—cultural preparation, or other missionary training for communicating the Gospel among non-Christians."[166]

Missionaries need to learn to adapt to situations of their hosts to whom they carry the Gospel. If that is done well they will cultivate many friends among their hosts. Paul Hiebert, a former missionary to Andhra Pradesh says,

> The extent we identify with the people and become bi-cultural, to that extent we find ourselves alienated from our kinsmen and friends in our home land... In time we find our closest associates among other bi-cultural people.[167]

Thomas and Elizabeth Brewster who trained more than 2000 missionaries in seventy nations in cross-cultural adjustments by teaching a language technique called Language Acquisition Made Practical (LAMP) suggested that a new missionary trained by another older missionary from the same background was not advisable. Being with an older missionary, the young new missionary might imbibe his prejudices against a new culture. The best situation places a missionary immediately with the local people where he can pick up the culture from an authentic source—the local people. The new missionary may thus form his own opinion of the place and the people.[168] The Brewsters suggested a new missionary should live with a local family, limiting personal belongings to twenty kilograms (the weight allowed in an aeroplane), travelling only by public transport, and learn the language in a local context with the encouragement of the hosts.[169] Indian missionaries do not usually follow these methods although some groups like the Frontier Servants and other short-term foreign groups have tried to carry out these suggestions.[170]

According to Vasantha Raj of CGAI, it was a mistake on the part of some missions to ordain their missionaries as pastors. He feels missionaries should continue as church planters while they groom local people as the leaders of their churches and then ordain them as pastors. If missionaries become pastors, they find it difficult to train local leadership to shepherd their churches. Also, missionaries might remain as pastors instead of moving on to plant more churches. Thus ordaining missionaries as pastors would impede the growth of the church in the long run.[171] This occurred in churches planted by cross-cultural independent workers, Pentecostal and Brethren. They tended to stay and shepherd the churches after planting them.[172] The goal of the missionary is to make himself unnecessary (for the growing church).[173]

Tensions Over Comity

The many emerging missions need clear demarcation of their work areas. This is not a new problem.

Among the early missionaries and Christians, the denominational feeling was so rigid ... sometimes (they) fought at the same territory. The need for comity, to settle matters between societies was felt. Comity means one accepting the ecclesiastical character of the

other. In several Indian missionary conferences the
principle of comity of missions was discussed. This
paved the way for agreement between missions for
cooperation ... and restrict their territories so that they
would not fight (but) support each other.[174]
When this occurs between missions associated with IMA, most
problems can be sorted out. However, unassociated missions
without accountability do not bother to make or follow comity
agreements. The dire consequences are illustrated in the following
incidents.

At Ettappalli, in the Nagpur diocese of Maharastra two mission stations belonged to FMPB and CGMM. Although they were
forty kilometres apart, the CNI Deputy Moderator Bishop wanted
one of them to leave. There was much tension. Both felt their good
links with the Nagpur diocese and wanted to continue. The issue
was sorted out after discussions.[175] This is maturity.

One mission leader complained that the members of Beersheba
church, excommunicated on moral grounds, were being absorbed
into a new church by XX movement at a district in MP, and this
caused problems.[176] In Mayurbhanj district, Orissa, church members of Mission YY were baptised by a worker of Mission ZZ. This
problem had to be sorted out between the mission heads.[177]

LL Mission faced struggles with NN Mission in their work
among the Lambady Thandas in Tamil Nadu. The problem was
not sorted out, as the NN Mission did not take action.[178] FMPB
complained that Corner Stone Ministry was disturbing their work
in Denkanikottai and Marandahalli area.[179] Little Flock Fellowship
had twenty churches, including El-Bethel at Nadarihat, North
Bengal. One missionary from El-Bethel, joining Siloam Mission
built, a children's home between El-Bethel and the Presbyterian
churches on the same street. Then, he declared the children's home
also to be a church. He stole six of the families from the El-Bethel
Church with promises of education for their children and homes
built for the parents. A worker of Vishwa Vani, made the split
more obvious. The Secretary of the Little Flock Fellowship requested Vishwa Vani to sort out this problem.[180]

Mission leaders willing to consider the Big Picture straightened
out some matters to the advantage of all. Some cases were not
simple. Some CEOs were torn between encouraging their own
workers and also keeping peace with other missions.

To clarify the working relationship, IMA member missions

agree to the definition of what is and what is not a mission station. EFI has an almost identical charter.[181]

> A mission station is defined as a place where one or more full-time paid missionaries of a particular mission reside permanently and work in and around that place in evangelistic / church planting / other allied ministries. An occasional preaching point or the residence of the honorary worker will not amount to a mission station.[182]

IMA associated missions have to agree on the following as they come into the association. a) They submit a list of the locations of their mission stations. They may not open a new station in a tribal or rural area within the working distance of another mission.[183] b) If a mission or church has been in existence for five years, but has not been involved in evangelism around the area, its working distance is zero. c) If there is a breech of this agreement, IMA will negotiate between the missions. d) A missionary who leaves one organisation to go to the next cannot carry his congregation to the next mission unless a mutual arrangement is arrived at by both the missions involved. e) Mission agencies must check with IMA whether another mission works in the area before they start a new mission station.[184]

Although, the IMA and EFI comity charters specify that no workers of two different missions work in the same PIN Code area or within the radius of 6 kilometres,[185] some leaders became confused over the distance. Some thought it was over twenty kilometres,[186] twenty-five kilometres,[187] forty kilometres[188] and fifty kilometres[189] which were the norms for other missions to keep away from their own work.

In a further complication, relatives in different missions in the same area became a threat to others in the region. Vinod Vishwas, the National Co-ordinator of KEF wrote, "I was warned and threatened by (the missionaries) of three other missions. They are all from one family trying to spoil our work at Dharamgarh, Orissa. I tried to fix the problems, but they are not willing."[190]

Sometimes the comity issues brought out animosities and distrust of missions for each other. In such difficult situations partnership did not work and it became a matter of self-survival and not wishing the best for each other. To highlight this, Hrudaya from Orissa Follow-up wrote,

> I regret to say that FFF has written to you for the second

time and it indicates to me that they are not comfortable with us and trying to push out our activities in the name of comity. ... After all, Tiring is over thirty Kilometres from Rairangpur. FFF should concentrate their man power at Rairangpur with a 2.5 lakh population.[191]

Some missions in Vyara region, Gujarat, misunderstood the Evangelical Churches in India and Vishwa Vani establishing churches. Ezra Sargunam, the President of ECI wrote of this,

In the name of comity let us not allow satan to hinder the ongoing work of the church planting in Gujarat region. Church planting in India is constantly thwarted by this outmoded idea of comity. Many denominations and missions claim the whole tribal belt or sections as their mission field. They do very little for the effective church planting followed by discipline, constructing places of worship etc. but scream in outrage when an aggressive church planting team gets things going. Let not satan use these obstacles to dissuade us from winning the winnable people in our life time. We are also prepared to welcome with open arms if FMPB will come forward and hand over a few groups to us.[192]

Emil Jebasingh, wearied by accusations of comity violations about Vishwa Vani wrote,

I give you (Sunder Raj) full freedom to go directly to the mission fields and contact any of our Vishwa Vani missionaries. Please go ahead and make a personal enquiry into the allegations. ... I shall be happy to bear your travel as well as accommodation expenses.[193]

Devadasan regretted the bad impression made by these fights over comity.

We have confused the poor Adivasi converts at Vyara area. We have created bad impressions in the minds of the Bishop and other church leaders in Gujarat. They think that these *Madrasis* are fighting with each other again and again in Vyara area even after a settlement. My prayer and plea is that ... this action should not be repeated.[194]

Eventually leaders met at Nagpur, 17 July, 1990 and sorted out the matter.[195] Often comity issues can be sorted out only when there is continuous dialogue and openness.

Some leaders took time to respond and clear misunderstandings on comity problems, and could then work in unison. One instance was a letter from Samuel Devadasan, FMPB field Director, to Raja Mohan Das, the IEM Secretary for Field Ministries and Field Communications.

Thank you for the letter dated March 14, 1994. You have mentioned about your ministry in certain districts of HP. One (large) ethnic group cannot be covered by a single organisation, as in Kukna, Kolami. We will carefully keep the minimum distance of twenty Kilometres between the fields of FMPB and IEM. We will work with good understanding and co-operation.[196]

When comity problems arise, the leaders of the concerned organisations are asked to meet and sort them out among themselves. When a comity problem arose between the Little Flock Fellowship and Vishwa Vani, Raja Samuel, the co-ordinator of Management Standard Cell (MSC) of IMA asked them to meet,[197] with an observer to help build relationship if needed.

R. Stanley, the President of Blessing Youth Mission wrote a pleasant letter to K. Francis, a missionary of FMPB who was starting a work afresh in Uriah, Keonjhar, Orissa.

We are happy to know that you have opened a new station in Keonjhar, Orissa. We were there a few years ago, but now we have cleared the place because of the trouble. We know some families there and our brothers know the place. If you are interested we can arrange one of our brothers to take your missionary to the place and introduce him to our old contacts. The following two persons are receiving our magazine, they may be of some help to you. God bless your work.[198]

Such letters and a sense of co-operation contribute much to build relationships, good feelings and a sense of partnership.

However reports indicate comity problems in Orissa more than in any other part of India. There is little evidence of this problem occurring in Andhra, Bihar, UP, Maharastra, Punjab and Haryana. Perhaps there is more scope for expansion of work in those areas before the problem of comity emerges.

Conclusion

Opposing strategies may impede or may facilitate mission work. Missions are still divided on HUP versus individual conversion where the solution is to balance people movements and individual conversion. This does not rule out the need for personal faith in Christ, for each person to be accepted by God through Christ and for faith in His sacrifice on the part of each individual. But, Christian society can be built more quickly by a mass turning to Christ.

Khushwant Singh's desire for a Christian Saint is fulfilled in Mother Theresa, but in following her example social work should not obliterate the Great Commission, to make disciples of Christ and establish them in the Church. Missions must watch the balance between proclamation of Christ and social uplift. Missionaries must not become like any other humanists and humanitarian organisations without the punch of bringing people to Christ. On the other hand, we should discourage just preaching the Gospel and entreating people to come to Christ, whilst turning a blind eye to social problems where Christians could help.

The progress in contextualising while avoiding syncretism is slow, too slow to attract the masses to Christ. Most traditional Christians find it anathema to change any external customs that the church has held dear for many years. The few who prompt innovation are sidelined as compromisers, syncretists or backsliders. Yet mission must adapt the message of Christ to new cultures without changing the essence of it. Contextualisation could effectively instil biblical values in a culture.

Missions must balance spirituality, theology and carrying out the Great Commission. Christians cannot camouflage laziness as spiritual life, but neither should they place activity ahead of walking with the Lord and seeking His face for guidance, especially in their mission work.

Missions have freedom to use the most effective tools to communicate, but they need to evaluate and research effectiveness. Then their efforts will not be wasted, and they will appreciate and pray for the differing methods of fellow Christians.

Missions need to integrate more completely within their own ranks by making their national offices more central, and treating all without partiality. This calls for conscious effort so that missions do not falter in integration and unity.

Partly-paid missionaries who depend upon "faith" need reconsideration. Sufficient salaries would avoid leaving them to fend for themselves and depend upon other Christians for their financial survival. It is not lack of faith when missionaries to unreached peoples receive a proper salary and have their needs met. A fully-paid missionary has fewer personal tensions and can function better. Missions must look after their missionaries if this nation is to be reached systematically, especially in targeting the real unreached people.

Training lay men and women is a significant strategy. They in turn can impart a vision for evangelism and missions. Short-term mission programmes are an asset. The exposure enlightens, enthuses, overcomes fears, trains, and brings some back for full time mission work. We can build such programmes as a special department within a mission. These programmes help Christians to support missionaries sympathetically and generate prayer for them.

The welcome to work as missionaries should remain open to foreigners, but with roles defined and mutual agreements reached. Thus world missionary enterprise is reciprocal. The Great Commission is for all disciples and not just for certain local people. Though foreigners have wider culture gaps to cross, they fulfil the Great Commission. In partnership and exercising spiritual gifts for world evangelism, neither a foreigner nor an Indian is better than the other person, though often foreign missionaries need to assume background roles. There are always things to learn from each other. The lessons of discipleship, brokenness, forgiveness and walking in the light are universal, to be exercised both by Indians and foreigners.

Indian missionaries must train *swarthics*, local workers, to take leadership as early as possible with a deadline. *Swarthics* do feel at times that *"madrasi"* missionaries dominate and try to make them *"madrasees"* in all areas of life. Yet with roles defined, partnership with *swarthics* could significantly aid the evangelisation of India.

We reiterate that Indian missionaries in new cultures within India need to learn well the new culture and language and integrate effectively. Their cross-cultural training should be in the place of their new work rather than their place of origin. Sending some to work with groups like OM and YWAM could prove useful. Indian missionaries will learn local customs quicker and better, enjoy the food more (even if it is cooked in mustard oil!), by living with local people rather than senior missionaries, where they may also absorb their prejudices.

As new missions emerge, tensions with comity will continue when missions do not plan, do not research well and leave the problems to the grassroots workers who may be less mature than the CEOs. Mission leaders must be big hearted even if the problem is not their own. Being willing to forgive, graciously giving up a field for the sake of others' growth, will produce better relationships, partnership and unity in future work. If concerned leaders meet and discuss issues, possibly with the people in the field, grassroots workers could learn reconciliation skills through openness and dialogue.

END NOTES

1 KC Joseph, "Water Forbidden", *OM India At a Glance*, October–November (1993) 2.

2 Kuknas live in the Vyara areas of Gujarat.

3 _____, "FMPB Entry in Kukna Region", *Friends Focus*, April (1997) 11–14.

4 Roberta Winter, "The Kingdom Strikes Back", Budelman, Ralph (Ed.), *Inheriting God's Perspective* (Bangalore: Mission Frontiers, 1996), p. 31.

5 Dr Houghton in discussion, SAIACS, Bangalore. September 2, 1997.

6 Donald McGavran, Seminar at the Allahabad Seminary in 1974. Donald A. McGavran, "The Bridges of God", Ralph Winter, Steve Hawthorne et al (Eds.), *Perspectives*, p. 285–286.

7 McGavran, "The Bridges of God", *Perspectives*, p. 276.

8 Neill, *The History of Christian Missions*, p. 128.

9 Stock, *People Movements in the Punjab*, p. 257.

10 Firth, *Indian Church History*, pp. 152–153.

11 Stephen Neill, *The History of Christian Missions* (London: Penguin Books, 1990), pp. 308–309.

12 Stock, *People Movements in the Punjab*, pp. 21–22.

13 McGavran, "The Bridges of God", *Perspectives*, p. 286.

14 Bishop Thoburn and his mass-movement leaders.

15 Stock, *People Movements in the Punjab*, p. 251. Quoted in *Twentieth-Century Perspectives* by Copplestone.

16 J. W. Pickett, *Christian Mass Movements in India*, (1933) and *Christ's Way to India's Heart*, (1938).

17 Neill, *The History of Christian Missions*, pp. 439–440.

18 Firth, *Indian Church History*, p. 158.

19 Firth, *Indian Church History*, p. 194.

20 John Abubakker, FFNI, inter-

view at Vellore, August 1, 1997.

21 Leighton Ford, *The Christian Persuader*, (London: Harper & Row Publishers, 1996), p. 32.

22 _____, "FMPB Entry in Kukna Region", *Friends Focus*, April (1997) 11–14.

23 Pickett, *Odyssey*, p. 29.

24 Jeyakaran, OM Graduate, interview, Tirunelveli, 1991.

25 John Vandayar, personal interview, real name withheld, Bangalore, September 1997.

26 Shunmugam, David and Karpagam & Abubakker, personal interview, Madras, July 1997.

27 Suresh, SABC, Bangalore, interview, January 1996.

28 Ravi Kumar, personal interview, Chennai, August 1997.

29 *Kristanugami Sangh* means An Association of the followers of Christ. This is based at Cannanore.

30 Ashok Kumar, personal letter to Rajendran August 1997.

31 John Abubakker, interview, Vellore, July 1997.

32 Pickett, *Christ's Way to India's Heart*, p. 108.

33 Winter, "The Kingdom Strikes Back", *God's Perspective*, pp. 32–33.

34 Soltau, *Mission at the Cross Roads*, p. 120.

35 Harold Fuller, *Mission – Church Dynamics* (California: William Carey Library, 1981), p. 13.

36 Frederick W. Norris, "God and the gods: Expect Footprints", Doug Priest Jr. (Ed.) *Unto the Uttermost*, (California: William Carey Library 1984), pp. 55–56.

37 Singh, *India*, pp. 76–76.

38 _____, "State Funeral will be on Saturday. PM going Today to Pay Tribute," *The Asian Age*, September 7 (1997) 1–2.

39 Neill with Joanne Anderson, *Daily in Christ* (Oregon: Harvest House Publishers, 1993), p. December 13.

40 HL Richard & Vishal Mangalwadi, "A Review Dialogue", *To All Men All Thing* (Vol. 7 No. 1 August 1997) p. 8.

41 Acharya Daya Prakash Titus, Executive Secretary's letter to IMA General Secretary, dated October 5, 1997.

42 Anderson, *Daily in Christ*. December 13.

43 Bruce Nicholls, "The Gospel in Indian Culture," Ezra Sargunam (Ed.), *Mandate*, p. 386.

44 Ponraj, *Church Growth Studies in Mission*, pp. 37–38.

45 Doug Priest, "A Massai Purification Ceremony", D. Priest, (Ed.), *Unto the Uttermost*, (California: William Carey Library 1984), p. 200.

46 Rao, *Some Concerns of the Indian Church*, p. 110.

47 Frederick W. Norris, "God and the gods," pp. 56–57.

48 Paul, *The Cross Over India*, p. 106.

49 Sunder Raj, GS, IMA, interview at Chennai for the magazine *Mission Frontiers*, September 12, 1997.

50 Soltau, *Mission at the Cross Roads*, p. 120.

51 Rao, *Some Concerns of the Indian Church*, p. 2.

52 Ponraj, *Church Growth Studies*,

pp. 37–38.

53 Ibid, pp. 37–38.

54 These non-essentials in Paul's terminology, were truly "lawful" yet for the higher purposes were "not expedient".

55 Rao, *Some Concerns of the Indian Church*, pp. 2–9.

56 Soltau, *Mission at the Cross Roads*, pp. 122–126.

57 S. Pillai, interview, Chennai, September 10, 1997.

58 Cornelius, SAIACS, interview, Bangalore, October 1996.

59 Pradip Ayer, OM Leaders' Discussion, Hyderabad, September 1992.

60 Discussion in the NCCI Mission Conference organised by Rev. Jeevan Babu at UTC, Bangalore, August 14–16, 1997.

61 Jayaprakash, *Missions of India*, p. 7.

62 Francis R. Steele, "The Roots of Two Missions Tensions," *EMQ* no.2, Winter (1973) 91.

63 Donald McGavran, "New Mission," in Arthur Glasser and McGavran, *Contemporary Theology of Missions*, (Grand Rapids: Baker Book House, 1983), p. 48.

64 Kim Sai Tan, *The Great Digression: World Evangelism from 1910: The Ecumenical Digression and the Evangelical Response* (Malaysia: Malaysia Bible Seminary, 1981), p. 14. Quoted in Harris, *The Theological Pilgrimage*, p. 69.

65 Rene De Visme Williamson, "Negative Thoughts about Ecumenism," *Christianity Today*, August 30, (1968) 14. Quoted in Harris, *The Theologi-cal Pilgrimage*, p. 69.

66 Wagner, *Whole Gospel*, pp. 121–122.

67 Ibid, p. 124.

68 Ibid, pp. 193–194.

69 [n.a], "Three Models of Mission," *Dristikone* No. 2. (1994) 7–8. Quoted from Samuel Escobar, "A Movement Divided. Three Approaches to World Evangelisation stand in Tension with one another", *Transformation*. Vol. 8 No. 4 Oct. (1991) 7–13.

70 Austin, (Real name withheld), interview, April 1997.

71 Ibid.

72 Yohannan, *Revolution*, p. 73.

73 Ibid, p. 97.

74 Ponraj, *Church Growth Studies in Mission*, pp. 72–73.

75 Ibid.

76 Austin, interview, April 1997.

77 Ponraj, *Church Growth Studies in Mission*, p. 73.

78 Ibid, p. 67.

79 Joseph D'Souza, "India Celebrates Fifty years of Independence", *OM Today*, Issue 22, July– September (1997) 3.

80 Refer to documents cited in chapters 1 & 2.

81 John Varghese, personal interview, SAIACS, Bangalore, September 1995.

82 D'Souza, personal interviews, Hyderabad, 1994, 95, 96.

83 D'Souza, discussions, Hyderabad, 1994, 95, 96.

84 Jayaprakash, *Indigenous Missions of India*, p. 20b.

85 Genesis 13: 1–14.

86 GW Peters, *A Biblical Theology of Missions* (Chicago: Moody Press, 1972), p. 214.

87 Orlando Costas, *The Church and the Mission: A shattering Critique from the Third World,* (Illinois: Tyndale, 1974), pp 168–169.

88 Ron Penny, Lecture at an OM seminar at Ranchi, 1973.

89 Ralph Winter, "The Two Structures of God's Redemptive Mission", Arthur Glasser, Paul Hiebert et al. (Eds.), *Crucial Dimensions in World Evangelisation* (California: William Carey Library, 1977), p. 327.

90 Rev. Jeevan Babu's fax to Dr. Dyanchand Carr at Hongkong dated November 1997.

91 This was written in 1984. Years have passed, but the mission in North East India has not taken off, for which both the Churches in the North East and the Indian mission leaders are collectively responsible. This needs attention.

92 PC Muathunga, "A Missiological Survey of the Church in North East India," *India Church Growth Quarterly,* Vol 6 No 2 April – June (1984), pp. 17–19.

93 Rev. Vijaya Kumar, Asst. Pastor, Richmond Methodist Church, Bangalore, personal interview, February 3, 1998.

94 Letter from Rev. Chandy, the former Pastor of the Lalbagh Methodist Church, Lucknow, August 14, 1997. Chandy has moved to an independent church in Lucknow from late 1997.

95 Letter from Rev. James Nathen, Executive Secretary for Council of Evangelism, Methodist Church in India, to Sunder Raj, IMA, July 7, 1997.

96 John MacQuarrie, "Prayer and Theological Reflection", John MacQuarrie, Cheslyn, Jones, Geoffrey Wain Wright (Eds.), *The Study of Spirituality* (London: SPCK, 1986), p. 587.

97 Rao, *Some Concerns of the Indian Church,* pp. 50–51.

98 Letter from Nathen to Sunder Raj, IMA, July 7, 1997.

99 FORUM at Nagpur, April 16–18, 1997.

100 James Kaiser's report on his visit to Delhi attending NIHNW meetings held in November 11–12, 1997.

101 Discussions with Juliet Thomas at several occasions, 1994–97.

102 Chacko Thomas, personal interviews, Bihar, 1972, 1994.

103 _____ "A Tract on the Road", *OM Today,* July–September (1997) 5.

104 Pam Ninan. Lecture, Writers workshop at Bangalore, March 1997.

105 OM orientation on Literature Evangelism.

106 Vishwa Vani India Believers' Movement, Bharathyia Vishwasi Sangathi and TWR Information Brochures, Jan 1997.

107 Emil Jebasingh, "Media, Missions and the Mandate," Ezra Sargunam (Ed.), *Mission Mandate,* p. 289.

108 PA Sundara Rajan, " Cassette-A Powerful Media." *Mission Mandate,* pp. 293–297.

109 Ron Beard, "Flipcharts an Old Tool for a New Day," *Mission*

Mandate, pp. 214–216.

110 Kathleen Nicholls, "The Traditional Media and the Gospel." *Mission Mandate*, pp. 298–307.

111 Muathunga, "The Church in North East India", *ICGQ*, Vol. 6 No. 2 April – June (1984)

112 Kaur, personal interview, July 1994.

113 Jacob King's report (real name withheld), Chennai, November 1997.

114 IMA Research Team (Eds.), *Go into All Karnataka,* (Madras: IMA, 1996), pp. 8–9.

115 Out of 22,000 PIN Codes in India only 7000 areas have any kind of Christian worker.

116 Sunder Raj, IMA, Interview, Chennai, July 17, 1997.

117 Shyam Winston, one of the speakers in the convention, personal interview, Chennai October 8, 1997.

118 Tent-Makers is a networking agency based in Delhi to encourage tent-making missionaries.

119 *Second National Consultation on Evangelism* held at Hyderabad, September 1996, (Madras: IMA, 1996), pp. 23–24.

120 Patrick Johnstone, answering questions about "tent-making missionaries" during a mission conference on board the ship M.V. Logos, while in Sydney, October 1979.

121 Raja Bahadur and Beulah Herbert, "Prayer Evangelism", *ICGQ, Vol. 6*, No 1. January - March (1984) pp. 1–2.

122 K. Imotemjen Aier, "A Local Church in Action", *ICGQ,* Vol.

6, No. 2. April – June (1984) 29.

123 CGAI, "A Strategy Paper on Harvest Training School – A Plan to Raise 10,000 Lay Leaders by AD 2000." [n.d]

124 Paul Gupta, CONS report for 1996–97, pp. 6–8.

125 DB Hrudaya, Director Orissa Follow-up, personal interview, Chennai, July 31, 1997.

126 JS Raja, OM Bihar, interview, Hyderabad 1994.

127 James Kaiser, personal interview, Chennai, July 1997.

128 C. Barnabas, CEO of Indian Institute of Management, personal interview, at IMA office at Chennai, August, 1997.

129 Madhu C. Singh & Alani, OM, interview, Dimapur, December 1993.

130 Glandion Carney, "Pathways Of Spiritual Growth," Bill Berry (Ed.), *The Short–Term Mission Handbook* (Illinois: Berry Publishing Services, 1992), p. 40.

131 Elouise Corwin, "Mission Motivating Factors: Then and Now," *EMQ*, Volume 17, No. 3, July (1981) 158.

132 Tim Gibson, "Planning Your Short-term Trip," Berry (Ed.), *The Short-Term Mission Hand-book*, p. 44.

133 OM "Project Light" pamphlet, p. 7.

134 K. Rajendran, "*Chai* in a Mud Cup. Testimony of a Cross-Cultural Worker" KC Joseph (Ed.) *OM India At a Glance. News and Prayer Bulletin from Bombay.* October - November (1993) 2.

135 Jose Thomas, a report to IMA, on SVP, August 3, 1997.

136 K. Rajendran, "Hello! Students Discover God's Plan for You." *Indian Missions*, January – March (1998) 27–28.

137 Steve Hoke, "Shape Up for Mission," Berry (Ed.), *The Short-Term Mission Handbook*, p. 48.

138 Pramila Rajendran, Lecture on "Team Work" in OM women's Conference at Lucknow, September 1994.

139 Robert McQuilkin, "Don't Let Expectations to Get You Down." Berry (Ed.), *The Short-Term Mission Handbook*, p. 65.

140 Conversation with Keith Danby, Lucknow, 1989.

141 Peter Maiden, OM Associate International Director quoted this in a conference at Europe, 1981.

142 OM "Project Light" pamphlet, p. 4.

143 OM Reports, 1997.

144 Mission Entry Orientation is for those who are entering into the mission field, preparing them mentally to cope in their work, cross-cultural relationships, motivation, discouragements, stress, low funds and other issues. Recommended orientation period is two to five days.

145 Mission Re-entry or Exit Orientation - This helps those who return to their homes to cope with their home and church situation. If this is not done some could become judgmental of their home churches. They need coaching on sharing the vision, discipling, supporting the missionaries on the fields and reevaluation of their time on the mission field. Some may have had good times of learning. It is good if they share this for the benefit of others, as there are many dimensions in learning. Some have become critical during their exposure trip due to culture shock, bad leadership, fiascoes in programmes, opposition and other factors. They need to hear the positive side from other people to balance their perspective. The exit orientation could also help the organisers to plan better next time, as there could have been some blunders.

146 Jose Thomas, UESI Mission Secretary, letter to K. Rajendran, Chennai, August 3, 1997.

147 Yohannan, *Revolution*, pp. 150–151.

148 Rao, *The Indian Church*, p. 72–73.

149 Yohannan, *Revolution*, pp. 145–52.

150 Ibid, p. 134.

151 The lowest wage set by the Government for a daily labourer is Rs. 38 per day, one dollar at time of writing, unless a person is employed illegally as a (bond) slave.

152 US $50 is solicited for a missionary, interview of GFA personnel by Jim Johnson, Nagpur, 15 February 1998.

153 IMA also receives US $30 per missionary as an additional grant for a missionary salary. This subsidy is dispersed

through the Cell for Assistance and Relief to Evangelists (CARE), a wing of IMA.

154 Sunder Raj, IMA, Interview, Chennai, 15 July 1997.

155 Ashok Kumar, a missionary to Singapore, Australasia Training Director, OM, interview, Calicut, November 16, 1997.

156 *swarthics* —local Christian workers who reach their own people.

157 E1 evangelism has no language or cultural barrier to overcome. E2 evangelism is done among the people who could be similar to the proclaimer, yet he has to cross some language and cultural barriers. E3 evangelism is distinctly cross-cultural with or without great crossing of distance as in the case of Marwadies from Rajasthan and Gujarat who are settled in Bangalore.
Wayne Gregory, "The Types of Evangelism – The E-Scale".
[n.a.], God's Perspective, p. 67.

158 Ibid, p. 67.

159 MVM Souvenir on the 50th year celebration, 1996.

160 Kulothungan, interview at Nagpur on October 30, 1996.

161 Edwin Simon, interview, Lucknow, UP, October 1989.

162 Houghton, *Dependency*, p. 246.

163 Roger Hedlund, *Evangelisation and Church Growth* (Madras: CGRC, 1992) p. 251.

164 Gopal Hembrom, interview, visiting Bangalore, Sept.14, 1997.

165 Bruce Graham, former Principal of Bethel Bible School at Danishpet, personal interview, Hyderabad, September 1996.

166 Hedlund, *Evangelisation and Church Growth*, p. 253..

167 Paul Hiebert, "Culture and Cross-Cultural Differences", *Perspectives*, p. 372.

168 Thomas and Elizabeth Brewster, "Bonding and the Missionary Task: Establishing a Sense of belonging," *Perspectives*, pp. 452–464.

169 Ibid, p. 458.

170 Graham Hulse, interview, SAIACS, Bangalore, October 1997.

171 Vasantharaj, interview, Chennai, December 20, 1996.

172 Benny Kurian, a missionary to Bastar, MP, interview at an IICCC course at Kotarakara, Kerala, October 29, 1997.

173 Soltau, *Missions at the Crossroads*, p. 110.

174 [n.a], *Missionary Conference*, (Madras, 1902), p. 159, quoted in Harris, "The Theological Pilgrimage" p. 50.

175 Correspondence between the parties in July –October 1997.

176 Letter from the pastor of the first church about XX mission, January 5, 1997.

177 Letter correspondence from YY and ZZ missions, March 3, 1994.

178 Correspondence from LL mission, June – October 1994.

179 JE Jeyakumar, FMPB, letter dated June 1992.

180 Chandra Singh Iswarary, Secretary, Little Flock Fellowship, letter to Executive Director of Vishwa Vani, April 5, 1994.

181 EFI Comity Arrangement.

182 IMA "Mission Field Comity Arrangement."

183 **Working distance** of another mission was defined as the distance rate by which a mission station is expanding now, in its church planting work, during five years. For instance, if a mission station planted congregations in the last five years up to a radius of two kilometres, another mission should not come with four kilometres of that mission station (twice the working distance). In cities the distance did not make any difference but the count of the people in thousands. If the working distance is a Postal Pin Code area which has about 30,000 people, the other missions/churches should avoid establishing similar work in that Pin Code Area. Or if in the same Pin Code area two missions work among two distinct people groups, then it is accepted as a norm.

184 IMA "Mission Field Comity Arrangement".

185 Ibid.

186 Devavaram Samraj, FMPB AGS for field, letter to General Secretary FMPB, February 18, 1994.

187 Rev. Bose Meiyappan's letter on Ettapally.

188 MJ Sukumaran, FMPB, letter to IMA, April 25, 1992.

189 Letter from the CEO of ZZ Mission to keep OO Mission fifty km from the ZZ field, March 3, 1994.

190 PM Thomas, KEF President's letter, Sept.. 28, 1993.

191 DB Hrudaya, CEO OFU, letter to AD Moses, IMA MSC coordinator about the comity grievances of FFF. October 19, 1992.

192 Ezra Sargunam, President of ECI, letter to Samuel Devadasan, FMPB Field Director and Emil Jeba Singh, Director Vishwa Vani, July 17, 1990.

193 E. Jebasingh's letter to Sunder Raj, July 13, 1990.

194 Samuel Devadasan's letter to leaders, July 9, 1990.

195 Patrick Joshua's letter dated July 12, 1990.

196 Samuel Devadasan, FMPB field Director's letter to Raja Mohan Das, IEM Secretary for Field Ministries, April 9, 1994.

197 Raja Samuel, IMA – MSC Coordinator's letter to the Secretary of Little Flock Fellowship, Bengal, April 14, 1994.

198 R. Stanley, BYM National coordinator's letter to ___ (addressee's name missing). Letter dated April 1986.

8

Issues for Mission Agencies

If a mission does not handle an issue when it is small, it may snowball into a major problem. Indeed all issues, large or small need procedures and strategy.

Dynamic and Institutionalised Missions

According to Ray Eicher, former Director of OM India, a mission passes through four stages in its lifetime. It starts with a few individuals who have a special ethos and vision. It becomes a movement and thrives on the move and achieves many things on the way. It is vibrant when it moves. Thirdly, it becomes an institution with norms, laws, policies, a certain amount of stability and consolidation. The last stage is monumental. It just stays and does nothing,[1] ineffective and mediocre.

The Student Volunteer Movement (SVM) began in 1888 in the United States of America. By 1945 it had turned out 20,000 full time missionaries to different parts of the world.[2] However, by 1950 no more missionaries enrolled. SVM had reached its monumental stage. In the same way Young Men's Christian Association (YMCA), Young Women's Christian Association (YWCA), Young People's Missionary Education Movement (MEM), The Laymen's Missionary Movement (LMM) and many other movements became monuments.[3] The same thing could happen to any of the missions, like OM, YWAM, CCC, IEHC, FMPB, IEM, WV, IMS, NMS and all the others, if the original vision is not kept alive. The Indian missions which are already about twenty-five years old have many difficulties. The newer generation looks at older leaders as belonging to another age. Some of the pioneering leaders were ousted with excuses like voluntary retirement and rest for the weary. One thriving mission suddenly found its leader unable to lead and cope with the pressure of leadership due to sickness. It lacked second level leaders who could comfortably step in and give dynamic direction.[4] Several missions had neither workers nor second-level leaders. The only things left standing were gigantic buildings and the members of the same family running it.[5]

The Need for Strategic Planning

William Carey was a strategic thinker.

Carey and his colleagues had clear ideas as to the lines which missionary endeavour should follow. The first step must be translation, printing and dissemination of the Scripture. In the second place dissemination of Christian knowledge by preaching. Thirdly, they believed that they should be organised (to mobilise Christians of other denominations for the task of evangelisation).[6]

"Slogans are there but strategic planning is missing till to-day".[7] Indian missions grew after 1947, but methods of evangelism and the needs are different now. Missions have had to re-think to revitalise their mid-term of life.

Some missions seem to be slowing in effectiveness, growth and in leadership-building. Some have internal struggles of ethos, leadership and materialism. Second and third generations perhaps are not familiar with the original thrust and the ethos. Each mission needs strategic planning to set the tone for the future. Soltau, a missionary to Koreans, says that if the missionary does not plan, he works on things of lesser importance.[8]

"Changing your thinking from 'being in the rail road business' to 'being in the transportation business' is a result of strategic thinking."[9] Missions need to re-evaluate their policies and methods, and place fresh emphasis on training national leadership, evangelism, and urgent use of Christian literature.[10] "A strategy is an overall approach, plan, or way of describing how we will go about reaching our goal or solving our problem."[11]

Several books in the past two decades[12] deal with strategic planning from a biblical perspective. David Frazer and Dayton argued that planning, strategising and being Spirit-led are not contrary to each other. Articulating goals in evangelism and Church planting are statements of faith in what God wants us to do. The same Spirit which leads the missions is also capable of giving the direction in which the mission should go. Frazer and Dayton plead for balance,[13] balance between strategising and Spirit-led ministries.

Goals and accountability frighten some who like spiritual phrases such as "Spirit-led", "results in God's time." Strategising would help missions to plan creative tools such as literature and radio programmes and perhaps experience tangible results. Ideally, strategising and prayer both result in waiting on the Lord. Dayton and Frazer described four types of strategy: Standard Solution Strategy, the Being-in-the-Way Strategy, Plan-so-far Strategy and Unique Solution Strategy.[14]

Consultant David Schmidt said strategy requires a mission statement telling the reason for the mission's existence; a vision, the mission direction for three or five years; philosophies, values and policies for the vision to be carried forward; planning; and analysis of strengths, weaknesses, opportunities and threats (SWOT). On the basis of the SWOT analysis, goals are set, a strategy formulated to achieve goals, and a system of monitoring set up to make sure goals are achieved. Part of monitoring is midway analysis, measuring progress and presenting rewards for performance.[15] The point of strategic planning is to invigorate each mission to streamline their organisation.

D'Souza from OM observes that the major missions in India have already strategised and most aim to win the winnable, that is, the tribals and the poor.[16] Patrick Joshua of FMPB affirmed that FMPB is targeting three hundred responsive people groups in the Hindi heartland and was hoping to raise 1000 new workers to reach them.[17] However, many smaller missions need a clearer purpose, goals and plan.

Theodore Srinivasagam advises three levels for effective cross-cultural evangelism - getting existing churches to evangelise their neighbourhood, Christians in secular jobs finding employment in areas that needs witnesses, and missionaries sent cross-culturally to establish new churches.[18]

The Energy of Vision and Variety

The range of visions and goals of missions is enormous.

- Each ethnic group has been identified and several new strategies have been made to reach them according to their needs and responsiveness.
- Portable schools aim to equip laymen to reach out to their own people.[19]
- George Verwer, founder of OM, wants globally to raise 200,000 fresh missionaries.[20] OM India plans to saturate India with a hundred million pieces of literature among one hundred peoples of India through a "Global Action" programme, and also recruit many workers for mission work.[21]

- Sunder Raj envisions at least one thousand students channelled to mission every year for exposure and cross-cultural experience, so some will become full-time missionaries and others become partners for mission ventures and their support.[22]
- NIHNW aims to train fifty thousand grassroots church planters. Their first target is preparing two thousand master trainers to achieve this.[23]
- Bogosian (USCWM) advocates reaching India's eighty-seven scheduled tribes that have only less than one per cent Christians.[24]
- Ponraj is producing books on church planting particularly among the tribals. Many grassroots institutions use the books for information on church-planting.[25]
- Maharastra Village Ministries have a training centre near Yavatmal, Maharastra to train Christian workers for villages in Maharastra.[26]
- ICPF is actively moving into college campuses across the nation with two full-time music teams in two buses (Angelos).[27]
- Arpana has women's Prayer network and reaching out to the women of India by the women.[28]
- "UESI seeks to evangelise post-matric students in India to make disciples of the Lord Jesus Christ and serve as spiritual leaders making their local, national and global impact."[29]
- IICCC trains literacy workers and Bible Translators.[30]
- Kerala Evangelistic Missionary Fund (KEMF) has set up at Kottayam with the sole purpose of helping missionaries across the nation.[31]
- The Timothy Project was designed for pastors to train their people as mentors (like Paul to Timothy) to help them to develop their spiritual lives and also help them to witness.[32]
- FEBA Radio launched a *Network* programme on issues deeply affecting India's well-educated youth.[33]
- Similar programmes are aired also by TWR for teenagers and young people.[34]
- Gospel Recording Association (GRA) distributes cassette players and cassettes for villagers to hear the Gospel.[35]
- Centre for Communication Skills (CCS) explores the secular media to influence the educated with Christian values.[36]
- People India produces graphic research information for different groups to educate people about the mission situation in

India.[37]

- FFNI helps seekers from Islam, spreads the vision to Christians to reach them.[38]
- For fifty years Child Evangelism Fellowship of India (CEFI) has reached out to children to lead them to Christ, and passed on that vision in many seminars.[39]
- *Krishtanugami Sangh* has a vision for a movement of Hindus-seeking-Christ, and to work hard in placing new believers in churches.[40]
- A campaign style of evangelism is followed by Robert Cunville and his team. Through this people come to Christ and the team follows them up.[41]
- The Evangelical Free Church movement around India has a strategy to reach out to the urban middle class and bring these people to the Church.[42]
- Project North West 2000 AD Network promotes a vision of one church in every village in Punjab by the year 2000, one church in every PIN code in Himachal Pradesh by 2000, and one church in every PIN code in Jammu and Kashmir by 2005.[43]
- Maranatha Revival Crusade reaches out to people who are deaf.[44]
- Living Light Ministries at Bangalore shares the Gospel and rehabilitates handicapped people. Several blind persons have come to Christ through it.[45] Similar ministries across the nation are handled by Mission to the Blind,[46] IFVH and others.

There are hundreds of other missions across the nation, and most began with a specific purpose. The number of Indian missionaries is enormous. More complementarity, networking and prayer for each can only help.[47]

Partnerships

"The task of fulfilling the Great Commission is much greater than most of us estimate. A refusal to work in partnership with others comes from a wrong sense of success,"[48] said George Ninan. Patrick Joshua said that to evangelise India five things are needed: personal prayer, commitment and renewal; sacrifice of personnel and funding for mission; more new missionaries; discipleship and incarnational lifestyle to the poor; and partnership.[49] Ponraj and Sue Baird indicated four areas for partnership: in prayer, in personnel, in research and information and in sharing resources.

Sunder Raj advises partnerships between Indian missions and the churches, partnerships among the missions, partnerships between Indian missions and international missions, and partnerships between evangelistic missions and development missions.[50]

John Richard, the former General Secretary of Asia Evangelical Fellowship (AEF) active in the AD 2000 movement said, "At a time such as this, there is no place for bickering, infighting and a spirit of competition. Rather we have to humbly seek the cleansing of the blood of the lamb and the empowerment of God, the Spirit."[51] Kingsley Arunothaya Kumar of FMPB and R. Billy of UESI offer similar sentiments, "No more lone rangers. We the evangelicals must seriously consider the concept of partnership. We must be consciously building the kingdom of God ... complementing, ... willing to learn to respect and empower one another."[52]

The partnerships between the Church and mission must be firm and tangible. They need work, and there were church-mission consultations in 1981,[53] 1994,[54] 1996,[55] and in 1998.[56] However, as Vasantharaj said, "the need for partnership among ministries with common goals is articulated in several conferences. But practically not much has been done. Mutual agreement and oral consent is not partnership.[57]

George Edward of FMPB, who translated the New Testament into Malto language in Bihar, appreciated the partnership of assistance by the Bible Society Translation Department.[58] A GFA "Training with the End in Mind", promoted partnerships to share information, resources, stewardship, and co-operation among Christian leaders, theological educators and mission leaders. Partnership also in global missions - concern for the diaspora Hindus, partnership with the Indigenous, international missions and the Church in India will help.[59]

Ponraj is endeavouring to form networks in every Indian state to help grassroots workers build partnerships in their local ventures. Recently such conferences took place in Bihar, Nagpur and Karnataka. Similar efforts come from North India Harvest Network, CONS and CGAI to facilitate grassroots workers.

NIHNW has encouraged grassroots workers to reach the low castes of North India.[60] CONS trains lay people through Portable Bible Schools.[61] The Church Growth Association of India encourages workers to consider Homogeneous Peoples of India.[62] At the grassroots workers networks in different States, Ponraj and others emphasise church planting in rural and tribal areas.[63] OM, partnered with missions and churches, mobilises prayer and trains workers for other missions in India.[64] YWAM has a similar vision.[65] Campus Crusade joins with and mobilises other agency's teams to screen the "Jesus" film across the nation to create a mass awareness of Christ. There are nearly one hundred such teams across India with different missions.[66] Kulothungan, General Secretary of MVM greatly appreciated CCC for lending a projector and Jesus film, and sponsoring some of his workers to carry the Gospel to the villages in Maharastra.[67] The Joshua Project 2000, explained, "the Project seeks to partner with the great power of emerging missionary movements within the country and outside".[68] NLCI has actively worked with IICCC for the past three years in surveying languages for scripture translation.[69]

IMA tried to establish partnerships across the country between the CEOs on the major issues of the nation for evangelisation.[70] Muanthanga, representing the North East Missions, said, "Partnership in evangelism and exchange programmes could help in widening the vision and commitment of (North East) Christians in this (missionary vision)." [71] We need partnerships, but with clear understanding of each other, to complement one another in evangelism across the nation.

In addition International and Indian partnerships are growing. "The phrase 'indigenous mission' was very attractive in the first twenty-five years of Independence but now it is a negative word to isolate it in the global scene."[72] Phil Butler, Director of Interdev International has fostered partnerships, through IMA and EFI.[73] Gene Davis promotes partnership at a national level, and has encouraged many joint ventures for the missions.[74] PR Misra of Advancing Native Mission has tried to get his organisation to assist worthy causes for Indian missions.[75] With IMA, South Asian Concern (SAC) partners with Indian missions in India by contributing to health care for missionaries.[76]

Jim Engel, the founder, and Jane Overstreet, the North American Director of Development Association International, work to set up Partnership for Non-Formal Leadership Development in India and across the world in conjunction with Development Association International (DAI)[77], MAF and GMI with Indian partners. IMA has been asked to discuss this further to help the member missions of IMA benefit.[78] Engel writes, "We are very excited about the possibility of taking important future steps together."[79] In similar vein William David Taylor, the Executive Secretary of Missions Commission, of WEF has proposed a joint consultation on missionary attrition, pastoral care and mission education accreditation due in 1999 in India.[80]

Partnership to strengthen Indian missions is positively on, in consultation with mission bodies in India, and working within a few stated reservations. Stan Nussabaum, the former Training Director of Global Mapping International (GMA) wrote, "GMI is not offering to hold training seminars with a pre-determined American agenda. We want to make trainers available who will assist Indians in applying GMI resources to your Indian agendas."[81] D'Souza commented, "However, the guideline for such Indian and international partnership should be on equal terms with a right to veto from the persons who live with the situation in India."[82] A rich International partner should not "hire" "agents" among the Indian missions. It should be on the equal basis of partnership and agreement. If agents and collaborators are sought, it will be disastrous. The major credible missions may not buy such unsuitable means for evangelism, but because of the buying power of some International partners, small and naive Indian missions could be charmed and bought, willing even to use means that may not be suitable for the country. For example, books could be used which totally miscommunicate the Gospel to the Hindus. This will only harm missionary work in India in the long run and could jeopardise all that God is doing. International partners must accept the advice and the boundaries of reputable associations that monitor and view the whole of India.[83]

Smaller partnerships have apparently decreased. More partnerships, open and trusting, could foster funding, education, training, and outlets for sending missionaries to neighbouring needy countries.

Creative partnerships such as teaching English in neighbouring nations[84] could be furthered by IMA and EFI. In Hyderabad, pastors and mission leaders meet once a month to share, fellowship and pray.[85] George Verwer realised many missions in the same region did not know what each other did. He recommended keeping informed with E-mail, videos and by other means, to cooperate with each other at both management and grassroots level.[86]

PM Thomas from KEF said, "If Martin Luther, Charles Wesley, William Carey or David Livingstone waited for the permission of their mother churches, we would have lost some precious opportunities in Church (Mission) history."[87] Leaders must overlook minor differences and get on with the job of evangelising India. PM Thomas has also rightly urged, "Churches and missions (must) humbly find out where we have failed God and contribute wherever possible with the principle, 'Unity in essentials and Freedom in nonessentials' and fight our common enemy together."[88] "Pray for unity among and effective Christian witness of national associations like NCCI, EFI, FECI, CMAI, PFI, CBCI and IMA."[89]

But partnership is delicate in India, in both Christian and secular organisations, because of mistrust and genuine concerns. Max Warren wrote,

> Partnership means involvement between real people in real situations. It means committal of oneself in trust to the genuine integrity of the other person. It calls for a responsible attitude to the other by each. It means acceptance of a host of liabilities. And all this is completely mutual or it is not partnership.[90]

Bishop Neill wisely said, "Suspicion of motive can be a painful source of division."[91] D'Souza said pessimistically that Indian partnership is good only at grassroots work level in projects. At national level this is not happening because donors would get confused. Most agencies are nervous about surrendering donor lists to others.[92] Real partnership takes hard work.

Two agencies working among one group of people did not want to co-operate because they disagreed on the philosophy of work. One encouraged new Christians back into the community to witness among their people, even if with severe persecutions. The other believed persecution could be so heavy that new believers could lose their lives, so brought them out of the community to settle elsewhere and be rehabilitated. Neither party was willing to have anything to do with the other. One accused the other of being a moneymaking racket. Both had valid points, but they failed to find any middle ground to work together. Such situations dissipate efforts to evangelise India. Neill said, "Partnership starts with the recognition that the source of fellowship is in a common obedience to the living Word of God, given once for all in Jesus Christ, yet given anew through the Holy Spirit in every generation."[93] Christian partnership will not function if the above basic belief is not at the forefront of all efforts made in the mission field.

Secular company executives describe a paradigm shift in the concept of partnership. Sundeep Khanna distinguished many fables and facts about partnership, as below.

Partnership: Fables and Facts.[94]	
FABLES	FACTS
Joint ventures are meant to be permanent.	Every joint venture has a scheduled life cycle, which will end sooner or later.
Joint ventures are terminated only because they have failed.	Every joint venture has to be dissolved when it has outlived its life cycle.
Joint ventures are doomed to failure from the beginning.	Changes in the environment force joint ventures to be redesigned regularly.
Joint ventures between Indian companies and transnationals cannot succeed.	Joint ventures between Indian companies and transnationals also follow life cycles.
Transnationals exploit their Indian joint venture partners.	Transnationals seek to absorb their partners' competencies.

Here are many principles to apply in missions. Partnerships may legitimately change with situations. With these precepts we may avoid many heartaches, accusations and mistrust.

Standards, Accountability and Spirituality

Growth (in missions) though a blessing, has also resulted in unregulated proliferation of missions, ambiguity of objectives, dilution of definitions, and duplication of service leading to declining standards. There has also been damage. Many emerging missions make mistakes out of ignorance.[95]

God expects excellence in missions, faithfulness, and profitable stewardship,[96] which means excellence in structure, finance, management, work and public relations."[97] "The major criticism is that (parachurch groups) lack accountability to anyone but themselves. Parachurch groups are religion gone free enterprise."[98] Occasionally leaders announced they were accountable to God alone.[99] By not having standards and accountability some missions have generated troubles for all the genuine missions in the country.[100] The newspaper *The Asian Age* reported the following.

> A pastor in the city, who is getting foreign funds for his
> orphanage ... allegedly using the money for his own
> comfort. ... He collects the slum children with a prom-
> ise of *Biryani*[101] lunch, and when they assemble to eat,
> he shows them to (foreign) visitors and claims they are
> his orphanage children.[102]

Another incident was reported in *India Today*. A fifty-two year old Father Joseph, alias Yesu of Marthandam, Tamil Nadu, had over five thousand frenzied disciples in his Charismatic Centre. Joseph and his aides had been charged with financial swindles, sex crimes and a trail of murder.[103]

Jerry White said,

> Most para-local church groups operate in complete
> independence and isolation from each other. Conse-
> quently many groups duplicate and overlap each other
> in their specialities. This happens even in the same
> geographical areas. Each group thinks that its approach
> is unique or more effective than others - and especially
> more effective than the local church.[104]

Lack of accountability and standards caused tensions and duplication. The CEO of one mission wrote to another CEO,

> You have lured away two of our young workers whom
> we have taught in our Bible School for three years and
> spent thousands of rupees for training them. It is really
> unfortunate that a senior leader like you are (sic)
> disturbing our work. I request you to refrain from this
> unhealthy practice of inflating the quantity and sacri-
> ficing quality. This affects us very much ... because of
> our limited resources. But the fact remains that your
> lucrative offers are an attractive temptation. This way
> we will never be able to evangelise India.[105]

Workers of one mission sold Bibles cheaply while the FMPB stock lay unsold. In an another incident, three *Swarthic* workers left the field because of a promised higher salary.[106]

Many ministries started with good intentions and reputation, ended with scandals due to a lack of accountability. Even if the scandals were rumours, the damage was done for the ministry of the Gospel. One concludes that voluntary accountability is better than scams.

The present socio-religious and political situation gives us enough warning that our performances are being watched closely. Every small mistake on our part can be exploited to curtail our freedom of functioning. In recent years, there have been attempts at state levels to bring Christian voluntary organisations under state control. The only way we can counter such trends is to develop our own Standards and Monitoring Cell, so that missions do not fail in the standards that will attract Government action.[107]

Let missions be open to each other for help and correction to have a clean image. Let there not be dishonesty, secrecy and jealousy. When missions have a clear accountability structure, with a clean slate regarding financial dealings, proper Boards and other checks and balances, the government will have little cause to point out mishandling in missions. For these purposes associations became important.[108] To become members of IMA the following minimum criteria are required:

- a balanced Board of about seven people who are not relatives.
- a minimum of five fully paid evangelists/missionaries.[109]
- the mission must have existed for at least three years.
- audited accounts, including for the last three years.
- a resolution from the Board to become a member of IMA.

The introduction of the Evangelical Council for Financial Accountability (ECFA) in the USA had a restraining and standardising effect on member organisations, especially in the financial areas.[110] Something similar will help member missions in India. Accountability must start with CEOs for whom IMA has started a Missions Standards Cell (MSC), a panel of Christian professionals expert in management, accountability and professional standards.[111]

Besides this the National Institute of Christian Management (NICM) commenced in an IMA general body meeting consisting of EFI, IMA, FECI, PFI, NACSC, AETEI, ECFI, IAE, ICMA, ETANI and ETASI. The goal is to train and equip missions with skills to professionally run their missions. This body would eventually act autonomously.[112] NICM is yet to emerge as a major force. Some CEOs of missions felt nervous of being controlled and "policed" by others, and many were reluctant to divulge their mission and individual finances.[113] MSC and NICM are yet to take effect, due to distrust and apprehension.

IMA has also initiated second level leadership training, a

management journal for the mission executives,[114] and a friendship and support meeting of CEOs. Small informal groups of CEOs meeting encourage openness, trust and genuine concern for each other. They an help CEOs unwind. Trust, confidentiality, patience, commitment, ability to confront and knowledge of one another are key to the success of these groups. Necessarily e-mail contacts alone are not adequate. These friendship groups must be face-to-face encounters and must involve some hours every two months or so. According to those who have tried, the benefits are worth it.[115]

The Contribution of Lay People

"The call of Christ for service in the world comes to all Christians."[116] Lay people need to take part in Church work and evangelism, trained, motivated and guided. Bishop Pickett said, "The Church is dependent upon the witness of unpaid lay Christians. We, therefore, recommend that all Churches and missions consider ways and means of securing a large increase in honorary evangelistic effort by laymen."[117]

> The witness of lay members, even of the new converts, when wisely directed and supported by a trained ministry, has proved unique value in arresting attention and winning a response among ... the unreached. Informal personal witness has proved effective among many who are inaccessible to more organised and official means of approach.[118]

Rao says,

> There is a dearth of trained ministers. Not even one third of the need of trained ministers is met by existing theological schools. Non-traditional churches can use matured lay-men to help fulfil the functions of trained ministers. The rural churches also can not (adequately) support full time trained pastors.[119]

Few missions have understood the awesome latent power of lay people. IEM, BYM and many others use lay people to mobilise in evangelism, spread the vision of mission, collect funds for mission work and conduct revival meetings to arouse Christian consciousness for the need to be involved in missions. They also recruit and channel young people into full-time mission work.

For people to hear Christ and be matured, training is a major factor.[120] FMPB has a strong department to train lay people and calls them Prayer Group Leaders. They mobilise Christians in prayer and raise a major part of FMPB's funds. It even enrols Prayer Group Leaders in an accredited study programme run by IIM.[121]

Similarly, UESI has a special emphasis among Christian graduates in secular work. It is known as Evangelical Graduates Fellowship (EGF). Through this, many key and committed lay people teach new students and witness effectively in their professions. EGF is a key factor in directing and supporting the local work of UESI in every town. These men and women, influenced by UESI while they were college students, want similar change in the lives of the youth in colleges.[122]

OM trains as many young people as possible in evangelism, without requiring them to become "full-time" Christian workers. Many trained in OM become witnesses for Christ through their professions. For example, Jyothis is an Engineer at the thermal Power Station of Barauni, Bihar.[123] Surendra Kisku is a professor at Ranchi Christian College and became a staff worker of UESI. Ramesh Hembrom is a forest officer at Ranchi, Bihar.[124] Benjamin Besra is with the ministry of Finance at Delhi. Premo Ecca works with a Bank in Bihar. The CNI Bishop of Bhagalpur, the Rt. Rev. Philip Marandi, received his exposure to ministry when he was with OM in early Seventies.

Realising this power and wealth, some specialise in training lay people. Hrudaya, the leader of Orissa Follow-up Ministries, JS Raja, the Director of OM Bihar use the "Portable Training Schools" (PTS), for lay people to plant churches. PTS was working well, recruiting lay people from any denomination for 200 lessons full-time in two months using the regional language to equip them to plant and strengthen churches. This programme can be emulated by other Churches and missions to teach their believers. If this concept works there will be a multiplication of lay workers who would do E1 and E2 and some would also eventually move to E3 evangelism and the dormant power of lay people could be a powerful tool.

Training Missionaries

"Raising money was easier than raising quality men for many jobs in mission work."[125] To provide adequate training before going to the field, mission training needs a Biblical basis, sound philosophy of training, and a curriculum to suit varied stages of training. After that continuing educational opportunities (CeO) while on the field must be provided. We need partnerships in training, proper evaluation, and accountability.[126]

Dr. Seth Anyomi, the African Chancellor for the World Link University (WLU) said learning was not confined to classrooms or lecture halls. He gave four contexts for learning and training: daily life and professions, the local church, the ministry team (in mission field) and in specialised training.[127] Giron advises integration between the sending church, training school and the receiving mission to give the missionary oversight and pastoral care.[128] There are three areas of training: learning the Word, learning ministry skills, and character development. Often training courses impart theology, few ministry skills and less character development. It is better to mentor people in small groups.[129] Training for a missionary should include: mission awareness theory and practice with on-the-job-training, starting with orientation. This could last one to two years. Then spiritual retreats under expert teachers. Thirdly, personal and group studies monitored on the field. Fourthly, leadership training, and lastly, specialised training according to the vision and spiritual gifts of the person.[130] This places the missionary in continuous training in different areas for a long period, with pastoral care also partially achieved. This fulfils the continuous educational opportunity (CeO) for the missionary.[131] These suggestions have largely been implemented in OM teams with a degree of success. The questions faced were accreditation,[132] accountability, better team trainers and frequent change of missionaries from one field to another. If field missionaries study a specially designed courses in small teams, they will benefit in motivation, skills, better evangelisation of India, and better relationships with the co-missionaries and missions other than their own.

Many missionaries during service feel a need for more study, or feel "burnt out". In a study on attrition, Frank Allen wrote, "Probably one of the keenest disappointments that the new missionaries face is that everyday life on the field is a far cry from what was told them."[133] For this reason Dr Graham Houghton suggested they take occasional courses in a seminary. He is open for such people to apply to SAIACS for one or two terms, calling it Continuing Educational Opportunities (CeO).[134] Johnny Desai of IEM and Ravi Antine of EGF, an Engineering lecturer and active witness in his college, studied counselling at SAIACS in this way.

Men and Women in Indian Mission

Women in India make up nearly fifty per cent of the population, and have an important place influencing their family in religious, cultural and social values. They are the custodians of religious faith. "The condition of women is the truest test of a people's civilisation. Her status is her country's barometer."[135] Traditionally, non-Christian women could be reached only by Christian women. Men cannot influence them as much as women.[136] Hence Christians must plan creatively. "Women are more receptive to the Gospel in most instances than men, and they are easily reached by the women missionaries."[137]

Most women in mission in India are prepared to be assistants and wives. Few people emphasise women winning women.[138] What God intended for the Christian woman was partnership with men in the ministry and mission of the church. However, those in charge of training programmes for women volunteers and full-time workers found the obstacles to partnership so many and so formidable that they kept wondering out loud what specifically they were training the women for.[139]

Patrick Joshua said that his wife was a great source of encouragement to him and their children. Now all their grown-up children are in mission field. Thus she over a period had influenced the family. Most Christian women did play their part in missions in indirect ways rather than in upfront ministry. Parrot Devasahayam, with UESI, helped her husband to reach out to students first in Patna, Bihar then in Delhi during the past few years. She has been personally involved in winning people to Christ and counselled girls who then came to the Lord. However, she has been a wife first and then, a Christian worker. Mercy Matthew with IEM has a fulfilling role in the mission field as a nurse and as a witness. She and her husband have influenced some of the Kolamis in Maharastra. Parrot and Mercy find fulfilment in their husband and wife team ministry. Most women trained for mission assist their husbands in the ministry, which has a very positive effect.

Most women recruited for missions work are involved as indirect evangelists in Christian schools, hostels or in mission offices. Few directly influence non-Christian women to Christ.[140] Some Principals and teachers had a great influence on girls in their schools and colleges and some led girls to Christ.[141] Sneha Maxwell testified that she became a Christian while she studied at the Lalbagh Methodist School, the first Christian in her home.

There has been no emphasis on reaching the women of India on a mass scale. OM has the highest number of women workers, many are trainees. However as trainees they do more than many other missions to reach women.[142] "Gospel in Action Fellowship and Blessing Youth Mission have extremely effective women's ministries.

According to the latest research,[143] seventy-two per cent of national women missionaries are working with Pentecostal-Charismatic missions,[144] but this is small in number compared to men reaching men. Juliet Thomas suggested as strategies, developing individual gifts of women to use for home base ministry, using the church as a centre to mobilise women, starting special studies to train women, and opening homes of refuge for women in distress.[145] There has been much talk and little action. Even if there were training centres, missions usually do not know how to employ trained women missionaries, especially if they are single. Hedlund aptly summarises, "The role of women in ministry has been a neglected theme among Indians. Significant conversion movements to Christ in Andhra Pradesh and other areas are led by women."[146] Since Muslim *Zenana* women and upper class Hindu women are out of reach of evangelism by men, Christians need women to reach them.

The paucity of work among women stems from confusion on the role of women. With so much argument on the place of women in the Church, many are afraid to encourage women to upset the status quo.[147] Culturally it is a taboo for Christian women to evangelise because of fear they will be labelled loose or immoral if they visit other women at home. Christian women are already seen by society as aggressive and free. Because of this wrong perception, Christian men want their wives to do household chores and not venture out. Even a prominent liberated Indian Christian woman worker heavily criticised Indian women distributing literature and visiting homes to meet other women, though she claimed India would be reached by concerned women. She seems to have no tangible strategy. Traditionally a woman helps her husband in evangelism. A noble concept but it lacks creativity for women to find their own methods to reach women.

Women as the co-leaders for evangelism is also unacceptable among many evangelicals. People are uneasy about working with women for fear women might take over and exercise a "non-biblical" leadership over men! However Jacob Kavunkal and F. Hrangkhuma write, "Our Indian culture has already accepted women as Prime Minister and cabinet ministers. We have many women Gurus now in Hinduism. It is a poor excuse to say our culture does not accept women as leaders."[148] If we continue with these beliefs, the women of India will remain unreached. Women themselves must design new creative ways to work, by themselves or in partnership with men.

Traditional Indian women, contrary to popular belief, are strong members of the family. They wield much power and influence the husband and children. If they are touched with the Gospel, they will influence the family more than many men.[149]

Global Indian Missionaries

Secular Indians feel the need to stick together in spite of their diaspora.

> In Kathmandu more than four hundred people of Indian origin gathered ... to discuss and deliberate on the challenges faced in their respective countries of adoption and in the world. Indians from Fiji, Indonesia, Malaysia, Mauritius, Burma, Nepal, South Africa and Thailand are attending the third Asia-Pacific regional conference hosted by The Global Organisation of People of Indian Origin, Nepal Chapter. (They discussed) the need to develop some sort of diaspora consciousness in regard to trade, investment and tourism.[150]

Indian Christians have the multiple responsibility of reaching their own in India, Indian diaspora, and also others.

Lack of money has deterred sending Indian missionaries to other countries of the world, particularly to economically well off countries where the cost of living is higher. However, the North African countries, the newly opened CIS countries and South Asia have become the focus in recent years.

> Indian missionaries abroad? Will it work? Why not? If Indian textile businessmen can flourish in Central Asia, if MARUTI and TATA can run in Central Asian roads, why can't we send missionaries there? Today there are unprecedented opportunities among Azeris, Kazaks, Kyrgys, Tajiks, Turkman, and Uzbeks who are hungry for spiritual things, but know little or nothing about the Lord Jesus. It is high time for India, a country that has been receiving for hundreds of years, to give in this new era of Christian missions.[151]

OM India has already sent Indians as short-term missionaries to many of the above nations, and a full-time worker to Egypt. There for several years now, the Indian worker in Egypt has adjusted well. He looks like an Arab, has learned the language well, and is not as conspicuous as non-Arab missionaries from Europe and East Asian countries. Another report said, "If all goes well the first batch of Indian missionaries will arrive in Central Asia in September 1997."[152] By October six had arrived.[153] Many missions such as CCC, SISWA, OM, IEHC, GFA, KEF, BCM, UESI, IEM are working in the same direction.

George Ninan, Director of Affairs in South Asia of Campus Crusade for Christ, and Ebenezer Sunder Raj, the General Secretary of IMA urged,

> Indian missions have grown in size and in vision. It is time for us to show concern for the rest of South Asia. With our resources, the manpower and the experience, the missions in India could contribute to South Asia and move forward. Internationally India is looked upon in that progression. There are already requests from the neighbouring nations for help. Culturally there are many similarities and in some cases the same people across the borders. Therefore, there is a need to provide a meeting point. Thus missions and Churches are encouraged to adopt "people groups" in the surrounding nations and target reaching them with prayer and evangelism.[154]

Sunder Raj suggested that when the basic information on South Asia was ready, partners within India and abroad could meet, plan and adopt the unreached in South Asia. The Forum has scheduled a gathering in January, 2000.[155] Some doors would unlock through teaching English.

Evangelicals and Liberals

Non-evangelicals say Evangelicals are cowards with a naive view of Theology who busy themselves "saving souls". They claim they are irrelevant to the needs around them, majoring on non-essentials. They are fundamentalists with a ghetto mentality, looking down on the rest with hallowed isolation. They are clannish, cliquish, individualistic and pro-capitalists.[156]

Evangelicals emphasise evangelisation of the 'heathen world.'[157] According to Pradeep Das, Indian Evangelicalism is a transplant of Western anti-ecumenism and theological distinctiveness. By contrast liberals and liberation theologians turn to social activism, giving less emphasis on spiritual change through the

Gospel. Some evangelicals are also drawn into this.

Still, Churches and missions are trying to figure out a partner-ship deal for evangelisation. Patrick Joshua of FMPB said in a gathering of missions executives, "By bringing the mainline churches we may influence them, or they may want this Forum to adopt some of their concerns like women's liberation and other."[158] Someone else said perhaps the Evangelical Fellowship (EFI) failed because it only related to "evangelicals".[159] Rajaiah said, "One great defect is that the Indian Church is not sufficiently evangelis-tic."[160] This tension has to be carefully analysed if it is to form a mission alliance with the liberals, some of whom believe in reli-gious pluralism.

Creating Future Leaders

A missionary from a major mission, complained while in a Bible College that he had not heard from his mission leader about his next posting until he graduated. He felt discouraged about the complacency of his leaders. A missionary attending an IMA organised mid-level leadership seminar at Hyderabad wished his leaders/CEOs were there to listen to the leadership sessions. He felt his leaders needed to hear about planning and counselling more than the rest in that mission. He felt disillusioned that some of his learning could not be practised in the field under his present leaders.

Many missions now express greater determination to raise more leaders for the future. IMA has appointed a leadership training co-ordinator to conduct mid-level leadership seminars for member missions.[161] OM emphasises training leaders with many-tiered programmes well planned and ably executed.[162] However, some felt that many missions, prepared mid-level leaders only from their own clan and thus the leadership was kept within the clan and family itself.

"Some training programmes appear mainly to inoculate graduates against further learning. Uninformed leadership and irrelevant teaching tend to produce closed minds."[163] Chacko Thomas remarked humorously that he was interrupted in his learning when he was at school.[164] Bible schools can be a drag. Pradip Ayer, the Director of OM North India, complained that some of his workers after training were unable to fit into their previous regular ministries.[165] Either the workers matured or the training was not appropriate to the needs of the mission.

Only large missions build potential leaders by giving them to senior leaders as apprentices to mentor— a powerful method. Smaller missions struggle both for good men and for funds to train them.

The Myth of Indigenous Funds

There is much discussion on indigenous and local funds. Some, especially foreigners, would like to know when the Indian Church is going to become responsible financially for the evangelisation of India. The answers are not simple in the light of the immense need in the nation. The Indian church is young as far as Indian missionary endeavour is concerned. But then some assume the Church in India is weak and irresponsible and does not see the necessity to give for missionary work.[166]

Though there may be some truth in this, the following factors have to be kept in mind. The Church in India has given much towards meeting the need for their own evangelism in the past fifty years.[167] The Church in India is small compared to the vast task of Indian evangelisation. The vast majority of the Church is from the lower, Dalit strata of society which is unable to bear the whole burden of the huge task. "Christians are from fourteen scheduled castes."[168] Ashish Massey, a Christian sociologist and journalist reflected, "The Christians are simply poor. They get little opportunity to seek employment outside church institutions. They have very little role in business."[169] This is reflected in the way the Indian missionaries are paid meagrely and the focus of missions is to the poor and the tribals. Large parts of Indian society have not been touched. The evangelical Church, responsible for most evangelisation, is small and is still emerging. And the Church is still being educated in giving for mission. Rajaiah Paul said, "the Indian Christian community has not yet learnt the importance of Christian giving."[170] Although this statement was made in 1952, the struggle to teach Christians continues. "Our Church members need to be informed of the unreached people of the world who have to be reached with the Gospel and remind them of their responsibility and privilege.[171]

Some missions claimed they were indigenised and there was great applause for their efforts. Most of these barely meet the needs of the missionaries. Their missionaries work with the ethos of "sacrifice"! The human cost of maintaining these missions is too high. A study in 1980 revealed that an average of thirty-five per cent of Third World missionaries did not receive their promised full salary.[172] Most of these missions paid very little to their missionaries. This is one of the main reasons why missionaries went to work among the tribals and villages. Of course the tribals and villagers are also unreached. But with the salary the missionaries received, they could not afford to live in the growing cities and towns. This also affected the missionaries' children's education. Most missions provide no pension, no medical insurance, no life insurance, no savings and no plans for future housing for the retiring missionaries. This is basically to do with the inability to manage with the paucity of funds. Although the vision of reaching India is large, the means to meet the needs are inadequate. Often money which should be spent on missionary welfare is spent on the social needs of those who do not know Christ.[173] Often the salary of the missionary is compared to that received by the poor of India. This is how some missions recruit more people for less money, at the cost of missionaries' welfare. Instead of looking after two missionaries with the funds available, ten missionaries are employed for the number games. Some, though not consciously playing the number games, feel such "burden" for unreached that they lose awareness of the cost of maintaining missionaries and their welfare.[174]

Missions which claim indigenised funding explain that their missionaries are supported by the Church in India. Apart from this there are funds raised from the non-Resident Indians (NRI). Many larger "indigenous missions" employ foreign funds through their sister organisations for social activities which sometimes support the evangelistic and the holistic activities in the mission field. Thus, some large indigenised missions have one agency for Indian funds and the other for foreign funds. Keyes says it is a good idea to separate missionary salaries from projects. "Perhaps the best policy, in the light of world nationalisation and missionary indigenisation, is to support special missionary projects, but allow the national churches to pay personal salaries."[175]

Thus, indigenisation is something of a myth and only partial. Massey said that, "Foreign sources are sizeably curtailed and the indigenised resources have not developed so far to fill the gap."[176] Consequently, the Indian Church may not be able to bear all the financial demands of the great needs of all the missions in India in all their evangelistic and the social activities. However, the Indian Church has the manpower which can be trained to evangelise

India and in the neighbouring countries. Therefore, by and large it is a good idea to support missionaries with Indian funds and use overseas funds for projects, training and other capital expenses.

The church has to be educated and that is slowly taking place. Gopal Hembrom, a Christian leader from Bihar said that the concept of mission in the minds of people in Bihar is the Lutheran Mission and its missionaries. They could only think of mission as a body set up by foreigners. The local Christians failed to see the local church as the place of mission and missionaries. Such concepts need changing by educating the Church in Bihar about what mission is and how to go about it.[177] To some extent this is true of the Church across India.

The Church must be educated on giving. Many did not know the difference between giving to a glamorous crusade speaker and missions which are quiet. The best and most worthy appeals have not raised all the needed funds. Some did not even know how to appeal for the credible work and structure of missions. As a result the wrong people received much money from Christians while credible missions suffered. Giving should be based on understanding and enlightenment and not excitement. Giving should rely on objective information rather than inspiration for the wrong cause. In other words, Christians should be taught to give to the right causes—credible missions.

Family Dynasty Missions

Many genuine missions across India have ended up without legitimate successors. According to one source, the majority of the Indian mission agencies are either led by clan members; or people of the same state, language or areas; or by the relatives. CV Mathew quoted the perception of some that, "Evangelicals are clannish. They are 'committed' to their families and endeavour to build their family empires or at least fiefdoms."[178]

Indians want to keep things in the family, as marriages when the alliance keeps the family fortunes. In *Business Today,*[179] fifty families were highlighted who monopolised the industries of India since 1947. Vinay Kamat said,

> Four hundred and sixty-one of the five hundred most valuable companies in the country were controlled by families. Thus, it is the business family that is the most powerful form of enterprise in corporate India even today.[180]

Business tycoons give their business to family members whom they trust more than others, passing on wealth to their own family. Christian dynasties too hand everything over to their family members to provide future security, work and continuity in the ministry. One Christian worker, in spite of knowing his children's weaknesses, commented that he would rather give the work to the known evil than to the unknown evil!

On the other hand, those who genuinely work in a mission – capable, more burdened and better able to guide the work – suffered, while the children and the relatives of the leader enjoyed themselves to an extent of making a mess of the ministry. The efficient bystander's job was only to sort and bailout the heirs of the boss from complicated situations. Some missionaries' children have become aware of the problem and left missions altogether, refusing to help the parents who aspired for the children to take over.[181]

Those who are neither the relatives or family members of the boss work with the "bonded labourer" syndrome and work hard to be graded as high as possible. Many, feeling disappointed, exploited, start their own ministries which could become prosperous and be passed on to their children. Thus, often a new ministry is not due to some new sense of burden, but to obtain a freedom from the exploitation of family enterprises. Often hurt pride and egoism made people start new ministries almost as competition with others.

Children of some family dynasty mission leaders end up overseas and settle, while the native missionaries can hardly pay fees for their children in ordinary schools. They feel the wide disparity and murmur. It can cause disunity. Some spiritualise that 'the Lord was good and met the needs,' while the same organisation starved its other employees. The children of many mission executives fare well, enjoying many facilities. At the other extreme people criticised some other executives for not caring enough for their families and children.

The question is not whether it is right or wrong to encourage family dynasties in missions and churches. In some cases, a member of the family could have come up with proper rank and file and was genuinely elected as the leader, but in many cases, the family member is the only one who has been trained to take over and the others were by-passed. This showed worldly selfishness.

The majority of Tamil missions are dominated by the Tamils, Malayalee by Malayalees and similarly with North Easterners.

Very few cross-cultural disciplings take place in the Indian missions. Indian missions have behaved no better than have some Western missions with hundreds of denominational and geographical differences. If India is to see national integration it has to truly start with Christian believers who honestly believe that all of them belong to the same family of God.

IMA does not accept any mission in to the association in which board members are relatives.[182] This is IMA's way to try and discourage family members on governing boards. However, after they became members, some missions elected relatives. This has not been scrutinised adequately by IMA. Unless a mission has an ethos of not allowing family members in on the governing body, it would be difficult for anyone to police the situation including IMA.

Conclusion

Missions need strategic planning or they will drift. Strategic planning must encompass national needs, not just on the winning the winnable, and leaving the majority of the people with no opportunity to respond to Christ. This would reinforce the idea that Christianity is only for the poor, low castes and the tribals. To enhance this strategic planning, it is better to call in a third person to view issues objectively. This may be a hard and painful process when missions may have to discard old ways. We recommend SWOT analysis led by an outsider for each mission or having a strategic planning consultant present to help them to move in the right direction.[183]

Partnerships between the missions are being cultivated, aiming to overlook minor differences. The differences of modes of work, personalities, philosophies and doctrines have to be understood in the light of the need of the nation and also in the light of the fact that all missions are pressing toward one goal of proclaiming the Gospel. We need trust without fear of filching workers and donors from each other. Even if wrong is done; openness, honesty, walking in the light, brokenness and forgiveness can foster partnership. Prayer, collaboration, accountability, and believing the best of each other will heal the present fears. Christian workers need larger hearts to understand, forgive and get on with the job. Partnership must be more than lip service. It can assist in evangelising India, and when we have partnership we must nurture and guard it.

Missions are still confused between standards, accountability and spirituality. At times even sloppiness and below standard work is mistaken for true spirituality. Poverty and simplicity is considered a virtue of spirituality, yet these virtues may appear in sloppiness. It comes in the form of second grade material for studies, bad food, poor hygiene, unacceptable organisational methods, dirty room service/class rooms and many others. It is also expressed by a dire financial status, voluntary work syndrome and an inability to control laziness.

Accountability may be lacking from top leadership to the grassroots workers. And in some places only fear of getting the sack makes people accountable in the lower cadre workers. Sometimes sloppiness is also not because of lack of money, but because of over delegation and poor follow-up of instructions. At times it is purely a lack of training and exposure by weak leadership. In these circumstances Christian programmes may lack effectiveness, punch, authenticity and closure, all excused as being spiritual. Some failures in accountability are soft-pedalled in the name of showing Christian love, and leaders who demand accountability are accused as tyrants, unspiritual, unchristian and purely "secular". In the same manner in the name of spirituality, workers may not "allow" the leaders to confront for corrective actions.

Lack of accountability stems from the theory that a person is debtor only to God, people may do their own thing—top leadership or grassroots—especially if they are paid very little and do not worry about being ousted. There are many exceptions to this and many have genuinely committed their lives to God only to eventually become frustrated in leading difficult people.

Missions need to think much further on mobilising a lay people's power for the cause of evangelisation. The sooner young people are exposed to cross-cultural and local evangelism, the faster they will catch the vision. UESI, ICPF, OM, YWAM, CCC, Navigators, Scripture Union, YFC, BYM, LEF and many others have made a very special input into the lives of these lay people. Let the churches encourage them.

Continuous Educational Opportunities (CeO) are a useful principle, on and off the field. By positive planning some attrition could be stopped, and ministries benefited. Study programmes designed by groups like TAFTEE, IIM, OM and others can offer group studies on the field for the missionaries. If an accreditation standard could be worked out, missionaries could study seriously to obtain credits, and at the same time be refreshed and better equipped.

The dichotomy of funds being received from India and abroad for the sake of just being called "indigenised" will be solved if the giving is channelled and accounted for. There is no double standard in acknowledging God's resources from God's people. One day, in God's timing the Indian Christians might disburse for the needs of evangelistic works in other countries. In fact, this is already happening to some extent. Teaching the Church to give is only a secondary step. The primary task is making the training programmes such that the leaders are informed of what went on to mobilise the Church. Often it is the pastor or the leader of the church who is the sticking point to a church taking part in evangelising this nation. More than the church the leaders have to be motivated.

Leaders should constantly look out for capable people to mentor. The folly of depending only on trained and ready-made leaders from a seminary will end up in disaster. Leadership has to be built over the years by finding and nurturing faithful people.[184]

Women's responsibility in the mission has to be looked at carefully in the light of the fact that the women in India can usually be reached only by women. Let us design creative strategies.

To avoid missions controlled by family members, we must groom new leaders. We should require separation of personal and mission property, so that work can move to others. We must trust and mentor disciples, including cross-cultural ones, so they will capably work even when the "founder President" is not around. Let us avoid having missions the property of a few families.

END NOTES

1 Ray Eicher, Lecture, OM Leaders' Meeting, Bombay 1986.
2 [n.a.], "The Awakening of Student and Laymen A Call for A Mission Renewal Movement", Budelman, (Ed.), *Perspective*, p. 49. It also had 80,000 people pledged as "crisis men" who were normal secular men committed to be supporters and advocates of the SVM missionaries and spread the vision at home.
3 Ibid, pp. 49–50.
4 Interview, the Mission's name withheld. July 1997.

5 Names withheld.

6 Neill, *Church in India and Pakistan*, pp. 67–69.

7 Vasantha Raj, CGAI, interview, Chennai, Dec. 20, 1996.

8 Stanley Soltau, *Facing the Field* (Grand Rapids: Baker Book House, 1959), pp. 107–109.

9 Bryant Myers, "Strategic Thinking as Christians" *MARC Newsletter*, No. 97–2. June (1997) 3.

10 Soltau, *Missions at the Crossroads*, pp. 174–178.

11 Dayton and Fraser, "Strategy", From Winter, Hawthorne et al (Eds.), *Perspectives*, p. 569.

12 Refer to the following books. Edward R.Dayton & David Frazer, *Planning Strategies for World Evangelisation* (Michigan: WB Eerdmans Publication Company, 1980); James F. Engel, *Contemporary Christian Communications Its Theory and Practice* (New York: Thompson Nelson Publishers, 1979); Robert E. Coleman, *The Master Plan of Evangelism* (New Jersey: Spire Books, 1984). Leighton Ford, *The Christian Persuader*, (London: Harper and Row Publishers, 1976).

13 Dayton & Frazer, *Planning Strategies*, p. 570.

14 Dayton and Frazer, "Strategy", in Winter, Hawthorne et al (Eds.), *Perspectives*, pp. 570–571. The Standard Solution Strategy works out a particular way, then uses the same approach in every situation. The Being-in-the-Way Strategy at first appears to be no strategy. This strategy has no specific goals for the future. The assumption is that God will lead. The implications of this strategy is that long-range planning is not very important because this is God's job. It also eliminates failure because that is God's problem. The Plan-So-Far Strategy assumes that after an initial plan God will take care of the rest of the plan. The Unique-Solution Strategy assumes that every situation is different, that each one requires its own special strategy. It works on the assumption that answers can be found for every question. It does not depend on standard solutions.

15 David Schmidt, a strategic planning consultant from Wheaten, lectures for Operation Mobilisation, London, 1993–94.

16 D'Souza, OM, interview, Hyderabad, April 15, 1997.

17 Patrick Joshua, FMPB, Reported at NCE, Hyderabad, September 25, 1996.

18 Theodore Srinivasagam, "The Need for Effective Cross–Cultural Evangelism," in *Mission Mandate*, p. 204.

19 JS Raja, OM Coordinator, Bihar, Interview, 1994.

20 Verwer, "Acts 13", Message–Audio tape, June 16, 1996.

21 OM *Project Light* pamphlet.

22 Ebenezer Sunder Raj, interview, Chennai, August, 1997.

23 Kaiser on NIHNW meet at Delhi, November 1997.

24 David Bogosian's letter, Frontier Mission Updates, November

26, 1997. Refer to Appendix 3. IMA letter to the CEOs of the member missions, 13, 14 November 1997. Refer to Appendix 4 for Unreached People >50,000.

25 Dr. Akbar, IOM, Nagpur, Interview, November 11, 1997.

26 MVM 15th Anniversary Souvenir, (1996), p. 23.

27 ICPF *Collegiate Fisherman*, Feb.–Mar. (1996) 1.

28 Arpana Pamphlet, 180 Jal Vayu Vihar, Bangalore 560084.

29 UESI Prayer Map, (1996).

30 IICCC pamphlet.

31 Editor, "Existing Missionary Funds", *Insight India*, April–June (1997) 15–16.

32 Timothy Project Booklet, (1994).

33 FEBA, "*Network* Shaping the Future," November (1996) 2.

34 TWR News, "The Life Line Connection," June 1997.

35 GRA Report, "In the Light of His return," (1996) 3–4.

36 CCS News Letter *Media Link*, December (1996).

37 Tony Hilton, *Maharastra Harvest Field Handbook, Field Series* (Chennai: People India, 1997).

38 FFNI Newsletter, *Neighbours Concern*, December (1996).

39 CEFI Newsletter, Jan–Feb 1997.

40 Ashok Kumar, interview, Calicut, November 16, 1997.

41 Billy Graham Evangelistic Association Prayer Letter from the head Office at Secunderabad, January 15, 1997.

42 Dr Booshan Raj Thomas, personal interview, May 1997.

43 Project North West 2000 AD News, "A Vision for a Saturation Evangelism in North West India." (1997).

44 Maranatha Revival Crusade pamphlet, "My Deafness – that Others May Hear."

45 Living Light Ministries Booklet, Bangalore.

46 Mission to the Blind Mission Update June 1996.

47 Patrick Joshua, interview, SAIACS, Bangalore, October 15, 1996.

48 George Ninan, South Asia Director of CCC, "Partnership," unpublished paper, Bangalore, April 1997.

49 Patrick Joshua, Interview at SAIACS, Bangalore, Oct. 15, 1996.

50 Ebenezer Sunder Raj, *Evangelism in India Today*, paper presented at NCE, Hyderabad from 25–29 September, 1996.

51 John Richards, "Partnership", a paper presented at the National FORUM at Nagpur on April 15, 1997.

52 Kingsley Arunothaya Kumar and R. Billy, "'Evangelical Mission Thought and Practice'– Could it be more Indian?" Arles & Benwati (Eds.), *Pilgrimage 2100*, p. 79.

53 Sponsored by EFI, interview with John Richard, Whitefield, Bangalore, January 23, 1998.

54 Thirty-five Christian leaders from all over India met at Nagpur for a unique historical church-mission consultation, 15–18 December 1994, to respond to the commonly felt national issues affecting the churches and missions in India. They represented the

major indigenous missions and church denominations of India, jointly organised by the IMA and NCCI. Rev. K. Lung Muana, Mr Ebenezer Sunder Raj and Rev. Jeevan Babu, "Partnership in Mission", Nagpur, December 18, 1994.

55 NCE at Hyderabad organised by IMA in September, 1996.

56 Church-missions consultation at Whitefield jointly organised by IMA and NCCI from 20–22 January, 1998.

57 Vasantharaj Albert, Editorial, *India Church Growth Quarterly*, Vol. 3, No. 2, July – September (1996), p. 2.

58 George Edward, FMPB, at SAIACS, personal interview, Bangalore, November 16, 1997.

59 GFA Committee Meeting Minutes of "Training with the End in Mind" held at Tiruvalla on August 18–19, (1997) 6.

60 [n.a.] *To the Uttermost Part: The Call to North India,* Colorado: AD 2000 and Beyond & Joshua Project 2000, 1997.

61 Paul Gupta, CONS report for 1996–97.

62 Vasantharaj Albert, Director of Church Growth Research Centre, personal interview, Chennai, 20 December 1996.

63 Ponraj, interview, SAIACS, Bangalore, Nov. 11, 1997.

64 [n.a] *OM India and You,* OM Publicity brochure.

65 Sam Dharam, Director of YWAM, interview, Nagpur, FORUM meeting, April 18, 1997.

66 George Ninan, Interview, CCC, Bangalore, March 1997.

67 Kulothungan, MVM, interview, Nagpur, October 31, 1997.

68 [n.a], "Joshua Project 2000", p. 12.

69 Jacob George, fax to Rajendran, June 19, 1997.

70 Sunder Raj, *Evangelism in India Today,* NCE at Hyderabad. September 25– 29, 1996

71 Muanthanga, "Survey of North East India," *IGCQ,* p. 19.

72 D'Souza, interview, April 14, 1997.

73 Phil Butler and Ebenezer Sunder Raj met at Madras and discussed partnership in October 1997. Also discussed with Dr Richard Howell and others in Delhi, September 1998. Since that date it has been resolved to have a partnership department under EFI. Interdev will facilitate that for the next few years.

74 Gene Davis, interview while visiting Bangalore, July 1997.

75 PR Misra, PR, Advancing Native Mission, Bhubaneshwar, Orissa, interview at Chennai, October 7, 1997.

76 Raju Abraham, discussion on health care for missionaries at Chennai, July 4, 1997.

77 Development Associates International (formerly known as The Centre for Organisational Excellence at Eastern College founded by Dr. James Engel) has in the last five years developed and tested curriculum to enhance the effectiveness of Christian leaders throughout the majority world. This curriculum includes strategic thinking, management, leadership, spiritual

formation, financial planning, working with boards and indigenous fund raising. This course could stimulate Indian mission CEOs to stretch beyond routine administration and crisis management to strategic planning. In February 1998, the initial training of trainers was attended by about thirty-five people at Hyderabad.

78 Jane Overstreet, DAI, North American Director. Letter to IMA General Secretary, October 15, 1997.

79 James Engel, letter to Rajendran, December 4, 1997.

80 William David Taylor, the Executive Secretary of Missions Commission, of WEF, letter Correspondence with IMA General Secretary and Asst. General Secretary, May 1997.

81 Stan Nussabaum, letter to IMA, January 27, 1997.

82 D'Souza, interview, April 14, 1997.

83 Discussion with Dr Houghton, SAIACS, December 12, 1997.

84 PTI, "India To Export 'English'," *The Indian Express*, Chennai, August 11, (1997) 9.

85 Rev. J. Samuel, leader from the Twin-cities Pastors and Missions network, interview, Secunderabad, April 1994.

86 Verwer, "Acts 13", audio message, June 16, 1996.

87 PM Thomas, "Some Thoughts on Churches and Missions", unpublished paper, 1997.

88 Ibid.

89 *My Prayer Guide*, IMA, p. 3.

90 Max Warren, *Partnership*, (Chicago: SCM Books, 1956), pp. 92–93.

91 Stephen Neill, *Christian Partnership*, (London: SCM, 1952), p. 31.

92 D'Souza, interview, April 14, 1997.

93 Neill, *Partnership*, p. 21.

94 Sundeep Khanna, "Partnering", *Business Today*, October 7–21, (1996) 80.

95 IMA pamphlet, Missions Standards Cell.

96 Matthew 25: 21–30.

97 MJ John, the Executive Director of FARMS India, Madras and Dr R. Chandrasekar, Director of Nave Jeevan Seva Mandal, "Excellence in Missions", a paper presented at the EFI National Convention in 1990 at Hyderabad.

98 Stephen Board, "The Greatest Evangelical Power-shift," *Eternity*, June (1979) 17. Cited in Jerry White, *The Church and the Parachurch. An Uneasy Marriage* (Portland: Multnomah Press, 1983), p. 90.

99 J. Allan Youngren, "Parachurch Proliferation: The Frontier Spirit Caught in Traffic," *Christianity Today*, November 6, (1981) 39. Cited in White, *The Church and the Parachurch*, p. 90.

100 IMA pamphlet, Missions Standards Cell.

101 *Biryani*—celebratory rice meal with meat.

102 S. Kushala, "Pastor Lures 'Orphans' for Show", *The Asian Age*, Bangalore, June 20, (1997) 1.

103 MG Radha Krishnan, "Unholy

Messenger", *India Today*, October 6, (1997) 46.

104 Jerry White, *The Church and the Parachurch*, p. 91.

105 CEO of KKK (identity withheld), letter dated January 27, 1993.

106 Lazarus, letter from Denkanikottai, June 10, 1992.

107 IMA pamphlet, Missions Standards Cell.

108 Discussion with Sunder Raj, Chennai, July 1997.

109 Raj Samuel, former IMA coordinator for MSC, letter to EK Emmanuel, GS, Junglighat, Port Blair Andamans, on his enquiry to become member of IMA, July 29, 1994.

110 White, *The Church and Parachurch*, p. 90.

111 Sunder Raj, interview at Chennai, July 31, 1997.

112 Letter to mission leaders from IMA, August 9, 1996.

113 Interview, requested to withhold name, July 1997.

114 IMA Journal Committee discussion, Chennai, July 1997.

115 C. Sekar, Abubakker, David Shunmugam and K. Rajendran. Discussions on the formation of FRIENDS, 1996–97.

116 [n.a], *The World Mission*, Thambaram Conference, p. 71.

117 Pickett, *Christ's Way to India's Heart*, p. 108.

118 Ibid, p. 48.

119 Rao, *Some Concerns of the Indian Church*, p. 29.

120 Verwer, "Acts 13" Message on Audio tape.

121 Barnabas, CEO, IIM, interview, Chennai, August, 1997.

122 Sunil, UESI, interview, Bangalore, November 11, 1997.

123 Jyothis Hembrom letter correspondence over the years.

124 Ramesh Hembrom at Ranchi, 1990.

125 Discussion with Sunder Raj. Chennai, 2 August 1997.

126 K. Rajendran, "Strategic Training Partnership for Effective Evangelisation of India," a paper presented at Interdev Conference at Larnaca, Cyprus on April 9, 1992.

127 Seth Anyomi, "Four Contexts for Learning and Training," *Training for Cross-Cultural Ministries*, Volume 96, No. 2, September (1996) 5.

128 Giron, "An Integrated Model of Missions," p. 1.

129 Dr Allan Adams, OM, Director of Pastoral Care, lectures to Small Group Leaders, on ship M/V Logos, 1982.

130 K. Rajendran, "Five Inputs – A Training Proposal for OM India", a Paper to OM Leaders at Hyderabad, September 1992.

131 K. Rajendran, "Strategic Training", pp. 3–4.

132 At present the accreditation has been sorted out with IIM. B. Min degree and diplomas are offered depending upon the studies completed by the members. Accreditation has also brought in a better discipline and accountability from the missionaries. OM celebrated their first graduation ceremony on the 6th of December 1997.

133 Frank Allen, "Why do they leave? Reflection on Attrition."

EMQ, April (1986) 121.

134 Discussion with Houghton, SAIACS, Bangalore, 1996.

135 Vedanayagam Samuel Azariah, *India and Missions* (Madras: CLS, 1915), p. 18. Cited from JP Jones, *India's Problem: Krishna or Christ*, [n.p].

136 Sakhi M. Athyal, *Indian Women in Mission* (Bihar: Mission Educational Books, 1995), p. 108.

137 PT Abraham, "Pentecostal-Charismatic Missionary Outreach," in Sam Lazarus (Ed.), *Proclaiming Christ*, p. 104.

138 Pramila R., a former women's leader of OM India, personal interview, November 1997.

139 MH Wigan, "Educated Christian Women and Missionary Vocation," *NCCR*, October (1948) 408–413, cited CB John & Ellen Webster (Eds.), *The Church and the Women in the Third World* (Philadelphia: The Westminster Press, 1984), p. 38.

140 Annathai, a former missionary with FMPB and OM, personal interview, October 1995.

141 Eva Shipstone, the former Principal of IT College Lucknow, personal interview at Lucknow, 1989.

142 Athui, one of the OM women leaders. Personal Interview, Hyderabad, December 1994.

143 Abraham Pothen, "Indigenous Cross-Cultural Missions in India and their Contributions to Church Growth." Ph.D. Thesis, (Pasadena: Fuller Theological Seminary, 1990), p. 255.

144 PT Abraham, "Pentecostal-Charismatic Missionary

Outreach," p. 104.

145 Juliet Thomas, "Role of Women in Christian Ministry," in Sam Lazarus (Ed.), *Proclaiming Christ*, p. 112.

146 Hedlund, "Introduction," in Sam Lazarus (Ed.), *Proclaiming Christ*, p. xi.

147 Pramila, "The Urban Christian Wife:" p. 75.

148 Jacob Kavunkal and F. Hrangkhuma, *Bible and Mission in India Today* (Bombay: St. Pauls, 1993), p. 283.

149 Pramila, *The Urban Christian Wife*, p. 47.

150 Ramyata Limbu, "People of Indian Origin Abroad Meet in Nepal," *The Asian Age*, August 24, (1997) 4.

151 OM India News, *India Area Communique*, July 1997.

152 Ibid.

153 Sagayaraj, interview, Bangalore, October 25, 1997.

154 George Ninan and Ebenazer Sunder Raj, a paper presented at the FORUM, Nagpur, 28 April, 1997.

155 Correspondence with IMA and AD 2000, Oct–Dec. 1997.

156 CV Mathew, 'Who are the "Evangelicals",' in Sam Lazarus (Ed.), *Proclaiming Christ*, pp. 15–16.

157 Pradeep Das, "The Evangelical Movement in India," p. 20.

158 Patrick Joshua, discussion during the preliminary planning of the FORUM to be held at Nagpur, Chennai, December 19, 1996.

159 Name withheld, discussion on preliminary planning of the NCE to be held at Nagpur,

Chennai, December 19, 1996.

160 Paul, *The Cross Over India*, p. 110.

161 IMA Introduction Brochure. At present the leadership training is conducted by the training director of OM for IMA.

162 K. Rajendran, "Five Inputs," September 1992.

163 Hedlund, *Evangelisation and Church Growth*, p. 252.

164 Chacko Thomas, interview, London, July 1994.

165 Pradip Ayer, OM North India Director, Personal discussion, Hyderabad 1993.

166 In an interview of Mr Ebenezer Sunder Raj, the question was: "Why don't Indian churches give money for evangelisation of this nation?" This question was loaded with the assumption that the Indian churches were not giving enough to reach the nation. Knowing this assumption is not true, he declined to comment. The churches need education and have to be coached.

167 Phuvei Dozo, "Awakening Resulting in Church Growth in the Hills," *ICGQ*, April – June (1984) 23.

168 Roger E. Hedlund, "Christianity in India," *ICGQ*, April–June (1986) 154.

169 Ashish K. Massey, "Challenges to Mission in North India," in Lazarus (Ed.), *Proclaiming Christ*, p. 89.

170 Paul, *The Cross Over India*, p. 110.

171 Massey, "Mission in North India," p. 89.

172 Lawrence Keyes, "The New Age of Cooperation," cited in Theodore Williams (Ed.), *Together in Missions* (Bangalore: WEF, 1983), p. 74.

173 Rajendran letter to Partners India, September 1997.

174 Discussion with Shyam Winston, Chennai, August 1997.

175 Keyes, "The New Age of Cooperation," p. 75.

176 Massey, "Mission in North India," p. 89.

177 Gopal Hembrom, interview, Bangalore, August 24, 1997.

178 Mathew, "Evangelicals," p. 15.

179 *Business Today* August 22– September 6, 1997.

180 Vinay Kamat, "Family Business", *Business Today*, August 22 – September 6, (1997) 17.

181 B. Abraham, personal interview, Bangalore, July 1995.

182 IMA policy documents.

183 SWOT—analysing Strengths, Weaknesses, Opportunities and Threats, a method followed widely for strategic planning around the world. If this process is done with the participation of employees, it helps them corporately own the Mission rather than leaving it to the CEO.

184 II Timothy 2:2.

9

Recommendations

Our evaluation of the impact of foreign missionaries in India, both positive and negative, and our survey of the challenges India presents help us understand our past and face the future. The sacrifices made by the early missionaries call us now to faithfully continue to bring the Gospel in word and deed. The Indian Church is no longer an infant. We must encourage and support Indian missionary endeavours with prayer and finances, and send and support Indian missionaries to other parts of the world. Where Christians have been accused of being agents and collaborators of the "West", Christians should interact with and befriend the accusers. In every way we must demonstrate increasing maturity. We must take up the challenge of a comprehensive commitment to the cause of Christ.

Firstly we must have a clearer grasp of the goal that God has for India the way it is and despite the way it is. We need a renewed grip on the purpose of the message.

A Call for a Comprehensive Vision

By Management and Accountability

The goal of missions is to influence the nation for Christ. Each Mission must have clear vision, a purpose statement and strategic planning, preferably with the whole of India in view, so, like a jigsaw puzzle, each complements its neighbour. Such plans are better reworked every five years, preferably with an outside consultant for objectivity.

We are still confused on many terms and meanings for words like evangelism, mission, social work. We need consensus to avoid divisions and further confusion. Perhaps a core group could compile consensus meanings and definitions. This is urgent so that there is clear communication between missions.

Missions must measure and evaluate, using proper reports and records.

Standards in Christian work must exceed those of secular work. We cannot excuse sloppy work by blaming lack of personnel and funds. If excellence is not the goal, we should not start the assignment.

Missions will do well to come under credible associations to protect them from isolation and not being answerable.

Mission leaders should voluntarily become accountable. Where the top-brass feel accountable neither to their organisation nor to the local people where they only go for "ministry", this must change.

Mission leaders must not wilfully neglect their own pastoral care. Without it they may feel lonely "on the top",[1] or fall into a crisis of morals—whether in family, or financial matters. The CEO must deliberately submit to a non-formal accountable group to share, pray, learn and receive counsel.

If social work is an entry point to people groups, plan it with boundaries and time limits.

Recruit people for identifiable tasks so that the person with a burden can work in that aspect.

A Call for a Comprehensive Vision

By Strategising

To accomplish the goal of mission, we have to think and strategise clearly. We need to know our nation well. Statistics of the massive population growth and the extent of the Gospel will help us sharpen our thrust.

We are always touched by human misery and the distress of the poor, marginalised Dalits, tribals and others. We immediately reach out to them and meet their physical needs. However, as missionaries we must remember to leave much of the task to the Government or NGO agencies. Missionaries must be clear that their primary task is alleviating the spiritual agony of people who will otherwise not be with the Lord Jesus Christ after this life. Making disciples of Christ has to be the highest priority, greater than alleviating poverty and injustice. Every mission must recognise that the key to a lastingly better society is people alive in Christ. However, no missionary should ignore the immediate misery of poor people. When there are disasters we must help. Social work could serve the ultimate goal of leading people to Christ.

We have been inattentive to the middle class and the rich. Let us find new strategies to reach them. Let us recruit and train missionaries for this single purpose, and pay them enough to live in the cities!

For the educated class, we have not provided attractive and appropriate reading materials. We are looking for more Indian Christian journalists both in secular and Christian publishing, and funding for Christian publishing. We need to consciously prepare more Indian Christian journalists and writers. We need books and magazines produced to the standards of secular books, distributed through sound marketing. Good music and movies will aid the task.

Missions do fairly well in communicating to illiterates with the Jesus movies, Gospel Recordings and other audio-visual methods. Yet nearly fifty per cent of India's people are illiterate and need much more attention.

Missions and Christians need to grasp the three main approaches for mission work: by PIN Code areas, by people groups or by language groups.

We need special, contextual efforts to reach Hindus, Muslims and other minority religious groups. We suggest two initiatives that have not been tried enough:

- Dedicate and train missionaries to reach particular people groups, and, because Muslims are fourteen percent of Indian population and few people reach out to them, they must take priority.
- Churches should stay open every day of the week, with some offering relevant discourses at hourly intervals, morning and evening, with more on Sunday. (This will attract Hindus, since in temples and in places of *Gurus* this is regular, and Muslims keep mosques open all day with prayers and discourses five times a day.) In contrast, churches are rarely open. Perhaps the church building should be simple to fit this. The synagogue mindset should change.

Have we thought enough about reaching politicians and Christians getting involved in Indian politics?

We need a large amount of salt to influence the society. In India we [Christians] are only 2.3 per cent of the population... Yet we are responsible for twenty percent of all primary education. Ten percent of literacy and community health care, twenty-five percent orphans and widows are looked after by us, thirty percent of the handicapped and lepers are looked after by Christians. Christians run some of the oldest and best colleges and schools in the country. All that is good, but we need to enter the spheres that we have avoided so far. Can we find some committed Christians as lawyers and magistrates? Can we influence the world of politics, armed forces, prisons, police force, municipal services, media, press, education, business, legislation etc.[2]

We need to use both the HUP principle of "one people at a time" and the PIN code geographical location method. Some groups can best be reached along language lines, but this will not apply for large groups like Bhojpuri in UP and in Bihar and Maithili in Eastern Bihar and Bengal. However, they are further divided in castes.

We must resolve the question of individual or mass conversion by a middle course. Individual conversion is important but it is easier to lead individuals to Christ in a less hostile situation after the whole family or many of the clan embrace Christianity. This will aid integration of new converts into the Church, for it is easier for a church to accept a group rather than an individual convert who often may feel lost in the church till he or she matures in Christ – or falls by the wayside.

We must teach church members to receive and care for converts, reaching also to marriage settlements. The church must receive people who are not of the majority clan or culture of that church.

We recommend churches and missionaries disciple lay-people as soul-winners to multiply effectiveness, and develop a sense of ownership and active participation with both church and mission.

Local workers at the place of mission are a major resource. We must treat them equally with the missionary, even avoiding ordaining a missionary as pastor of the church, because that might hamper the growth, training and appointment of local leadership.

There is definitely room to encourage short-term missionaries, but it needs competent planning and capable leaders to train young short term missionaries on the field. The goal of a 1000 students every year could be encouraged.

Missionaries must distinguish culture from religion, and accept what they can of the first while excluding non-Christian elements of the second. The goal of such contextualisation is to encourage biblical lifestyles. It is never a question of being Western or Eastern.

South Indian and North East Indian missionaries should not dominate the local people, becoming "bosses" with a colonial mentality. Cross-cultural missionaries must adapt as much and as early as possible, not mixing only with their own diaspora people and holding services in their own original tongues.

Missions clearly need more women workers and leaders, for the sake of the women of our nation. We have done little for the women, fifty per cent of the population. The absence of programmes focused on them is appalling.

It is time for Indian missions to think wider about sending missionaries to other parts of the world, firstly to the diaspora Indians – USA, Trinidad, Canada, Surinam, UK, South Africa, Mauritius, Kenya, Fiji, Australia, Nepal, Malaysia, Singapore, Sri Lanka, Myanmar and the middle Eastern nations have a high number of Indians.[3] "Currently, over twenty million persons of Indian origin are dispersed throughout the world."[4]

Indian missionaries must also go, full-time or tent-making, to other peoples of the world starting with countries close by. Missions like CCC, SISWA, OM, IEHC, GFA, KEF, BCM, UESI, IEM are progressing in that direction. New missions with this vision, could partner with them to learn.

The second major thrust of this chapter is that we need to demonstrate the unity of the body of Christ in mission. We need to integrate the efforts of the messengers.

A Call for Comprehensive Co-operation

Between Missions and Churches

Missions and churches must educate church members. Perhaps prospective pastors should go for a year of mission before they are ordained.[5] Then churches themselves may grow by the E1 and E2 mission activities.

Churches should automatically encourage their young people in some kind of short-term mission exposure, and offer church members a reading programme of missionary biographies and mission histories.

Leaders should plan missionary speakers to interact with church members, encouraging every church to support missionaries with a defined percentage of church funds.

Churches could support missionaries of a variety of missions and learn about various visions and needs, tangibly involving church members in such decisions.

Frequent regional Church and Mission consultations could

encourage practical contributions for partnership between the Church and Missions,[6] mobilising lay men and women and young people in various activities. This could proliferate into great partnership if competition, jealousy, selfishness and mistrust are tempered.

The Portable School concept for laymen should be adapted for all congregations.

Missionaries and Christians should be aware of the many superstitions of India and together stand against them.

By working together we should show to the country that Christ can break the barriers between the people of different cultures and communities. Too many of us are yet too clannish in our thinking.

Christian missionaries must learn to live in the midst of the tensions in this country and not give up witnessing in difficult situations.

A Call for Comprehensive Co-operation

Between Missions

Grasping the complexity of the goal of reaching all peoples, we need to recognise the complementary contribution made by the different activities of missions. We should foster a spirit of unity not of pulling one another down. As the number of missions and missionaries increased, it necessitated setting up associations and networks. This was and is to better organise efforts in reaching the whole nation with the Gospel. As missions associations and networks came into being, supporting agencies also developed for various needs. Each mission should come under one of the credible missions associations. This will enhance co-operation, effectiveness of each mission and the credibility of the corporate voice.

We must respect other missions and not interfere in each other's work areas, especially in the pretext of "the Lord's leading". Instead we can bless those who reap well and work with them or encourage them alongside us. The harvest field is large enough for all of us and much waits to be done in most parts of India.

Mission leaders must solve their differences with humility and empathy, believing the best of others. It can be done. Missions must work within agreed comity policies. Yes, there have been difficulties, but thankfully they have been ironed out.

Some missions plan in solidarity, notably GRCP, CONS,

IMAAN, IICCC, NIHNW. Others could learn from them. They must tap ideas and resources from organisations like Interdev, DAI and individuals like Gene Davis. They could work through existing credible bodies like IMA, EFI and others.

Missions would be wise to agree on similar standards in salaries, training, pensions, housing schemes and health insurance. Then people could join a mission or move from one to another according to their vision and calling, instead of on the basis of the remuneration and benefits. This would help prevent personnel switching from mission to mission. It would develop stability, experience and future leadership.

Leaders and members of diverse missions could build trust between each other by meeting and talking. This is effective especially when small informal groups of up to ten CEOs from different missions meet. The atmosphere must be one of commit- ment, communication, confidentiality and trust. The group should be composed of people from different cultures, languages and missions, yet equally committed to the discipline of meeting regularly, perhaps monthly, to share, pray, evaluate and build each other up. There are some examples of these friendship groups. Greater trust is slowly beginning to be built and this will foster real partnership in the future.

A Call for Comprehensive Co-operation

Between Indian and Global Missions/Partners

Since the Great Commission is for all, we have no interest in a moratorium on foreign partners. Indeed we can welcome interna- tional partners to assist existing missions on mutually agreed terms, which may be limited by any or all of geography, time, finance, or personnel.

Thank God for the indigenous funds, prayer, power and personnel for missions in India. Let us aim to raise adequate salaries of missionaries here. However international partners could 'come alongside' with some projects and capital expenses without attaching too many strings.

Missions must repeat vision statements, print them in all publications, gather workers periodically and inform them where the mission is heading.

With IMA leading the PIN Code research, NIHNW, GRCP, GFA, GEMS and a few other supporters are trying to get missions to concentrate on placing missionaries in each PIN Code area. In each PIN Code the missionaries could have the freedom to adopt to any of the above approaches of HUP or language or HUP division in a PIN Code where the missionary is working.

Substantial finance and some projects are funded from the country. This is especially true of missionary salaries, though they are not yet adequate. Nevertheless the proportion of funds generated from within India needs to rise. NRI Indians contribute already, but could contribute more.

The third major thrust of this chapter is that we must have a holistic concern for the care and development of the messengers. If we do not, missions will die.

A Call for Comprehensive Care

Missionary Welfare

Few missionaries as yet are provided with medical insurance, pension and housing. Few are assured of provision if there were to be major medical expenses. These issues must be confronted and solved.

Missionaries and their children struggle for lack of funds for good schools and colleges. This is short-sighted. We must provide for children's education or people will leave the mission.

Missionaries need pastoral care to face personal pressure, but this is often missing. We need more teams responsible for pastoral care. We need more training in counselling and human resource development.

We question the need for the wide disparity between leaders and grass root workers, and fear it could increase attrition among Indian missionaries. Discomfort is already apparent and may be lowering recruitment.

Training institutions should consciously train people to shed their own culture while in the host culture. This includes at least speaking the local language, eating local food and using local transport.

It would be healthy if missionaries came from the many different cultures of India. Then they could not impose their own culture on the converts. This would become a testimony to co-operation.

We must balance time spent in prayer, strategy and work. Action without enough prayer loses motivation and focus, and may lead to spiritual dryness and inter-personal conflicts. Action without strategy may be wasted effort. Conversely, too much time on prayer could be an excuse for laziness.

A fully paid missionary will be better than a partly paid or independent missionary. Being full-time with a mission organisation will help them to develop their skill, act accountably and accept leadership.

Tentmakers also should ascertain whether they will have time and freedom to do evangelism. If not, the energy will be wasted.

A Call for Comprehensive Care

Continuous Education for Missionaries

To properly train missionary candidates, most Bible seminaries need enhanced mission education. The Indian Institute of Missiology (IIM), working on this, needs much input in structure, facilities and in content. Most colleges evaluate and accredit students for their academic work, but they also need to evaluate practical training in mission work, character development and spiritual life.

Missions need to plan on continuous education for missionaries while they are on the field. These studies should preferably be accredited to increase commitment and accountability from the missionary, and should come with practical field guidance and testing, be written by former missionaries and include a workbook and discussions. This will also enhance inter-personal relationships among the missionaries.

Once in six months missionaries of a region should meet for a week of feedback, encouragement and motivation. The expense will be well worth it if the retreat is well organised. The missionary must not feel spiritually starved.

Missions should send missionaries for appropriate short-term courses to strengthen their spiritual gifts and widen their exposure. Courses are available.

Some missionaries, especially those with leadership potential, will profit from extended study in a training college like SAIACS, UBS, YCLT and others. Some may need a break from mundane routine for their own and the organisational well being.

CEOs need a broad outlook. In addition to magazines and reports, they need input in strategic planning, in writing for journals and in higher level of management and pastoral care. Highly focused three-day courses with top class practical leaders, not just a college professor from a developed country, should fit their needs. Some missions already have this provision, but many others lack it when intensive training for the CEOs is crucial.

A Call for Comprehensive Care

Development of Future Leadership

Missions have a duty to develop the people they direct. Missions should not wait till they have a need, but develop future leaders now. This takes time, and unselfishness.

After a careful selection, senior leaders should let new leaders work in apprenticeship for a while and then step aside. Interference from an ex-leader is detrimental to the ministry. The former leader should physically move elsewhere, remaining available on call for reference.

In Christian work in India selecting new leaders just from the same clan has to go. This means local leaders for a local ministry, and for a broader ministry there has to be leaders included from other parts of India also.

Conclusion

These recommendations need to be carefully considered. Indian missions will continue to grow, but so will the general population. The challenges are great but so are the opportunities. Change is certain however success is not. Carefully managed change is essential for effectiveness in sharing Christ.

The depth of the challenges, the variety of the dilemmas, the size of the workforce, and the urgency of the gospel message all call for a comprehensive commitment to fulfil Christ's Great Commission. We need a comprehensive vision of the goal of the message, comprehensive integration of the efforts of the messengers and comprehensive care for the messengers themselves.

Let us work for this clarity of vision, co-operative effort and care for missionaries to strengthen Indian missions. Then we may, with the Lord's help, see the day of a living and vibrant church among all the people groups and classes of India.

END NOTES

1 D'Souza, "Leadership—Lonely at the Top." *OM Today*, Issue 22, October–December (1997) 1.

2 Stanley Mehta, "Christian Influence on Society", *Light of Light*, February (1997) 11–13.

3 Johnstone, *Operation World, (1993)*, pp. 278–279.

4 [n.a.] *30 days Hindu Prayer Focus*

(Surrey, UK: South Asian Concern, 1997), p. 38.

5 Suggestion from church leaders in Church-mission Consultation, ECC, Whitefield, January 20–22, 1998.

6 Church & Mission, ECC, Whitefield, Jan. 20–22, 1998.

APPENDIX ONE

OM's BOOK OF STANDARD DEFINITIONS[1]

INTRODUCTION

We in OM have made a commitment to establish a "people and people group missions strategy. We will also be making a concerted effort to measure the results of our overall world-wide efforts.

While developing our strategy plan "Forward to 2001", it became clear that while we use common terms to describe what we do, we often mean different things. If we fail to take this weakness seriously we believe it will prevent us from measuring our overall effectiveness with any reasonable level of accuracy and consistency. We also believe this will hinder our ability to establish realistic strategies and ministry goals.

To begin to address this problem we have agreed to adopt standard definitions for several key terms. These terms either appear in our purpose statement or we believe they directly relate to the types of results we want to accomplish. We will use the *brief definitions* contained in this booklet when describing our key ministry activities and when measuring our overall effectiveness.

PURPOSE STATEMENT

OM's role in the body of Christ is to *motivate, develop* and *equip* people for world *evangelisation* and to *strengthen* and *help plant churches*, especially among the *unreached* in the Middle East, South and Central Asia, and Europe.

GLOSSARY OF STANDARD DEFINITIONS
INDEX

1	Church;	11	Mission;
2	Church Planting;	12	mission;
3	Contextualization;	13	Mobilize;
4	Conversion;	14	Motivate;
5	Develop;	15	People;
6	Equip;	16	People Group;
7	Evangelisation;	17	Plant;
8	Evangelism;	18	Reached/Unreached ;
9	Globalization;	19	Strengthen;
10	Help;	20	Tent-making.

1. CHURCH

Brief definition:

A local church is a body of Christian believers who are committed to meet corporately under established leadership for worship, to witness, and to live in accordance with the Word of God.

Amplification:

A normally-functioning church; - gathers together regularly - adheres to the historical biblical faith; - teaches and proclaims the Scriptures; - practices baptism and participation in the Lord's Supper; - gives a contextually appropriate, visible demonstration of spiritual life; - is locally led; - seeks growth, and

- is financially self supporting and caring for its own community. OM planted churches should be missions-minded.

Source of brief definition:

Modification of definition found in *Planting Churches Cross-Culturally,* by David K Hesselgrave, 1980

2. CHURCH–PLANTING

Brief definition:

The whole process of evangelising, discipling, training, and organizing a group of believers to a level of development permitting it to function as a viable church independent of the (human) agent(s) who brought it into being.

Amplification:

"Church-Planting" is not a term used as such in the New Testament. It may have been derived from Paul's comments in 1 Cor. 3:6 concerning his role in planting the seed and the role of Apollos in watering the seed. However, the term, like many other theological terms not explicitly found in the New Testament, is apt in describing an essential part of the missionary task.

Source of brief definition:

Planting Churches in Muslims Cities: A Team Approach, by Greg Livingstone, 1993

3. CONTEXTUALIZATION

Brief definitions:

The effort to understand and take seriously the specific context of each human group and person on its own terms and in all its dimensions - cultural, religious, social political, economic - and to discern what the gospel says to people in that context. (Taber)

It is "the attempt to communicate the message of person, works, Word, and will of God in a way that is faithful to God's revelation, especially as it is put forth in the teachings of Holy Scripture, and that is meaningful to respondents in their respective cultural and existential contexts." (Hesselgrave and Rommen)

Amplification:

Proper contextualization means that "old beliefs and customs are neither rejected nor accepted without examination. They are first studied with regard to the meanings and places they have within their cultural setting and then evaluated in the light of biblical norms." (*Anthropological Insights For Missionaries,* by Paul Hiebert, 1985)

This takes place by the process of

1. gathering information about the old, 2. studying biblical teachings about the event, 3. evaluating the old in the light of biblical teachings, and 4. creating a new contextualized Christian practice. (Hiebert)

The process of contextualization must involve people of the culture for which contextualization is being done. But, as reflection on the Scriptures is carried out, insights and correctives are needed from the wider Christian community, including those of earlier years.

Source of brief definition:

Contextualization: Indigenization and/or Transformation, by Charles R. Taber, in *The Gospel And Islam: A compendium* abridged edition, 1979, edited Don M. McCurry, and *Contextualization: Meanings, Methods, And Models* by David Hesselgrave and Edward Rommen, 1989.

4. CONVERSION

Brief definition:

The entry into the Christian life. It is an act of God, brought about by the Holy Spirit. It is also a human action, enabled by God, described in the Bible under such terms as turning to the Lord, repenting, confessing, and believing.

Amplification:

As with many missiological terms, "conversion" should be used with caution in certain contexts. In India it has been reported that the terms "conversion" and "a convert" create more derision than reverence among non-Christians. Spiritual conversion is not understood by most people, taking instead a social meaning. "Converts" are no longer considered to be 100% Indian.

Source of brief definition:
Introduction to Missiology, by Alan R. Tippet, 1987.

5. DEVELOP

Brief definition:
To bring about growth in the individual through character formation and spiritual maturation.

Source of brief definition:
Modification of definition found in *Missionary Care: Counting The Cost For World Evangelization,* edited by Kelly O'Donnell, 1992.

6. EQUIP

Brief definition:
To fit an individual for ministry through recognition and development of gifts, and skill acquisition.

Amplification:
The Greek word *katartizo* of Ephesians 4:11 is translated as "to make someone completely adequate or sufficient for something, ... to cause to be fully qualified." (From *Greek-English Lexicon Of The New Testament Based On Semantic Domains,* by Johannes P. Louw and Eugine A. Nida, edited 1988, New York, United Bible Societies)

Source of brief definition:
Agreed by OM Area Leaders

7. EVANGELISATION

Brief definition:
The total process of announcing the gospel and bringing people into discipleship, and of spreading the good news about Jesus Christ as God's salvation so that men and women have a valid opportunity to accept him as Lord and Saviour and become responsible members of his church.

Amplification:
See under Evangelism

Source of brief definition:
Planning Strategies For World Evangelization, revised edition, by Edward R. Dayton and David A. Fraser, 1990.

8. EVANGELISM

Brief definition:
The 1974 Lausanne Congress on World Evangelism declared that evangelism is "the proclamation of the historical, biblical

Christ as Saviour and Lord, with a view to persuading people to come to him personally and so be reconciled to God."

Amplification:

The complete reading of the definition is:

To evangelise is to spread the good news that Jesus Christ died for our sins and was raised from the dead according to the Scriptures and that as the reigning Lord he now offers the forgiveness of sins and the liberating gift of the Spirit to all who repent and believe.

Our Christian presence in the world is indispensable to evangelism and so is that kind of dialogue whose purpose is to listen sensitively in order to understand. But evangelism itself is the proclamation of the historical, biblical Christ as Saviour and Lord, with a view to persuading people to come to him personally and so be reconciled to God.

In issuing the Gospel invitation we have no liberty to conceal the cost of discipleship. Jesus still calls all who would follow him to deny themselves, take up their cross, and identify themselves with his new community. The results of evangelism include obedience to Christ, incorporation into his church, and responsible service to the world.

Source of brief definition:

Let The Earth Hear His Voice, by J.D. Douglas, edited 1975.

9. GLOBALIZATION

Brief definition:

The process by which organisations move beyond operating on the field from a single or dominant base to operating trans-nationally, not tied to any particular country.

Globalization in missions involves not only carrying out ministry across cultures, but also accomplishing the resourcing, governing, planning, and organising of missions by involving the church in diverse regions of the globe.

Source of brief definition:

Modification of definition found in *Globalization As A Model For Contemporary Missions: A Case Study Of Operation Mobilization*, by David Hicks, 1992.

10. HELP

Brief definition:

To add one's own action or effect to that of others so as to make them more effectual.

Amplification:

In phrases such as "help plant churches" this definition does not imply that OMers only serve a secondary role to that of others who have already begun the work of church planting. To help plant churches in a given country may mean joining with those already engaged in efforts to plant a church, or it may mean commencing an effort toward the establishment of a distinct church. Both roles are within the scope of existing OM policy. (See OM Policy Manual, 3.3.24)

Source of brief definition:
Oxford English Dictionary, 1989.

11. MISSION

Brief definition:

A 'Mission' is a particular organised body with the specific objective of reaching people with the Gospel of Christ. In the plural, 'Missions', represents a number of such groups.

Amplification:

Generally in this book, the word 'mission' has been uncapitalised unless there is possible confusion with the task of 'mission' (see clause 12), in which case, where the word is used in the sense of organised body, the word is capitalised—'Mission'.

12. Mission

Brief definition:

Christian 'mission' describes all that God has called the church to do in the world to help people to become followers of Christ. This includes preaching the Gospel, living in the community as witnesses and being involved in the social work of helping people according to their needs.

Amplification:

Mission is not just lecturing/preaching the Gospel. Mission is not just meeting the social needs of people. Mission is not just converting people of other religions to Christianity. Mission is not just doing social upliftment and bringing justice.

Refer to clause 11 for note on capitalisation in this book.

13. MOBILIZE

Brief definition:

The process of convincingly, in concert with the Holy Spirit, informing Christians of needs of service and motivating them to action.

Source of brief definition:
Agreed by OM Area Leaders

14. MOTIVATE

Brief definition:
To stir / inspire / convince a person to personal involvement.
Source of brief definition:
Agreed by OM Area Leaders

15. PEOPLE

Brief definition:
A missiological term used to describe the broadest possible group that would be distinguished by ethnicity, linguistics, geo-politics, ideology, and geography. When one or more of these factors significantly distinguishes one group of humans from another it is called a 'people.'
Amplification:
Ron Rowland further elaborates on the above factors, explaining the elements making up each factor as follows:
Ethnicity: People clusters, clans, kinship groups, family
Linguistics: Language family, language clusters, languages, dialects
Geopolitics: Region, nation, province, district
Ideology: Religion, politics
Geography: Rivers, mountains, deserts, jungles
Source of brief definition:
Presentation by Ron Rowland at Adopt-A-People Consultation II, Colorado Springs, Colo., April 1993.

16. PEOPLE GROUP

Brief definition:
A significantly large grouping of individuals who perceive themselves to have a common affinity for one another, because of their shared language, religion, ethnicity, residence, occupation, class or caste, situation or combinations of these.
Amplification:
Since the 1982 meeting sponsored by the Lausanne Committee for World Evangelisation at which this definition was established, it has become the standard in missiological literature.
In *Operation World* (1993) Patrick Johnstone identifies three types of people groups.

♦ Ethno linguistic people groups, of which there are some 12,000, are defined by language or ethnicity and are alternately referred to by Johnstone as "people".

♦ Sociological people groups do not have a self-contained culture or ethnic identity but are defined by a long-term relation to the rest of society such as class.

♦ Incidental people groups are casual associations "which may be temporary and usually the result of circumstances" such as drug addicts and occupational groupings.

Source of brief definition:

Planning Strategies For World Evangelization, revised edition, by Edward R. Dayton and David A. Fraser, 1990.

17. PLANT

Brief definition:

A figurative term describing the process of establishing a new church.

Amplification:

This term is traced to Paul's comments in 1 Corinthians 3:6 regarding the role he and Apollos played. See also "church-planting".

Source of brief definition:

Agreed by OM Area Leaders

18. REACHED / UNREACHED

Brief definition:

These are comparative terms useful in describing the extent of exposure and affirmative response of a population to the gospel. The common use of these terms is to define a people as "reached" when there is a cluster of indigenous churches among that people with sufficient resources to carry out the remaining tasks of evangelisation and discipleship among that people without outside missionary assistance.

Amplification:

Important response and exposure factors to be considered in evaluating "reachedness" of a segment of population include, but are not limited to; 1. the size of the Christian community, 2. the number of churches formed, 3. the development of indigenous church leadership, 4. the extent of missionary involvement, and 5. the availability of evangelistic resources in appropriate languages, including the scriptures, other media, and broadcasting.

A strategy decision based on "reachedness" would take these

factors into consideration.

No single variable gives a sufficient description of the spiritual state and need of a selected population segment. In determining the "reachedness" of some population it is suggested that both exposure and response be considered.

Further, in speaking of " reachedness" one must be precise in defining population segments. In Chad, for example, 13.3% of the total population of the country are reported to be evangelicals, yet there are more unreached peoples in Chad than in any other African nation. (Johnson 1993, 157/158). Comparing with other populations, and in attempting to make a more absolute statement on "reachedness", one must carefully define the population, geographic region, country, city, people, or people group concerned.

Caution must be used in employing in an absolute way rather than a comparative way the terms "reached" and "unreached".

Even if a comparative high percentage of individuals are Christians in the population in question, of those who are still in need of salvation and should not be considered as being of less eternal value than individual members of a remote tribe never penetrated by Christian witness.

On the other hand, in declaring that a population is "unreached" one must, while recognising the biblical mandate to humans to carry out the evangelisation of the world, also consider the sovereign initiatives of God, including His work through humans unknown to those attempting to evaluate a peoples' "reachedness".

In the literature one occasionally finds "reachedness" defined in terms of the evangelical percentage of the population. This has the advantage of simplicity and measurability. However, such a definition can be perceived as reductionist in its simplicity, failing to take into account the complexities within and in making comparisons between contexts. Further it would be very difficult to reach consensus (other than by decree) on what percentage should be established as the benchmark.

Source of brief definition:
Agreed by OM Area Leaders.

19. STRENGTHEN:

Brief definition:
In the context of "strengthen churches", to provide encourage-ment and to assist in the spiritual and character growth of the

congregation in evangelism and world mission.

Amplification:

The following are various related definitions found in the
Oxford English Dictionary (1989):

a. To give moral support, encouragement, or confidence (to a
person); to encourage and hearten in spirit, fix in resolution

b. to give defensive strength; to make strong against attack, to
fortify...

c. to make more effective or powerful by reinforcement of numbers
of resources.

Source of brief definition:

Agreed by OM Area Leaders.

20. TENT MAKER

Brief Definition:

A Christian who works in a cross-cultural situation, is recognised by members of the host culture as something other than a
"religious professional", and yet, in terms of his or her commitment, calling motivation, and training is a missionary in every
way.

Source of brief definition:

*Working Your Way To The Nations: A Guide To Effective Tent
Making*, by Jonathan Lewis, edited, 1993. This booklet is produced
by: Operation Mobilisation International, PO Box 27, Carlisle,
Cumbria, CA1 2HG England. (June 1994).

END NOTES

1 Modified by the addition of
    definitions for the words
    'Mission' and 'mission'.

APPENDIX TWO

Shalom Advisory on Finance for Evangelists

SAFE is a business entity with the specific vision of providing welfare schemes to Christian ministries and ministers to meet their special financial needs through small savings. It also assists in making secure and profitable investment of funds available with the minister and the ministries for various purposes and needs.

Principles

* *SAFE* is a business entity, using professional skills to assist Christian Ministry and ministers.
* Service exclusively to Christian Ministries and their staff.
* Consultancy is offered only on invitation. No soliciting of business. In recommendations, benefits to clients will be the objective rather than income generation to *SAFE*.
* Service will be of professional quality.
* Service will conform to high ethical standards, both secular and spiritual.
* Service will be rendered with a ministerial attitude and not as business.
* All information that comes into the hands of *SAFE* in the course of its business will be kept in strict confidentiality.
* *SAFE* provides personal services and is not aimed at institutionalising their professions.
* *SAFE* aims to be a model to many Christian professionals to consider similar services to the Lord.
* *SAFE* caters to Christian Ministries and Ministers financial needs in following areas.

Event	Scheme
Death	Life Insurance Schemes
Retirement	Pension Schemes
Sickness	Medical Insurance Schemes
Children education and marriage	Investment Schemes
Other special needs	Investment Schemes

While *SAFE* will be glad to provide services to enrol you in these schemes, *you are welcome to choose other agencies.* Our desire is that Christian ministers are secured financially to help in their times of need.

- *SAFE* has provided services so far and continues to do so to the following Christian Institutions: Union of Evangelical Students of India, India Missions Association, Indian Evangelical Mission, Missionaries Upholders Trust, Church Growth Association of India and InterMission.
- Proposals have been made to provide Health and Life Insurance to the 15,000 staff of member missions of IMA and 1000 staff and project staff of World Vision.
- Many schemes in Insurance and investments are being designed by *SAFE* for many other organisations.
- Apart from the above many Christian ministers individually have joined in Insurance and Investment schemes through *SAFE.*

APPENDIX THREE

India's 87 Scheduled Tribes that are less than 1% Christian.

Source: Frontier Mission Update, David Bogosian, 1997

"Let my heart be broken with the things that break the heart of
   God" Dr. Bob Pierce

There are 82 million members of Scheduled Tribes in India today,
   representing the highest population of tribal people in the
   world. We can rejoice that over 8% have come to know Christ
   and represent 35% of India's Christians. 40 Scheduled Tribes
   have experienced "people movements" in past years, in which
   large numbers of extended families have made group decisions
   to follow Christ. Today, 12 tribes are experiencing people
   movements and 34 are on the way. Praise God! Even so a great
   deal of work remains to be done. Of the 232 Scheduled Tribes
   over 10,000 in population, 87 are still less than 1% Christian.
In many states witness to these tribes is very difficult. Militant
   Hindu political groups have often used economic pressure and
   police threats to prevent the gospel from spreading among
   responsive tribes. Many villages have been forced to give up
   any open sign of following Christ. Please pray for the protection of God's pioneers among the tribal groups in India and
   that one day people movements would bring every tribe into
   the Kingdom. Listed below are India's 87 Scheduled Tribes
   that are less than 1% Christian.

Tribe	Language	Population
Kori	Hindi	3,500,000
Bhil	Mina, Wagri	2,910,000
Naikda	Naikadi	2,180,000
Bhuiya	Magahi	1,595,000
Tipera	Kakbarak	990,000
Rabari	Gujarati	920,000
Kawar	Chhattisgarhi	800,000
Varli		778,000
Bhilala	Bhil	760,000

Tribe	Language	Population
Bhumij		730,000
Dubla	Gujarati	680,000
Halba	Marathi	658,000
Dhodia	Gujarati	653,000
Koya		653,000
Kol	Hindi	453,000
Thakur	Marathi	444,000
Yenadi		440,000
Saharia	Hindi	416,000
Paroja	Parji	393,000
Dhanka	Dhanki	350,000
Charan	Hindi	340,000
Bhottada.	Basturia	340,000
Andh	Marathi	327,000
Kadu Kuruba	Kannada	288,000
Malayali	Tamil	287,000
Biar	Chhatisgarhi	257,000
Korku		251,000
Koli Dhor	Marathi	248,000
Kathodi	Marathi	248,000
Koli Malhar	Marathi	244,000
Konda Dhora	Konda	215,000
Bathudi	Oriya	205,000
Kolam	Kolami	192,000
Pardhan	Gondi	182,000
Irular	Tamil	171,000
Garasia		163,000
Pardhi	Gujarati	159,000
Dhanwar	Chhattisgarhi	144,000
Jatapur	Kuvi	144,000
Mahli	Sadri	141,000
Binjihal	Sambalpuri	135,000
Binjhwar	Chhattisgarhi	135,000
Tharu		131,000
Bedia	Panchpargania	127,000
Bagata	Telugu	124,000
Marati	Marathi	121,000
Konda Reddi	Telugu	120,000
Gaddi	Gadiali	105,000
Saur	Hindi	93,000
Sounti	Oriya	93,000
Mahali	Sadri	85,000
Kaniyar	Kannada	76,000

Tribe	Language	Population
Chik Baraik	Nagpuria	72,000
Sonr	Bundhelkhandi	66,000
Kanaura	Kinnauri	65,000
Kuruman	Kannada	63,000
Bhaina	Chhattisgarhi	55,000
Karmali	Khotta	55,000
Kammara	Telugu	52,000
Laccadive	Arabic	50,000
Kattunayakan	Kannada	49,000
Jenu Kuruba	Jenu Kuruba	47,000
Buksa	Hindi	43,000
Mali	Oriya	42,000
Konda Kapu	Telugu	40,000
Malai Arayan	Malayalam	34,000
Bhot	Ladakhi	31,000
Nagesia	Nimari	31,000
Yerava		26,000
Manna Dhora	Telugu	26,000
Meda	Kodagu	26,000
Dal Kui		25,000
Kudiya		23,000
Khairwar	Chhattisgarhi	23,000
Koraga		23,000
Soligaru	Soliga	23,000
Kadar		17,000
Pangwala	Pangwali	15,000
Mawasi	Hindi	15,000
Hasalaru	Kannada	15,000
Padhar	Gujarati	15,000
Badra	Marathi	14,000
Keer	Mandiali	14,000
Adiyan	Kannada	13,000
Holva	Halbi	12,000
Swangla	Manchat	10,000
Malaikudi	Tulu	10,000

APPENDIX FOUR

THE TOTALLY UNREACHED PEOPLES OF INDIA

The India Missions Association in a letter to all member missions dated 14 November 1997 announced measures aimed at encouraging efforts to reach the totally unreached of India including financial assistance to member missions provided these were used to reach the totally unreached.

The relevant portion of the letter is as follows:

A)THE 85 TOTALLY UNREACHED LANGUAGES: If any of you begin working with a totally unreached language and begin a Socio-Linguistic survey or Bible translation, IMA will be able to assist with Rs. 1000–3000 per month for a single person and more for a couple. To know what the TOTALLY UNREACHED languages are, read the book *Languages of India* published by IMA or visit the IMA Bulletin Board Website at http://www.inmissions.org (or) http://www.ad2000.org/ima. Also see the list of languages identified by the Socio-linguistic Survey Team of IICCC. IMA (IICCC) will take the responsibility to provide full information, give all necessary training and technically guide the work done by your translator.

B) THE 21,000 TOTALLY UNREACHED PIN CODE AREAS: Read the IMA books on PIN code areas or visit IMA Website or access IMA- BBS. If you send your missionary/evangelist to a TOTALLY UNREACHED PIN code area, IMA may be able to assist with Rs. 1000 per month (funds permitting). IMA will give information and guidance as to where to go.

C)THE 204 TOTALLY UNREACHED PEOPLE GROUPS with a population of greater than 50,000: Read the IMA book *Peoples of India* (or visit IMA Website or access IMA- BBS) to know which are the totally unreached People groups of India. If you send your missionaries/evangelists to work exclusively among one of these TOTALLY UNREACHED people groups, IMA will be able to assist with Rs. 1000–3000 per month for a single person and more for a couple.

For further information, contact IMA, Post Box 2529, 48, First Main Road, East Shenoy Nagar, Chennai 600 030; Telephone: 044 644 4602; 644 4603; Facsimile: 044 644 2859; E-mail: ima@pobox.com

The following table lists all the TOTALLY UNREACHED PEOPLE GROUPS in India with a population of greater than 50,000.

THE TOTALLY UNREACHED PEOPLE GROUPS
NUMBERING MORE THAN 50,000

Peoples of India, India Missions Association, November 1997
Used by permission

No	People Name	Religion	Status	Pop. 2001	Location of the People
1	Garia	M	BC	13,183,353	AS
2	Koiri	H	BC	10,660,050	AS, BH, MH, TR, UP, WB
3	Chotra Bansi	H	BC	6,432,871	AP, HP, HR, MP, OR, PN, RJ, TR
4	Khandelwal	H	BC	5,453,981	BH, DL, MH, MP, RJ, UP
5	Bhenrihar	H	BC	4,027,392	BH, DL, GJ, HP, HR, PN, RJ, TR, UP, WB
6	Kachhi	H	BC	3,890,165	DL, GJ, MH, MP, RJ, UP
7	Faqir	M, S	BC	3,529,263	AP, BH, CH, DL, GJ, HP, HR, JK, KR, MH, MP, OR, PN, RJ, TN, UP, WB
8	Bahna	A, M	SC	3,500,921	AS, BH, CH, DL, GJ, HP, JK, KR, MG, MH, MP, MZ, OR, PN, RJ, UP, WB
9	Sadgop	H	BC	3,253,428	BH, WB
10	Pod	A	SC	2,809,318	WB
11	Lewa	H	BC	2,749,860	GJ, MH
12	Kaikolar	H	BC	2,513,052	AP, KL, KR, PD, TN
13	Sutar	H	BC	2,346,506	GJ, MH, RJ
14	Koshti	H	BC	2,000,624	AP, BH, GJ, KR, MH, MP, OR, RJ, UP
15	Jhiwar	H, S, M	BC	1,819,363	AN, CH, DL, HP, HR, JK, PN, RJ, TN, UP
16	Bharbhunja	H, M	BC	1,803,961	AP, BH, CH, DL, GJ, HP, HR, JK, MH, MP, OR, PN, RJ, UP, WB
17	Kanet	H, B	BC	1,727,079	HP, HR, PN
18	Khati	H, M, C	BC	1,726,453	AP, CH, GJ, HR, KL, KR, MH, MP, OR, RJ
19	Kunjra	M	BC	1,492,944	BH, MP, OR, RJ, UP, WB
20	Qassab	M	BC	1,403,422	AP, BH, CH, DL, GJ, HP, HR, KR, MH, MP, PD, PN, RJ, TN, UP, WB
21	Kadwa Patidar	H	BC	1,317,585	GJ
22	Bohra	M	BC	1,215,097	AP, DD, GJ, HP, KL, KR, MH, MP, OR, RJ, TN, WB
23	Moghal	M	BC	1,208,216	AN, AP, AS, BH, DL, GJ, JK, KL, KR, MG, MH, MN, MP, OR, RJ, UP, WB
24	Thakarda	H	BC	1,143,971	GJ
25	Qazi	M	BC	1,134,783	AS, BH, GJ, MP, RJ, WB
26	Daroga	H	BC	1,127,319	MP, PN, RJ
27	Mawalud	M	BC	1,050,669	AP, KR, MH
28	Taga	H, M	BC	1,018,778	CH, DL, HR, PN, UP
29	Tipera	A	ST	988,998	AS, MG, MN, MZ, TR, WB

No	People Name	Religion	Status	Pop. 2001	Location of the People
30	Chhimba	M, H, S	BC	947,563	CH, DL, HP, HR, JK, PN, UP
31	Bant	H	BC	896,149	GJ, KL, KR, MH, RJ
32	Ramdasia	S, H	BC	889,012	HP, HR, PN
33	Gangauta	H	BC	880,740	BH, WB
34	andhabanik	H	BC	880,497	WB
35	Owari	H	BC	872,589	MH, MP
36	Kirar	H	BC	849,334	MH, MP, RJ, UP
37	Agri	H	BC	838,429	DN, GJ, MH, UP
38	Manihar	M, H	BC	826,848	BH, DL, GJ, MH, MP, RJ, UP, WB
39	Mangala	H	FC	822,698	AP, DD, GJ, MH, OR, PD, TN
40	Arakh	H	BC	787,274	MH, MP, UP
41	Sainthwar	H	BC	780,304	MH, MP, UP
42	Chain	H	BC	764,435	BH, WB
43	Ghirath	H	BC	746,405	CH, HP, HR, JK, PN
44	Bishnoi	H	BC	738,749	HR, MP, PN, RJ, UP
45	Sadh	H	BC	734,455	GJ, JK, MH, MP, OR, PN, RJ, UP
46	Raju	H	BC	708,494	AP, BH, OR, TN, TR, WB
47	Lohana	H	BC	702,730	AP, DL, GJ, MH
48	Kunchatiga	H	BC	700,497	KR
49	Ramoshi	H	BC	689,819	GJ, KR, MH, MP
50	Kasar	H	BC	677,809	AP, BH, DD, DL, GJ, GO, KR, MH, MP, OR, WB
51	Karan	H	BC	653,454	BH, MP, OR, WB
52	Aguri	H	BC	625,731	AP, BH, MH, OR, WB
53	Mairal	H	BC	600,026	MH, WB
54	Bhisti	M	BC	585,726	AN, AS, BH, DL, GJ, HP, MH, MP, RJ, UP
55	Chunari	H, M	BC	578,311	AS, GJ, MN, NG, UP, WB
56	Awan	M	BC	558,738	HP, HR, PN
57	Memon	M	BC	514,131	GJ, KL, KR, MH
58	Turk	M	BC	489,619	GJ, JK, RJ, UP
59	Satani	H	BC	471,667	AP, KR, MH, MP, OR, PD, TN
60	Chaturtha	H	BC	467,281	MH
61	Bunt	H	BC	466,813	KL, KR, MH
62	Makhmi	M	BC	465,219	JK
63	Dhimal	H	BC	441,430	WB
64	Chasot	H	BC	426,514	WB
65	Kadia	H	BC	425,817	GJ, KR, MH, MP
66	Sudhan	M	BC	412,573	JK
67	Rangrez	H, M	BC	409,901	AP, BH, DL, GJ, JK, KR, MH, MP, OR, RJ, UP, WB
68	Sirvi	H	BC	409,570	MP, RJ
69	Ravalia	H	BC	407,529	GJ, KR, MH, UP
70	Mal	A	SC	374,481	WB
71	Jhalo Malo	A	SC	360,452	AR, AS, MG, MZ, WB
72	Talabda	H	BC	358,872	GJ

No	People Name	Religion	Status	Pop. 2001	Location of the People
73	Devanga	H	BC	353,210	AP, KL, KR, MH, OR, PD, TN
74	Mussalli	M	BC	340,961	HR, JK, PN
75	Charan	A	ST	340,826	BH, DL, GJ, MH, MP, RJ
76	Keora	A	SC	330,841	WB
77	Dusar	H	BC	326,524	AS, MP, UP, WB
78	Thathera	H	BC	322,050	BH, CH, DL, HP, HR, JK, MP, OR, PN, RJ, UP, WB
79	Mahtam	H, S	BC	319,787	CH, HP, HR, PN
80	Kapali	H	BC	316,664	BH, OR, TR, WB
81	Kharva	H	BC	303,378	DD, GJ, KR, MH, PD, TN
82	Bafinda	H, M	BC	299,965	JK
83	Kadu Kuruba	A	ST	288,351	KR
84	Balti	M	BC	284,650	JK
85	Baidya	H	BC	278,190	BH, MH, MP, OR, RJ, TR, WB
86	Ilavaniyar	H	BC	275,402	KL, PD, TN
87	Swami	H	BC	268,690	RJ
88	Mangar	H	BC	264,742	BH, MP, SK, TR, WB
89	Thulukkan	M	BC	243,462	KL
90	Rawther	M	BC	241,849	KL, PD, TN
91	Bhatiara	M, H	BC	239,356	BH, DL, GJ, MP, PN, RJ, UP, WB
92	Bhansala	H	BC	234,330	GJ, KR, MH
93	Barela	H	BC	231,667	MP
94	Nagar	H	BC	225,347	BH, OR, RJ, TR, WB
95	Mahur	M	BC	225,041	BH
96	Yashkun	M	BC	217,490	JK
97	Deshwali	H, M	BC	211,109	MP, OR, PD, RJ
98	Karnam	H	BC	210,541	AP, OR, TN
99	Mangrik	H	BC	206,189	JK
100	Segidi	H	BC	201,704	AP, OR
101	Nayinda	H	BC	192,241	KR
102	Gondhali	H	BC	190,691	GJ, KR, MH, MP
103	Devadiga	H	BC	187,796	KL, KR, MH, PD
104	Dakaut	H	BC	185,434	DL, HR, RJ, UP
105	Gandla	H	BC	184,899	AP, KL, KR, MH, PD
106	Majji	H	BC	177,044	GJ, MP
107	Bhatia	M, H	BC	176,346	CH, DL, GJ, HR, KR, MH, PN, RJ, UP, WB
108	Kir	H	BC	173,804	GJ, HP, HR, MP, RJ
109	Ahar	H	BC	163,164	UP
110	Aheria	A	SC	162,963	CH, DL, HR, MP, PN, RJ, UP
111	Jhojha	M	BC	162,329	UP
112	Alia	H	BC	162,260	MP, OR
113	Khetauri	H	BC	161,118	BH, OR, WB
114	Rautia	H	BC	157,951	AS, BH, MG, MH, MN, MP, NG, OR, WB
115	Pundari	H	BC	157,595	TR, WB

No	People Name	Religion	Status	Pop. 2001	Location of the People
116	Kabliger	H	BC	148,930	KR, PD, TN
117	Naiya	H	BC	146,099	BH, KR, TR, WB
118	Kamkar	H	BC	145,314	BH
119	Rahghar	H	BC	144,898	HP, UP
120	Dhanwar	A	ST	144,848	MH, MP, OR
121	Korama	A	SC	144,776	KR
122	Jatapur	A, M, S	ST	144,344	AP, OR
123	Sargara	A	SC	141,121	RJ
124	Marasari	H	BC	140,923	KL
125	Mayra	H	BC	140,270	AS, MG, WB
126	Bhatta	H, M	BC	139,699	AS, GJ, JK, MH, OR
127	Mahimal	M	BC	139,271	WB
128	Kalavantulu	H	BC	137,412	AP, MH
129	Sanyasi	H	BC	136,938	AP, BH, GJ, KR, MH, MP, OR, PN, WB
130	Kaparia	H	BC	136,438	BH, OR, UP
131	Nikari	M	BC	136,384	OR, WB
132	Pondara	H	BC	136,151	AP, OR
133	Kalota	H	BC	135,058	KR, MP
134	Sood	H	BC	132,756	CH, DL, HP, HR, PN
135	Samanthan	H	BC	129,824	BH, KL, OR, WB
136	Sherugar	H	BC	128,053	GJ, KR
137	Baloch	M	BC	127,652	AR, CH, GJ, HP, HR, MH, MP, RJ, UP
138	Giddidki	H	BC	125,685	KR
139	Merat	H	FC	124,550	GJ, MP, RJ
140	Markande	H	BC	122,703	AS, BH, WB
141	Mallik	M	BC	121,130	BH, GJ, JK, OR, RJ, TR, WB
142	Marati	A	ST	121,042	KL, KR
143	Somvanshi Kshatriya	H	BC	120,901	AP, KR, MH
144	Pattanavan	H	BC	120,456	PD, TN
145	Molesalam	M	BC	118,887	GJ, MH
146	Moger	A	SC	117,526	KL, KR, TN
147	Satia	H	BC	116,455	MP, PN, RJ
148	Maraikayar	M	BC	115,134	PD, TN
149	Kalu	M	BC	113,618	BH, TR, WB
150	Manne	A	SC	112,637	AP, KR, MH
151	Nayadi	A	SC	111,715	GJ, KL, KR, PD, TN
152	Eluthassan	H	BC	111,488	KL
153	Raj	H	BC	108,295	DL, GJ, PN, RJ, UP, WB
154	Soiri	H	BC	107,760	BH, UP
155	Dhund	M	BC	105,393	JK
156	Prabhu Kayastha	H	FC	105,138	AP, GJ, KR, MH, MP, RJ
157	Samagara	A	SC	103,433	AP, KL, KR, TN
158	Chasadhobi	H	BC	103,422	WB

No	People Name	Religion	Status	Pop. 2001	Location of the People
159	Ganaka	H	BC	102,516	AS, KL, MN, MZ, NG
160	Pargha	H	BC	98,876	BH
161	Holar	A	SC	97,950	GJ, KR, MH
162	Valan	H	BC	96,190	KL, KR, PD, TN
163	Gachha	H	BC	91,265	MP
164	Arab	M	UC	91,122	AP, GJ, KL, KR, MH, RJ
165	Bandi	H, M	BC	90,305	AP, KL, KR, MH, OR, TN, UP
166	Shin	M	BC	85,039	JK
167	Mare	H	BC	81,767	AP
168	Brukpa	M	BC	78,815	JK
169	Nuniya	A	SC	75,947	WB
170	Udaiyar	H	BC	74,811	PD, TN
171	Bhabra	H	BC	74,116	PN
172	Kadera	H	BC	74,011	DL, MH, MP, RJ, UP
173	Krishnanvak	H	BC	72,369	KL, PD, TN
174	Benita Odia	H	BC	71,845	OR
175	Lawd	H	BC	69,872	AP
176	Ahirwasi	H	BC	68,036	UP
177	Baraik		BC	67,993	BH
178	Magar	H	BC	67,691	AR, AS, MG, MN, MP, MZ, NG
179	Jimdar	H	BC	66,886	WB
180	Payak	H	BC	65,500	MP, RJ
181	Nanbar	M	BC	65,221	KR
182	Kapewar	H	BC	62,704	AP, MH, MP
183	Kharol	H	BC	61,583	MP, RJ
184	Garpagari	H	BC	61,582	MH, MP
185	Koracha	A	SC	60,153	KR
186	Beriya	A	SC	59,991	MP, UP
187	Muli	H	BC	59,875	AP, KL, KR, OR, TN
188	Arasu	H	BC	59,156	KR
189	Sonowar	H	BC	59,046	AR, AS, MG, MN, MZ, NG, SK, UP, WB
190	Kanai	H	BC	58,844	GJ, KR, MH
191	Byagara	A	SC	58,840	AP, KR, MH
192	Kudumi	H	BC	57,799	KL
193	Saloi	H	BC	56,721	AS, MG, NG
194	Bhaina	A	ST	55,596	MH, MP
195	Jhora	H	BC	54,384	BH, OR
196	Nayata	M	BC	54,063	GJ, KL, KR, MP, TN
197	Bandawat	H	BC	54,008	BH, UP, WB
198	Targala	H	BC	53,868	GJ, KR, MH, RJ
199	Rajpur	H	BC	53,043	KR
200	Rana	H	BC	52,263	RJ
201	Narsinghpura	H	BC	51,216	GJ, MH, RJ
202	Laccadive	M	ST	50,918	LK
203	Dharhi	M	BC	50,748	BH, UP, WB
204	Miana	H	BC	50,436	GJ, MH, RJ, UP

APPENDIX FIVE

MEMBER MISSIONS OF
INDIA MISSIONS ASSOCIATION
August 1998

No	Missions	Year	Place of Work	Staff	Ministry
1	AGNI MINISTRIES	1972	Pondichery, Kerala, Tamil Nadu.	26	Church Planting, Outreach & Teaching Seminars.
2	AL BASHIR	1989	Delhi, Uttar Pradesh, Jammu & Kashmir, West Bengal, Assam.	10	Evangelism among Neighbours, Rehabilitation, Bible Correspondence Course and Training.
3	AMAR JYOTI INDIA	1979	Several states of India	36	Church Planting, Bible Correspondence Course, Follow-up, Seekers Conference and Discipleship.
4	ASSOCIATION FOR GARHWAL'S ADVANCEMENT, PROSPERIY AND EVANGELISATION	1980	Uttar Pradesh Mountains	38	Evangelism, Church Planting, Schools, Medical work, Vocational Training and Literature.
5	BEHALA HUMAN CARE MISSION	1991	West Bengal	14	Church Planting, Mission Research and Community Development.
6	BETHANY FELLOWSHIP	1983	Tamil Nadu, Kerala.	20	Evangelism, Literature, Job-oriented Projects for Poor and Childrens' Home, and Church Planting, Training.
7	BETHEL BIBLE INSTITUTE	1976	Tamil Nadu	11	Missionary Training, Church Planting, Discipleship Camps and Prisoner Camps.
8	BHARATIYA CHRISTI SEVA DAL	1991	Bihar	12	Church planting, Child care, Development and Bible School.
9	BIBLE SOCIETY OF INDIA	1811	All states of India	200	Scripture Translation, Publishing and Distribution.

No	Missions	Year	Place of Work	Staff	Ministry
10	BLESSING YOUTH MISSION	1971	Assam, Andhra Pradesh, Gujarat, Kerala, Karnataka, Madhya Pradesh, Maharastra, Orissa, Rajasthan, Uttar Pradesh, Tamil Nadu.	256	Revival, Evangelism, Bible Seminars, Church Planting, Youth, Medical, Literacy, Relief, Tribal Development and Publishing Books.
11	CENTRAL INDIA CHRISTIAN MISSION	1984	Madhya Pradesh	42	Church Planting, Children's Home, Audio-Visual and Radio Ministry, Correspondence Course, Medical work, Evangelism and Disciple-making.
12	CHILD EVANGELISM FELLOWSHIP		All over India	71	Child Evangelism and Training.
13	CHANDRAKONA ROAD NUTAN AALO	1986	West Bengal	10	Church Planting, Film and Orphanage.
14	CHRIST FOR INDIA MOVEMENT	1981	Maharashtra, Madhya Pradesh, Andhra Pradesh, Orissa, Karnataka, Tamil Nadu and Kerala.	417	Rural & Tribal Ministry, Ministry to Neighbours, Church Planting, Literature, Film, Bible School and Social Uplift.
15	CHRISTIAN ACADEMY FOR RURAL WELFARE AND EVANGELISM	1980	Uttar Pradesh Mountains.	67	Evangeliam, Church Planting, Medical Ministry, Children Homes, Bible School, Literature Evangelism.
16	CHRISTIAN BELIEVERS' ASSEMBLY FELLOWSHIP	1981	Rajasthan, Andhra Pradesh, Uttar Pradesh.	1800	Evangelism, Church Planting, Literature, Missionary Training and Social Uplift.
17	CHRISTIAN FOUNDATION FOR THE BLIND		Madras	12	Literature Ministry through Braille and Rehabilitation of Blind women.
18	CHRISTIAN LIFE SERVICE	1993	Karnataka	17	Church Planting, Training, Teaching on Missions.

No	Missions	Year	Place of Work	Staff	Ministry
19	CHRISTIAN MISSIONS CHARITABLE TRUST	1978	Tamil Nadu	35	Youth Evangelism, Orphanage, Uplift of Poor through Handicraft Centre, Sunday School and Bible study.
20	CHRISTIAN OUTREACH FOR MISSION AND EVANGELISM	1988	Madras, Chengleput.	18	Slum Ministry, Counselling, Adult Literacy.
21	CHRISTIAN OUTREACH UPLIFTING NEW TRIBES	1978	Andhra Pradesh, Madhya Pradesh, Maharashtra, Orissa, Gujarat.	160	Church Planting, Tribal Childcare, Orphanage, Healthcare, Bible Training, Vocational Training and Film.
22	CHURCH GROWTH MISSIONARY MOVEMENT	1975	Andhra Pradesh, Gujarat, Maharashtra, Tamil Nadu.	136	Church Planting, Evangelism and Social Work.
23	CROSS BEARERS MISSIONARY MOVEMENT	1982	Tamil Nadu.	5	Tribal Outreach Evangelism and Cross-Cultural Evangelism.
24	DIOCESAN MISSIONARY PRAYER BAND	1962	Andhra Pradesh, Tamil Nadu, Orissa, Karnataka, Gujarat.	145	Evangelism to Tribals, Church Planting, Childrens' Home, Medical work, Social Uplift and Educational Institutions.
25	DYING SEED MINISTRIES	1989	Tamil Nadu	22	Missionary training, Urban Slum Evangelism, Youth Ministry
26	EVANGELICAL FELLOWSHIP OF INDIA COMMISSION ON RELIEF	1980	Maharashtra, Bihar, Rajasthan, Karnataka, Orissa, New Delhi, Uttar Pradesh.	75	Community Development, Relief and Health Care.
27	EVANGELICAL FREE CHURCH URBAN MOVEMENT INDIA	1993	Tamil Nadu, Karnataka, West Bengal, Uttar Pradesh.	38	Urban Church Planting, Evangelism of Educated and Follow up.

No	Missions	Year	Place of Work	Staff	Ministry
28	EVANGELICAL MEDICAL FELLOWSHIP OF INDIA		Several states of India	10	Medical Fellowship and Evangelism.
29	FAITH OUTREACH	1986	Orissa	460	Evangelism, Church Planting, Bible College, Educational Institutions Children's Home and Day Care Centre.
30	FELLOWSHIP FOR NEIGHBOURS INDIA	1984	Assam, Bihar, Tamil Nadu, West Bengal.	15	Evangelism and Rehabilitation among Neighbours, Training Programme.
31	FELLOWSHIP OF EVANGELICAL FRIENDS	1975	Delhi, Kerala, Tamil Nadu.	35	Evangelism, Ministry among Tribals, Slums and Childrens' Home.
32	FRIENDS MISSIONARY PRAYER BAND	1968	All over India	714	Evangelism, Church Planting, Bible Translation and Social Uplift.
33	GILGAL GOSPEL MISSION	1979	Andhra Pradesh and Tamil Nadu, Orissa, Pondichery.	73	Bible Seminary, Church Planting, Counselling, Social Uplift, Adult Literacy and Tribal Ministry.
34	GOSPEL ECHOING MISSIONARY SOCIETY	1972	Bihar, Madhya Pradesh, Tamil Nadu and Uttar Pradesh	300	Evangelism, Orphanages, Day Care Centres, Schools, Training Programme and Church Planting.
35	GOSPEL IN ACTION FELLOWSHIP INDIA	1982	Andhra Pradesh, Bihar, Karnataka, Kerala, Punjab, Madhya Pradesh and Tamil Nadu.	180	Among Slums and Beggars, Medical Camps, Literacy, Rehabilitation and Missionary Training.
36	GOSPEL RECORDINGS ASSOCIATION	1961	All over India	20	Gospel Messages in Disc. Records and Cassettes.
37	GOSPEL RESOURCE CENTRE	1990	Tamil Nadu		Mass Evangelism through Audio Visual Media.

No	Missions	Year	Place of Work	Staff	Ministry
38	GREAT COMMISSION MOVEMENT TRUST	1990	Gujarat, Andhra Pradesh, Madhya Pradesh, Orissa, West Bengal, Rajasthan, Maharastra.	60	Evangelism, Church Planting and Social Work.
39	HILL GOSPEL FELLOWSHIP, THE	1973	Tamil Nadu	7	Church Planting and Development work.
40	HIMALAYA EVANGELICAL MISSION	1975	Bihar, Himachal Pradesh, Jammu & Kashmir, Madhya Pradesh, Maharastra Punjab, Orissa, Uttar Pradesh, Bhutan & Nepal	170	Evangelism, Church Planting, Missionary Training and Educational Institutions.
41	INDIA BIBLE LITERATURE	1950	All over India	100	Publishing and Distribution of Scriptures, Schools of Evangelism, Adult Literacy and Children Bible School.
42	INDIA BIBLE TRANSLATORS	1978	Karnataka, Madhya Pradesh, Orissa, Tamil Nadu and Uttar Pradesh.	50	Bible Translation, Evangelism and Literacy, Church Planting.
43	INDIA CAMPUS CRUSADE FOR CHRIST	1968	Most of the states in India.	1270	Evangelism, Discipleship, Training, Mass Evangelism through Jesus Film and Music.
44	INDIA CHURCH GROWTH MISSION	1979	Tamil Nadu, Madhya Pradesh.	50	Church Planting, Evangelism and Training the Church Planters, Bible Translation, Social Uplift.
45	INDIA EVANGELISTIC ASSOCIATION	1983	Orissa, Assam.	160	Pioneering Evangelism, Church Planting, Literature Distribution and Community Development.

No	Missions	Year	Place of Work	Staff	Ministry
46	INDIA EVERY HOME CRUSADE	1964	All over India.	800	Literature, Evangelism, Bible Correspondence, Follow-Up, Formation of Christ Groups and Church Planting.
47	INDIA FELLOWSHIP FOR VISUALLY HANDICAPPED	1983	Assam, Andhra Pradesh, Maharashtra, Tamil Nadu, Gujarat, Karnataka, Orissa, Goa, Kerala, Uttar Pradesh, West Bengal.	30	Evangelism and Integration of the Handicapped people in the Church and Church based Rehabilitation.
48	INDIA FOR CHRIST MINISTRIES	1988	Punjab, Rajasthan, Bihar, Kerala, Tamil Nadu, Andhra Pradesh, Karnataka.	49	Outreach, Church Planting, Literature, Children and Youth Ministry.
49	INDIA GOSPEL LEAGUE	1930	Bihar, Maharashtra, Karnataka, Tamil Nadu.	99	Evangelism, Church Planting, Childcare, Schools, Leprosy Rehabilitation, Bible School and School for Blind.
50	INDIA GOSPEL OUTREACH AND SOCIAL ACTION	1984	Andhra Pradesh, Orissa.	30	Evangelism, Church Planting and Social Work.
51	INDIA OUTREACH MISSION	1989	Maharashtra, Andhra Pradesh.	15	Evangelism, Training, Church Planting, Literature, Audio / Video Library, Social Uplift and Orphanage.
52	INDIAN CHRISTIAN MISSION CENTRE	1988	Tamil Nadu	50	Evangelism, Church Planting, Orphanage, Gospel Teams, Literature, Social Uplift and Seminary.
53	INDIAN EVANGELICAL TEAM	1977	Most States of India	1260	Church Planting, Children's' Home, Social Uplift and Revival, Bible Schools.

No	Missions	Year	Place of Work	Staff	Ministry
54	INDIAN EVANGELICAL FELLOWSHIP	1992	Uttar Pradesh	1	Gospel work in cultural context through Sat Sangh, Literature, Seminars and Training.
55	INDIAN EVANGELICAL MISSION	1965	Most States of India and 5 countries abroad.	430	Literature, Church Planting, Bible Translation, Training Programmes, Medical Work and Social Uplift.
56	INDIAN INSTITUTE OF MISSIOLOGY	1994	All Over India	2	To facilitate and coordinate missionary training.
57	INDIAN MISSIONARY SOCIETY	1903	Rajasthan, Uttar Pradesh, Bihar, West Bengal, Orissa, Kerala, Karnataka, Maharastra, Gujarat, Madhya Pradesh, Tamil Nadu.	350	Church Planting, Social Development, Literature Evangelism, Children's Homes.
58	INTER MISSION	1964	Arunachal Pradesh, Bihar, Gujarat, Maharashtra, Orissa, Rajasthan, Sikkim, Tamil Nadu, Uttar Pradesh.	175	Evangelism, Orphanage, Rehabiltation of Prostitutes and the Destitute (women) and Day Care Centre, Micro enterprising development.
59	INTERSERVE (INDIA)	1987	All over India and Outside India.	60	Discipling, Education, Evangelism, Tent makers' Ministry, Health Ministry, Student and Youth Ministry, Social Uplift. Discipling and Education.
60	JATIYO KRISTIYO PROCHAR SAMITY	1976	Assam, Orissa, West Bengal.	110	Outreach, Literature, Children Work, Social Work, School Ministry, Church Planting and Bible School.
61	KING OF KINGS MINISTRIES		Tamil Nadu	20	Church Planting, Social Uplift and Radio Ministry.

No	Missions	Year	Place of Work	Staff	Ministry
62	LEADS OUTREACH	1988	Maharashtra	7	Church Planting, Youth/Student Evangelism, Discipleship & Leadership Training.
63	LIFE IN CHRIST MINISTRIES	1991	Kerala and Tamil Nadu	17	Evangelism, Education and Relief.
64	MAHARASHTRA VILLAGE MINISTRIES	1981	Maharashtra	40	Church Planting and Social Uplift of Tribals.
65	MARANATHA FULL GOSPEL ASSOCIATION		Andaman & Nicobar, Bihar, Andhra Pradesh, Haryana, Karnataka, Tamil Nadu.	130	Church Planting, Bible School, Radio Programme, Social Uplift, Youth Ministry and Children's Home.
66	MESSENGERS FOR CHRIST IN INDIA	1969	Andhra Pradesh, Madhya Pradesh, Maharastra.	60	Church Planting, Social Uplift, Evangelism to drug addicts, Children's home, and others.
67	MISSION FOR ANDAMAN & NICOBAR	1986	Andaman and Nicobar Islands	15	Evangelism, Church Planting, Missionary Training and Social Uplift.
68	MISSION TO THE BLIND	1992	Gujarat, Maharashtra, Kerala, Tamil Nadu, Rajasthan.	24	Discipleship, Evangelism to the Blind and Community development.
69	MISSIONARY SPONSORS' FELLOWSHIP	1989	Several States of India.	Nil	Sponsoring Missionaries through various Mission Agencies.
70	MISSIONS INDIA	1991	Kerala, Rajasthan, Haryana, Andhra Pradesh, Jammu & Kashmir.	143	Church Planting, Social Uplift, Training.
71	NAGALAND MISSIONARY MOVEMENT	1971	Arunachal Pradesh, Bihar, Nagaland, Nepal, Sikkim, Uttar Pradesh, West Bengal, Cambodia, Burma, Andaman & Nicobar Island.	85	Tribal Ministry, Evangelism and Revival, Training.

No	Missions	Year	Place of Work	Staff	Ministry
72	NATIONAL FELLOWSHIP	1988	Assam, Bihar, Orissa, West Bengal	32	Pioneer Evangelism, Follow-up, Church Planting, Training, Research Prayer Networks, Seminars & Consultations and Leadership Courses.
73	NATIONAL MISSIONARY SOCIETY	1905	All over India	285	Evangelism, Church Planting and Children's Homes.
74	NATIVE MISSIONARY MOVEMENT	1981	Bihar, Rajasthan, Madhya Pradesh, Gujarat.	575	Evangelism, Social Uplift, School, Bible College and Literature Ministry.
75	NAVJEEVAN SEVA MANDAL	1984	Many parts of India	200	Rural and Tribal Ministries, Children's Home and Development Projects.
76	NAVJEEVAN VIKAS SANGATI	1994	Rajasthan	8	Church planting, adult literacy, community development.
77	NEW LIFE FELLOWSHIP MISSIONS DEPARTMENT	1995	Many States	54	Church Planting and outreach.
78	OPERATION MOBILISATION	1964	Most parts of India	400	Literature, Church Planting, Evangelism, Training & Community Development.
79	ORISSA FOLLOWUP MINISTRY	1982	Orissa	64	Evangelism, Follow-up, Church Planting, Social Uplift, Childcare, Film and School of Evangelism.
80	POCKET TESTAMENT LEAGUE INDIA, THE	1986	Uttar Pradesh, Haryana, Delhi, Punjab, Tamil Nadu, Orissa, Rajasthan.	190	Evangelism, Team Training, Follow-Up, Missionary Training, Church Planting and Social Concerns.
81	QUIET CORNER INDIA	1974	Tamil Nadu, Karnataka.	30	Church Planting among Tribals, Medical Centres, Vacation Bible School and Prayer Ministry.

No	Missions	Year	Place of Work	Staff	Ministry
82	RAINBOW EVANGELICAL ASSOCIATION	1986	Tamil Nadu	20	Evangelism, Church Planting, Camps and Prayer Ministry.
83	RASHTRIYA SUSAMACHAR PARISHAD	1992	Haryana, Uttar Pradesh.	22	Evangelism, Church Planting and Networking.
84	REACHING HAND SOCIETY	1994	Orissa	18	Cross Cultural Church Planting, Health Care and Community Development.
85	REVIVAL LITERATURE FELLOWSHIP	1973	Karnataka	5	Evangelism, Literature, Discipling and Worship Groups.
86	RURAL BLESSINGS MISSION	1989	Maharashtra.	25	Evangelism, Church Planting, School, Children's Home and Adult Literacy.
87	SADHU SUNDERSINGH EVANGELISTIC ASSOCIATION		Madras	8	Publication, Tracts, Audio Visual Tools, Education and Innovative Evangelism.
88	SOURASHTRA GOSPEL MOVEMENT	1994	Tamil Nadu	5	Evangelism
89	SOUTH INDIA SOUL WINNERS ASSOCIATION	1975	Tamil Nadu, Kerala, Andaman & Nicobar Islands, Burma, Bungladesh, Nepal, Sri Lanka.	325	Evangelism, Church Planting, Orphanage, Handicapped Children's Home and Bible College.
90	TAMIL VILLAGES GOSPEL MISSION	1985	Tamil Nadu	30	Village Evangelism and Church Planting.
91	TRIBAL MISSION	1980	Rajasthan, Tamil Nadu, Kerala, Orissa.	76	Church Planting, Outreach, Orphanage, Health Care and Film Ministry.
92	TRIBAL OUTREACH MISSION	1985	Rajasthan, Karnataka, Kerala, Tamil Nadu.	11	Evangelism, Church Planting and Translation.
93	UESI MISSIONS DEPARTMENT	1954	Most states of India	120	Students Ministry.

No	Missions	Year	Place of Work	Staff	Ministry
94	UNITED FELLOWSHIP FOR CHRISTIAN SERVICES	1954	Uttar Pradesh	50	Hospital, Bible School, Educational Institutions and Training for women.
95	VISHWA VANI	1987	All over India.	410	Radio Ministry, Follow up and Church Planting.
96	WORLD CASSETTE OUTREACH OF INDIA	1982	Several States of India	10	Scripture in Cassettes, Mission Studies on Cassettes.
97	YAVATMAL COLLEGE FOR LEADERSHIP TRAINING	1984	Maharashtra	54	Training for Evangelism, Church Planting and Home for Missionaries' Children.
98	YOUTH WITH A MISSION	1985	All over India	505	Evangelism, Church Planting, Social Work, Training and Research.
99	ZELIANGRONG BAPTIST MISSIONARY MOVEMENT	1987	Manipur, Assam, Arunachal Pradesh and Burma	27	Evangelism, Church Planting and Missionary Training.
100	MISSIONARY UPHOLDERS TRUST	1993			Upholding mission and missionaries. Providing welfare measures.
101	GRACE COUNSELLING	1982	Kerala	29	Literature evangelism, drug addicts and counselling and counsellor training.
102	BIBLE BELIEVING CHURCHES AND MISSIONS	1988	Karnataka, Gujarat, Orissa, Tamil Nadu, Manipur, Madhya Pradesh and Punjab	24	Church planting and training church planters and pastors.
				15613	

APPENDIX SIX

RESOURCES FOR FIELD STUDIES

Field Studies for missionaries is a part of their continuing education and is vital for long term stamina and refreshment.

OM India and OM Ships pioneered field studies for OM missionaries. Then OM World took up the idea. This model could be duplicated.

Refer to the following books:

[n.a.], *Discipleship Manual* (Bombay: OM, (1970). Many reprints.

OM Training Team, *Ministry Training Record Book* (Secunderabad: OM, 1993).

OM Training Team, *OM India Team Trainers Manual* (Secunderabad: OM, 1990).

Richard Briggs (Ed.), *Global Action—Operation Mobilisation's Core Study Manual* (UK: OM Publishing, 1997).

There are also other studies designed for the missionaries on the field which are available in book or booklet forms. Some of them are: *Spiritual Problems, Spiritual Maturity, Studies on Missions from the Acts of Apostles, Studies on the book of Romans, Core Studies for the month Programme Candidates, Studies on Judges, Tips on Leading Small Group Studies* and many others.

All of the above are discussion style studies, suitable for individual or group interaction and participation.

For further information write to Training Director, Logos Bhavan, Medchal Road, Jeedimetla, Secunderabad 500 855, India.

TAFTEE & IIM also have materials which could be used for field studies for missionaries.

GLOSSARY

acharya   The master, teacher and the *Guru* of the Ashram.

anna   One sixteenth of an Indian rupee. The *anna* went out of use in the mid 1960s.

archaha   A Hindu priest.

Arya Samaj   Arya Samaj[1] was founded by Dayanand Saraswati around 1870. He opposed the caste system, idolatry and some superstitions. Arya Samaj grew popular mainly because of its social reforms, educational and national as well as social welfare activities.

avatars   Incarnations. This is a Hindu concept of divine visitation. Ram is supposed to be one of the ten incarnations of Vishnu according to the *Ramayana*.

bandhs   Closing of shops and institutions called by opposition parties. When this becomes too frequent, the morale of the people drops. They also cause confusion in industries and loss of revenue due to non-productivity.

biryani   Indian rice delicacy with meat in it.

BJP   *Barathyia Janatha* Party - this means the Indian Peoples' party. This party strongly supports Hinduism as the basis of Indian nationalism.

CARE   Cell for Aid and Relief to Evangelists. It is a department of India Missions Association to help the member missions in dire need. Member missions could apply for salary assistance of Rs. 1000 per person in their mission. IMA raises this money from the donors for salary for the missionaries, and for Church buildings in pioneering areas.

Darithra Narayana   The god of the poor. Vivekananda claimed to be the worshipper of *Darithra Narayana*.

Dharmappallikkudam   (Tamil) Charity school

E1 evangelism   This is evangelism that has no language or cultural barrier to overcome.

E2 evangelism   Evangelism done among people who could be similar to the proclaimer, yet he or she has to cross some language and cultural barrier.

E3 evangelism   Evangelism that is distinctly cross-cultural with or without great crossing of distance as in the case of Marwadies from Rajasthan and Gujarat who are settled in Bangalore.[2]

goondas   Thugs.

Ganga Jal   Holy water from the sacred river Ganges.

Hindu Shatabdi celebrations - The century of Hindus' celebrations.

HUP — The Homogeneous Unit Principle, articulated by Donald McGavran, a former missionary to India. It states that for people to follow Christ there are less obstacles if they do so as a whole group than if they do so as individuals from many groups conglomerated into a new (cultural) group.

In my opinion, this principle has worked in many places. It is opposed by those who feel it keeps people in their own culture and opposes the Christian teaching of brotherhood and oneness. However, the principle is a good one and need not prevent eventual multi-cultural unity. Indeed the word 'nation' in the Great Commission may refer to a group of people who were homogeneously bound.

Jan Jagran — The awakening of people.

Krishtagraha — A movement aimed at reorienting Christianity away from being pro-Western and toward achieving a soul of its own, tied closely to Mother India. According to Ralph Templin, Jones influenced him to begin *Krishtagraha*

madrasi — Pertaining to missions or missionaries originating in South India (often from the city of Madras). Refer also *swarthics*.

Manavadvaita Vada — Humanistic monism, such as the philosophy of Swami Vivekananda.[3]

Mission Re-entry or Exit Orientation — This process is to help missionaries that return home to cope with their home and home church situation. If not done these returnees can become judgemental of their home churches. They need assistance in how to share about missionary vision, discipling and supporting the missionaries on the fields. It is also an opportunity to evaluate their time on the mission field.

OBC — Other Backward Castes. The Indian Constitution lists certain castes under Article 341 as Scheduled Backward Castes. This has given rise to the name OTHER Backward Castes (OBC) for those castes which come under Article 340.

PIN code — Postal Index Numbers. India is divided into 28,000 PIN codes, each representing a geographical area. About 20,000 of these PIN code areas do not have any evangelist or a pastor.[4]

RSS — Rastriya Swayam Sevak, a Hindu revivalist group.

sannyasin	a female sage.
sati	This was a Hindu practice of burning the widow with their dead husband. It was outlawed in 1829 by the British Viceroy through the efforts of William Carey and Raja Ram Mohun Roy.
Satyagraha	The passive resistance non-cooperation movement against the then British rulers of India.
Sikh	The third largest religion in India with a population of 1.92 percent.[5] Sikhism rose as a result of Hindu Bakthi (devotion) cult combined with Islamic teachings. It is a compromise religion between Hinduism and Islam. Their instructions have come from their religious teachers and leaders who are called *Gurus*.
Shiv Sena	A militant Hindu Party of India.
swarthics	Local workers or Christians who try to reach their own people. Refer also *madrasi*.
SWOT	Acronym for the process of analysing an organisation's Strengths, Weaknesses, Opportunities and Threats.
Varnashrama Dharma	India's caste system. The four castes stratify society and exclude those with no caste from any influence.
Vaastu	Superstitious tradition regarding the optimal placement of houses, seats in an office and many other things.
Vishwa Hindu Parishad	Hindu World Federation, a militant Hindu movement.
Waqfh Board	Islamic mosque management board.

END NOTES

1 Vable, *The Arya Samaj*; Introduction Pages in Zachariah, *Religious and Secular Movements*.

2 Wayne Gregory, "The Types of Evangelism - The E-Scale". [n.a.], *Inheriting God's Perspective*, (Bangalore: Mission Frontiers, 1996), p. 67.

3 This is the opinion of Dr. Rama Chowdri, quoted in Zachariah, *Religions and Secular Movements*, p. 96.

4 Prayer Resources Based on Research done by IMA, *Indian Missions* (January – March 1997), p. 24.

5 Johnstone, *Operation World*, p. 274.

BIBLIOGRAPHY

Abraham, PT, "Pentecostal-Charismatic Missionary Outreach," from
    Sam Lazarus [Ed.], *Proclaiming Christ*, Madras: CGAI,
    1992.

Albert, S.Vasantharaj, A *Portrait of India III*, Madras: CGAI, 1995.

Anantharaj, E., Neemkathana, "Longings of a Missionary," *Mission
    and Vision Who and What?* Bangalore: MUT, 1996.

Anderson, Gerald H, *Future of the Christian World Missions*,
    William J. Danker (Ed.), Grand Rapids: Eerdmans 1971.

Anderson, Neill with Joanne, *Daily in Christ,* Oregon: Harvest House
    Publishers, 1993.

Andrews, C. F., *What I owe to Christ*, New York: Abingdon Press,
    1932.

Arles, Siga & Benwati, I, (Eds.), *Pilgrimage 2100*, Bangalore: Centre
    for Contemporary Christianity, 1995.

_____, "Evangelical Movement in India—An Evaluation," Siga
    Arles & I. Benwati (Eds.), *Pilgrimage 2100*. Bangalore:
    Centre for Contemporary Christianity, 1995.

Arunothaya Kumar, Kingsley and Billy, R, "'Evangelical Mission
    Thought and Practice'—Could it be more Indian?" Siga
    Arles & I. Benwati (Eds.), *Pilgrimage 2100* Bangalore:
    Centre for Contemporary Christianity, 1995.

Athyal, Sakhi M, *Indian Women in Mission*, Bihar: Mission Educa-
    tional Books, 1995

Azariah, Vedanayagam Samuel, *India and Missions*, Madras: CLS,
    1915.

Bagchee, Moni. "Christian Missionaries in Bengal," in [n.a.], *Christi-
    anity in India*, Madras: Vivekananda Prakashan, 1979.

Barlett, Samuel Colcord, *Historical Sketches of the Missions of the
    American Board,* New York: Arno Press 1876 & reprinted in
    1972.

Beard, Ron, "Flipcharts An Old Tool for A New Day," Ezra
    Sargunam (Ed.), *Mission Mandate*, Madras: Mission India
    2000, 1992.

Beaver, R. Pierce, *All Love Excelling,* Michigan: Eerdmans, 1968.

_____, "The History of the Mission Strategy," from Ralph Winter,
    Steve Hawthorne et al (Eds.), *Perspectives on the World
    Christian Movement—A Reader*, California: William Carey
    Library, 1981.

Bebbington, David, *Evangelicalism in Modern Britain: A History*

from the 1730's to the 1890's, London: [n.pub.] 1989, p. 3.
Cited in Pradeep Das, "The Evangelical Movement in India."
Siga Arles & I. Benwati (Eds.), *Pilgrimage 2100,* Bangalore:
Centre for Contemporary Christianity, 1995.

Benerjee, Brojendra Nath, *Struggle for Justice to Dalit Christians,*
New Delhi: New Age International (P) Limited, 1997.

Bennis, Warren G, "Theory and Method in Applying Behavioural
Science to Planned Organisational Change," Alton C.
Bartlett and Thomas A. Kayser (Eds.), *Changing Organisa-
tional Behaviour,* New Jersey: Prentis–Hall, Inc, 1973.

Boyd, Robin, *Church History of Gujarat.* Madras: CLS, 1981.

Briggs, Richard, (Ed.), *Global Action—Operation Mobilisation's
Core Study Manual,* UK: OM Books, 1997.

Brock, Charles, *Indigenous Church Planting,* Tennesse: Broadman
Pub., 1981.

Budelman, Ralph, "The Awakening of Student and Laymen A Call
for A Mission Renewal Movement," Budelman, Ralph (Ed.),
Inheriting God's Perspective. Bangalore: Mission Frontiers,
1996.

Campolo, Anthony, *The Success Fantasy,* Illinois: Victor Books,
1988.

Carey, William, *An Enquiry Into the Obligations of Christians to Use
Means for the Conversion of the Heathen,* ([n.Pub.], [n.d.])

_____, excerpted from William Carey—*An Enquiry in to the
Obligations of Christians to Use Means for the Conversions
of the Heathen,* New Facsimile (Ed.), (London: Carey
Kingsgate Press, London, 1792, 1962), Winter, Hawthorne et
al (Eds.), *World Christian Movement.*

Carney, Glandion, "Pathways Of Spiritual Growth," Bill Berry [Ed.],
The Short-Term Mission Handbook, Illinois: Berry Publishing Services, 1992.

Clark, MM, *A Corner in India,* Gauhati: C. L. Centre, 1978.

Clarke, Alden H, "Should Mission Carry on Social Work?" in
Fennell P Turner and Frank Knight Sanders (Eds.), *The
Foreign Missions Convention at Washington 1925,* New
York: Fleming H. Revell Company, 1925

Coleman, Robert E, *The Master Plan of Evangelism,* New Jersey:
Spire Books, 1984.

Collins, Marjorie A., *Manual for Today's Missionary,* Pasadena:
William Carey Library, 1986.

Cornelius, John Jesudason, "Movements Towards Christ in India," from Fennell P. Turner and Frank Knight Sanders (Eds.), *The Foreign Missions Convention at Washington 1925*, New York: Fleming H. Revell Company, 1925.

Costas, Orlando. *The Church and the Mission: A Shattering Critique from the Third World*, Wheaten, Illinois: Tyndale, 1974.

Cressy, Earl H, *Christian Missions Meet the Cultures of East Asia*, New York: Friendship Press, 1948.

_____, *Christian Missions Meet the Cultures of East Asia*, New York: Friendship Press, 1948.

Das, Pradip, "The Evangelical Movement in India Its Roots and Motivations: 1793–1966". Siga Arles & I. Benwati (Eds.), *Pilgrimage 2100,* Bangalore: Centre for Contemporary Christianity, 1995.

David, Nirmala, " The Birth of a MUF Group," J. J. Ratna Kumar & Krupa Sunder Raj [Eds.], *Mission and Vision, Who and What?* Bangalore: MUT Publishers, 1996.

Davis, Rupert E., *Methodism*, Middlesex, U.K.: Penguin Books, 1963.

Dayton, Edward R, "To Reach the Unreached," from Ralph Winter, Steve Hawthorne et al (Eds.), *Perspectives on the World Christian Movement— A Reader*, California: William Carey Library, 1981.

_____, and Frazer, David, *Planning Strategies for World Evangelisation*, Michigan: W.B.Eerdmans Publishing Company, 1980.

_____, "Strategy," from Ralph Winter, Steve Hawthorne et al (Eds.), *Perspectives on the World Christian Movement—A Reader*, California: William Carey Library, 1981.

Dodge, Ralph E, *The Unpopular Missionary*, New Jersey: Fleming H. Revell Company, 1960.

Douglas, JD, [Ed.], *The New International Dictionary of the Christian Church*. Michigan: Regency Reference Library, 1994.

Downs, Frederick S, *Christianity in N. East India*, Delhi: ISPCK, 1983.

Dusen, Henry P. Van, *For the Healing of the Nations*, New York: Friendship Press, 1941.

Engel, James F, *Contemporary Christian Communications Its Theory and Practice*, New York: Thompson Nelson Publishers, 1979.

Ernsberger, Margaret Carver, *India Calling*, Lucknow: Lucknow Publishing House, 1956.

Escobar, Samuel, "A Movement Divided: Three Approaches to

World Evangelisation Stand in Tension," *Transformation*. Vol. 8. No. 4 Oct (1991) 7–13.

Fenton, Horace, *Myths about Missions*, Illinois: IVP, 1973.

Firth, CB, *An Introduction to Indian Church History*, Madras: CLS, 1961, 1983.

Ford, Leighton, *The Christian Persuader*, London: Harper & Row Publishers, 1996.

Fuller, Harold, *Mission—Church Dynamics*, California: William Carey Library, 1981.

Gibson, Tim, "Planning Your Short-term Trip," Bill Berry [Ed.], *The Short-Term Mission Handbook*, Illinois: Berry Publishing Services, 1992.

Gillquist, Peter E, *Let's Quit Fighting about the Holy Spirit*, London: Lakeland, 1971.

Gnanadasan, A. *Mission Mandate*, pp. 461–492. This list is quoted from Pate, *Every People Directory*, 1998.

Gregory, Wayne. "'Nations' and 'Countries,'" [n.a.], *Inheriting God's Perspective*, Bangalore: Mission Frontiers, 1996.

_____, "The Types of Evangelism—The E-Scale," [n.a.], *Inheriting God's Perspective*. Bangalore: Mission Frontiers.

Hedlund, Roger E, *Evangelisation and Church Growth*, Madras: CGRC, 1992.

_____, "Introduction," from Sam Lazarus [Ed.], *Proclaiming Christ*, Madras: CGAI, 1992.

Headland, Isaac Taylor, *Some By-products of Missions*, New York: The Methodist Book Concern, 1912.

Hicks, David, *Globalising Missions*. Miami: Unilit, 1994.

Hilton, Tony, *Maharastra Harvest Field Handbook, Filed Series*, Chennai: People India, 1997.

Hminga, C. Lal, "Churches in Mission, A Voice From the North," from Sam Lazarus [Ed.], *Proclaiming Christ*, Madras: CGAI, 1992.

Hodge, JH, *Salute to India*, London: S.C.M. Press 1944.

Holcomb, Helen.H., *Men of Might in India Missions—1706–1899*, New York: Fleming H. Revel Company, 1901.

Houghton, Graham, *The Impoverishment of Dependency*, Madras: C.L.S. 1983.

IMA Research Team (Eds.), *Go into All Karnataka*, Madras: IMA, 1996.

_____, *Go into All Tamilnadu*, Madras: IMA, 1996.

_____, *Languages of India—Present Status of Christian work in*

Every Indian Language, Second Edition, Chennai: India Missions Association, June 1997.

_____, *Peoples of India,* Second Edition, Chennai: India Missions Association, May 1997.

Jayaprakash, L. Joshi, *Evaluation of Indigenous Missions of India,* Madras: Church Growth Research Centre, 1987.

Jebasingh, Emil, "Media, Missions and the Mandate," Ezra Sargunam (Ed.), *Mission Mandate,* Madras: Mission India 2000, 1992.

_____, "Introduction", *Mandate,* 1992.

Johnstone, Patrick. *Operation World,* Carlisle: OM Books, 1993.

Jones, John P, *India's Problem: Krishna or Christ,* New York: Fleming H.Revell, 1903.

_____, *India Its Life and Thought,* New York:The Macmillan Company, 1908.

_____, *The Modern Missionary Challenge,* New York: Fleming H.Revell, 1910.

Jones, E. Stanley, *The Christ of the Indian Road,* Lucknow: Lucknow Publishing House, 1964.

Kane, J. Herbert, *Life and Work on the Mission Field,* Michigan: Baker Book House, 1980.

Kavunkal, Jacob and Hrangkhuma, F., *Bible and Mission in India Today,* Bombay: St. Pauls, 1993.

Kesler, Jay, "Foreword" in Anthony Campolo, Jr., *The Success Fantasy,* Illinois: Victor Books, 1988.

Keyes, Lawrence E, "The New Age of Cooperation," cited in Theodore Williams (Ed.), *Together in Missions.* Bangalore: WEF, 1983.

Kurian, CT, *Mission and Proclamation,* Madras: CLS, 1981.

Latourette, Kenneth Scott, *Missions Tomorrow,* New York: Harper and Brothers Publishers, 1936.

Lehmann, Arno, *It Began at Tranquebar,* Madras: CLS, 1956.

Lewis, James, *William Goudie,* London: Wesleyan Methodist Missionary Society, 1923.

Khan, Mumtaz Ali, *Mass Conversion of Meenakshipuram,* Madras: CLS, 1983.

Koola, Paul J, *Population and Manipulation,* Bangalore: Asian Trading Corporation, 1979.

MacQuarrie, John. "Prayer and Theological Reflection," MacQuarrie, Cheslyn, Jones, Geoffrey Wain Wright et al (Eds.), *The Study of Spirituality,* London: SPCK, 1986.

Mangalwadi, Vishal, *Missionary Conspiracy: Letters to a Post-*

modern Hindu, Mussoorie: Nivedit Books, 1996.

Mangalwadi, Ruth & Vishal, *William Carey—A Tribute by an Indian Woman*, New Delhi: Nivedit Books, 1993.

Manikam, Rajaiah B., *Christianity and the Asian Revolution*, Madras: CLS, 1955.

Mathew, CV, 'Who are the "Evangelicals"' From Sam Lazarus [Ed.], *Proclaiming Christ*, Madras: CGAI, 1992.

_____, *Neo-Hinduism: A Missionary Religion*. Madras: CGRC, 1987.

Mathews, James K, "The Mission to Southern Asia", James A. Engle & Dorcas Hall (Eds.), *The Christian Mission Today*, New York: Abingdon Press, 1960.

Matthew, KM, (Ed), *Manorama Year Book 1995*, Kotayam: Manorama Publications, 1995.

Mason, Caroline Atwater, *Wonders of Missions*, London: Hodder & Stoughton Limited, 1922.

Massey, Ashish."Challenges to Mission in North India." Sam Lazarus [Ed.], *Proclaiming Christ*, Madras: CGAI, 1992

McGavran, Donald, "New Mission," in Arthur Glasser and McGavren, *Contemporary Theology of Missions*. Grand Rapids: Baker Book House, 1983.

McMahon, Robert J, *To God Be the Glory: The Evangelical Fellowship of India 1951–1971*, New Delhi: MSS, 1971.

McQuilkin, Robert, "Don't Let Expectations Get You Down." Bill Berry [Ed.], *The Short-Term Mission Handbook*, Illinois: Berry Publishing Services, 1992.

Mische, Gerald and Patricia, *Towards a Human World Order*, New York Paulist Press, 1977

Misra, B.B. *The Indian Middle Classes, Their Growth in Modern Times*, London: Oxford University Press, 1983.

Murdoch, John, *Indian Missionary Manual: Hints to Young Missionaries in India*. London: Selay, Jackson, & Halliday, 1870 2nd Edn. Cited in Houghton, *The Impoverishment of Dependency*, Madras: C.L.S. 1983.

[n.a.] *Directory of Indian Missions*, Chennai: India Missions Association, January, 1996.

_____, *Discipleship Manual*, Bombay: OM, 1970.

_____, *Training Record Book*, Seconderabad: OM, 1993.

_____, *OM India Trainers Manual*, Seconderabad: OM, 1990.

_____, "India's Neo-karma Generation," excerpted from an article by Kevin Murphy in the *International Herald Tribune*;

Manorama Year Book 1995, Kottayam: Malayala Manorama, 1995.

_____, *India People Prayer Diary*, Madras: Church Growth Association of India, 1996.

_____, "Longings of a Supporter," *Mission and Vision; Who and What?* Bangalore: MUT, 1996.

_____, "The Awakening of Student and Laymen, A Call for A Mission Renewal Movement," Budelman, Ralph (Ed.), *Inheriting God's Perspective*, Bangalore: Mission Frontiers, 1996.

_____, *The World Mission of the Church. Findings and Recommendations of the International Missionary Council*, London: International Missionary Council, 1939.

_____, *30 Days Hindu Prayer Focus*, UK: South Asian Concern, 1997.

_____, "Missionaries in India: Focus on Madhya Pradesh", in [n.a.], Christianity in India, Madras: Vivekananda Kendra Prakashan, 1979.

_____, *Towards a Theology for Interfaith Dialogue*, London: Anglican Consultative Council, 1988.

Naipaul, VS, *India, A Million Mutinies Now*, London: Minerva, 1990.

Neill, Stephen, *Builders of the Indian Church*, Westminster, London: The Livingstone Press, 1934.

_____, *Call to Mission*, Philadelphia: Fortress Press, 1970.

_____, *Christian Partnership*, London: SCM, 1952.

_____, *Colonialism and Christian Missions*, London: McGraw Hill Book Company, 1966.

_____, *The Christian Church in India and Pakistan,* Michigan: Eerdmans Publishing Company, 1970. Quoted from the original translation by O. Wolff, *Christus Under den Hindus – Christus der Asiat.*

_____, *A History of Christian Missions*, England: Penguin Books, 1990. Quoted from [n.a.] *Religious Thoughts and Life in India*, 1983.

_____, *The History of Christian Missions*, London: Penguin Books, 1990.

_____, *Under Three Flags*, New York: Friendship Press, 1954.

Newbigin, Lesslie, *The Good Shepherd*, Madras: CLS, 1974.

_____, *Mission in Christ's Way*, Geneva: WCC Publications, 1987.

Nicholls, Bruce. "The Gospel in Indian Culture," Ezra Sargunam (Ed.), *Mission Mandate*, Madras: Mission India 2000, 1992.

Nicholls, Kathleen, "The Traditional Media and the Gospel," Ezra Sargunam (Ed.), *Mission Mandate*. Madras: Mission India 2000, 1992.

Niles, DT, *That They May Have Life*, New York: Harper, [n.d.].

Norris, Frederick W., "God and the gods: Expect Footprints," Doug Priest Jr. (Ed.) *Unto the Uttermost*, California: William Carey Library 1984.

O'Richards, Lawrence, *A Practical Theology of Spirituality*, Michigan: Academie Books, 1987.

Orr, J. Edwin, *Evangelical Awakenings in Southern Asia*, Minneapolis: Bethany Fellowship, 1975.

Padwick, CE, "Henry Martyn," JD Douglas [Ed.], *The New International Dictionary of the Christian Church*, Michigan: Regency Reference Library, 1994.

Page, Jesse. *Henry Martyn of India and Persia*, London: Pickering and Inglis [n.d.].

Parshall, Phil, "God's Communicator in the 80's," from Ralph Winter, Steve Hawthorne et al (Eds.), *Perspectives on the World Christian Movement–A Reader*, California: William Carey Library, 1981.

Pate, Larry D. "The Dramatic Growth of Two-Thirds World Missions," Taylor, William, (Ed) *Internationalising Missionary Training*, Grand Rapids: Baker House, 1991.

Paul, Rajaiah D., *The Cross Over India*, London: SCM Press LTD, 1952.

_____, *They Kept the Faith*, Lucknow: Lucknow Publishing House, 1968.

Pentecost, Edward C., *Issues in Missiology*, Michigan: Baker Book House, 1982.

Peters, GW, *A Biblical Theology of Missions*, Chicago: Moody Pub., 1972.

Pickett, J. Waskom, *Christ's Way to India's Heart*, Lucknow: Lucknow Publishing House, 1938.

_____, *My Twentieth Century Odyssey*, Bombay: Gospel Literature Service, 1980.

Pinto S. J. Ambrose, *Dalit Christians. A Socio-Economic Survey*, Bangalore: Ashirvad, 1992.

Ponraj, SD, *Church Growth Studies in Mission*, Madhupur, Bihar: Institute of Multi-cultural Studies, 1991.

_____, "The Relevance of Cross-Cultural Mission In India." [n.a.], *Inheriting God's Perspective*, Bangalore: Mission Frontiers,

1996.

Ponraj, SD & Baird, Sue.[Eds], "Major Networking Agencies," *Reach India 2000*, Madhupur, Bihar: Mission Educational Books, 1996.

_____, "Partnership in Reaching the Unreached," *Reach India 2000*, Madhupur, Bihar: Mission Educational Books, 1996.

Prabhu Rayan, RZ, "Ministry Among the Visually Handicapped People," [n.a] [Ed.], *Changing World*, Madras: UESI, 1990.

Premsagar, Victor, "Forward," *Mandate*, 1992.

Priest, Doug. Jr. "A Massai Purification Ceremony," Doug Priest [Ed.], *Unto the Uttermost*, California: William Carey Library 1984.

Rao, OM, *Some Concerns of the Indian Church*, Guwahati: Christian Literature Centre, 1983.

Rao, S. Madhav. "Organisational Set Up of Missions—Formation of A Society/Trust—Legal Obligations", from Ebe Sunder Raj and Team (Eds.), *Management of Indian Missions*, Chennai: India Missions Association, 1992.

_____, "Managing of Properties," from Ebenezer Sunder Raj and Team (Eds.), *Management of Indian Missions*, Chennai: India Missions Association, 1992.

RatnaKumar, JJ & Sunder Raj, Krupa [Eds.]. *Mission and Vision, Who and What?* Bangalore: MUT Publishers, 1996.

Richard, HL, *Christ-Bhakti: Narayan Vaman Tilak and Christian work among Hindus*, Delhi: ISPCK, 1991.

Sachdeva, SK, (Ed.), "Newspapers," *Competition Success Review Year Book 1995*, New Delhi: Competition Review Pvt.Ltd. 1995.

Sagar, Allan H., *Gospel Centred Spirituality*, Minneapolis: Augusburg Fortress, 1990.

Sargent, John, *The Life and Letters of Henry Martyn*, Edinburgh: The Banner of Truth Trust, 1985.

Shourie, Arun, *Missionaries in India*, New Delhi: ASA Publications, 1994.

Singh, Andrea Menefee, "Rural-Urban Migration of Women: Some Implications for Urban Planning" in Alfred de Souza [Ed.], *Urban Growth and Urban Planning*, New Delhi: Indian Social Institute, 1983.

Singh, Khuswant, *India: An Introduction*, New Delhi: Vision Books, 1992.

Smith, Oswald J, *The Challenge of Missions*, Bromley: STL Books, 1983.

Srinivasagam, Theodore, "The Need for Effective Cross-Cultural Evangelism," in *Mission Mandate*, 1992.

Soltau, Stanley, *Facing the Field*, Grand Rapids: Baker Book House, 1959.

_____, *Missions at the Cross Roads*, Illinois: Van Campen Press, 1954.

Sterk, Vernon J, "Territorial Spirits and Evangelisation in Hostile Environments," C. Peter Wagner [Ed.], *Territorial Spirits*, Chichester, England: Sovereign World Limited, 1991.

Stillman, Sue, "Ministry to the Handicapped (Deaf)," ____ [Ed.], *Changing World*, Madras: UESI, 1990.

Stock, Frederick and Margaret, *People Movements in the Punjab*, Bombay: Gospel Literature Service, 1978.

Sundera Rajan, PA, " Cassette—A Powerful Media," Ezra Sargunam (Ed.), *Mission Mandate*, Madras: Mission India 2000, 1992.

Sunder Raj, Ebenezer, *Demand for Restoration of Equal Rights for Christian Dalits*, Madras: [n.pub.], November 1996.

_____, *The Confusion Called Conversion*. New Delhi: TRACI, 1986.

_____, *Reservation Or Dalit Christians! Why?* New Delhi: National Coordination Committee for SC Christians, November 1995.

_____, Moses, Danapal., and Samuel, Lynda., (Eds.), *Management of Indian Missions*, Madras: IMA, 1992.

Tan, Kim Sai, *The Great Digression: World Evangelism from 1910: The Ecumenical Digression and the Evangelical Response*, Malaysia: Malaysia Bible Seminary, 1981.

Taylor, Richard, *The Contribution of Stanley Jones*, Madras: CLS, 1973.

Theerthan, Swami John D., *Choice Before India: Communism—Catastrophe; Sarvodya—Christ*, Trichur: Mission to Hindus, [n.d.].

Thiessen, John Caldwell, *A Survey of World Missions*, Chicago: Moody Press, 1961.

Thomas, Juliet, "Role of Women in Christian Ministry," from Sam Lazarus [Ed.], *Proclaiming Christ*, Madras: CGAI, 1992.

Thomas, MM, *The Acknowledged Christ of the Indian Renaissance*, Madras: CISRS-CLS, 1970.

Thompson, EW, *The Call of India*, London: The Wesleyan Methodist Missionary Society, 1912.

Thorpe, John K., *"Other Sheep" of the Tamil Fold, The Centenary Story of the Strict Baptist Mission 1861–1960*, London: SBM Publications, 1961.

Tucker, Ruth, "William Carey Father of Modern Missions," John Woodbridge (Ed.), *Great Christian Leaders*, Chicago: Moody Press, 1988.

Tudu, MM, "Appreciation," *Mandate,* 1992.

Vable, D, *The Arya Samaj; Hindu without Hinduism*, Delhi: Vikas Publishing House PVT. Ltd, 1983.

Waack, Otto, *Church and Mission in India*, Delhi: ISPCK, 1997.

Wagner, C. Peter, *Church Growth and the Whole Gospel,* Kent: MARC Europe, 1987.

Warren, Max, *Partnership*, Chicago: SCM Book Club, 1956.

Wati, I. Ben, "Forward", in Esther Williams, *Sacrifice or Investment*, Bangalore: IEM Outreach Publications, 1990.

Webster, John CB, "Assumptions about Indian Woman Underlying Protestant Policies, 1947–1982," John CB & Ellen Webster (Eds.), *The Church and the Women in the Third World*, Philadelphia: The Westminster Press, 1984.

_____, *From Indian Church to Indian Theology*, Madras: Dalit Liberation Education Trust, 1992.

White, Jerry, *The Church and the Parachurch, An Uneasy Marriage*, Portland: Multnomah Press, 1983.

Wigan, M H, "Educated Christian Women and Missionary Vocation," *NCCR* , October (1948) 408–413.

Wilder, Harriet, *A Century in the Madura Mission–South India 1834–1934*, New York: Vintage Press, 1961.

Williams, Colins, *Where in the World? Changing Forms of the Church's Witness*, New York: N.C.C., USA, 1963.

Williams, Esther, *Sacrifice or Investment*, Bangalore: IEM Outreach Publications, 1990.

Winslow, JC, *Narayan Vaman Tilak*, Pune: Word of Life Publications, 1996 [third edition].

_____, *The Eyelids of the Dawn*, London: Hodder and Stoughton, 1954.

Winston, Shyam. "Wanted: Life Savers," JJ Rathnakumar and Krupa Sunder Raj, [Eds.], *Mission and Vision Who and What?* Bangalore: Missionary Upholders Trust, 1996.

Winter, Ralph D, "The Task Remaining: All Humanity in Mission Perspective," Ralph Winter, Steve Hawthorne et al (Eds.), *Perspectives on the World Christian Movement,* California: William Carey library, 1981.

_____, "The Two Structures of God's Redemptive Mission," Arthur Glasser, Paul Heibert et al, *Crucial Dimensions in World*

Evangelisation, California: William Carey Library, 1977.

_____, "The Long Look: Eras of Missions History," from Ralph Winter, Steve Hawthorne et al (Eds.), *Perspectives on the World Christian Movement–A Reader*, California: William Carey Library, 1981.

Winter, Roberta, "The Kingdom Strikes Back", Budelman, Ralph (Ed.), *Inheriting God's Perspective*, Bangalore: Mission Frontiers, 1996.

Yohannan, KP, *Revolution in World Missions God's Third Wave*, Altamonte Springs, Florida: Creation House, 1986.

Zachariah, Alayamma, *Modern Religions and Secular Movements*, Bangalore: Theological Book Trust, 1990.

Index